D0457414

Reducing Delinquency

A Strategic Planning Approach

Reducing Delinquency

A Strategic Planning Approach

Gregory P. Falkin
U.S. Department of Justice

LexingtonBooks
D.C. Heath And Company
Lexington, Massachusetts
Toronto

Library of Congress Cataloging in Publication Data

Falkin, Gregory P.
    Reducing delinquency.

    A revision of the author's thesis, Cornell University.
    Bibliography: p.
Includes indexes.
    1. Juvenile delinquency—United States, Prevention.
2. Juvenile delinquency—California—Prevention.
3. Juvenile justice, Administration of—United States.
4. Juvenile justice, Administration of—California.
I. Title.
HV9104.F34   1979   364.4'4   78-3127

Published simultaneously in Canada.

Printed in the United States of America.

International Standard Book Number: 0-669-02318-3

Library of Congress Catalog Card Number: 78-3127

To Deb and Patience

Contents

List of Figures

List of Tables

Foreword

One of the more overworked clichés in criminal justice is the claim that the criminal justice system is a "nonsystem." That characterization is intended to suggest that the different parts of the criminal justice system—the loose aggregation of agencies society charges with dealing with crime, suspects, defendants, and offenders—are not only poorly coordinated, but that they often work at cross purposes. Indeed, that conflict is intended, since the different parts of that system are supposed to serve as checks on each other, especially in their decisions regarding those individuals who are the clients of the system. Thus, with respect to individual decisions, the criminal justice system is an intentional "nonsystem," in the sense that our democratic society does not want a single "system manager" who would be able in an unchecked way to direct the large array of government power and resources against those accused of criminal acts.

This intentional internal fragmentation with regard to individual decisions need not be translated into comparable fragmentation in the policy decisions made by and about the various parts of the system. Because the decisions made at any stage of the system can affect the nature and magnitude of the problems and workloads imposed on the others, it is clearly necessary that those influences be taken into account when policy changes are being considered and when resources are allocated.

Furthermore, each part of the system contributes to the combined objectives of controlling crime and doing so with justice, due process, and regard for individual rights. Resources allocated to one part of the system may conserve more resources in another part, while advancing these objectives. It is thus most important to consider such system-wide planning at the managerial level, and certainly at the strategic level.

The President's Commission on Law Enforcement and Administration of Justice, in its 1967 report, made an urgent plea for such planning for the criminal justice system. That planning was supposed to be grounded in solid theory, based on valid data, and was to consider the system-wide implication of policy choices made about any element of the criminal justice system. That plea was translated into a legislative mandate with the passage by Congress of the Omnibus Safe Streets and Crime Control Act of 1968, which created the Law Enforcement Assistance Administration and called for the creation of criminal justice planning agencies in each state. To provide some resources for those planning agencies to implement their plans, each was given federal LEAA funds in the order of 5 percent of their states' expenditures on the criminal justice system—not many dollars in absolute terms but a reasonable increment with which to be effective if they could.

The creation of that LEAA program initiated an era of naïve optimism regarding the prospects of rational planning for the criminal justice system. Now, over ten years later, most observers have concluded that most of the planning efforts have been notoriously weak and ineffectual, and the allocation of the LEAA funds has been characterized much more by a highly political and often arbitrary process, with very little contribution from system-wide planning or from the rational analysis initially envisioned.

A major reason for this failure is the inadequacy of the knowledge base on which to develop rational planning, and of the tools available for planners to carry out their assigned tasks. I have been involved in trying to provide such tools, first with Richard Larson with a batch-process model of a total criminal justice system, and subsequently with Jacob Belkin and William Glass in translating those concepts into an interactive model adapted to meet the needs of the nontechnician. Those models, JUSSIM I (which depicts the downstream flow in the criminal justice system) and JUSSIM II (which deals with the feedback of recidivists), have been widely distributed, but one could not validly claim that they have been widely used. The reasons for this are complicated, but they include the difficulties in generating data for even these simplified models, suspicion of the validity of the theoretical underpinnings and the consequent calculations in the models, antipathy by nontechnical users toward calculations with which they are not totally familiar, and a reluctance among many decision makers to become too rational about issues that are so inherently political as those involved in decisions about crime and punishment.

In his book *Reducing Delinquency: A Strategic Planning Approach,* Gregory Falkin follows in this tradition. He attempts to illuminate the various aspects of the issues that must be addressed in pursuing a strategic approach to planning. He properly identifies the kinds of objectives which the criminal justice system pursues, and relates these to the limited approaches available to the criminal justice system, as well as preventive approaches outside the system. These various categorizations are useful, partly because the different disciplines and professions involved with the criminal justice system can use the same construct to mean very different notions. For example, major debate centers around "recidivism rate": the police argue that the "recidivism rate" is over 75 percent, while corrections officials disagree vigorously, and insist that the "recidivism rate" is under one-third. It is entirely possible, of course, that both could be right, because police focus on a *re-arrest* recidivism rate, whereas corrections officials focus on a *re-institutionalization* recidivism rate, causing an arrest not to result in an imprisonment. The entire field of criminal justice needs much more precise definitions of its basic concepts to avoid such silly disagreements, and Falkin's chapters 2 and 3 move in that direction.

Because the criminal justice system has no individuals or agencies charged with overall managerial responsibility, most of the individuals who function within the system become victims of organizational myopia. Most such functionaries know intimately the operation of their own agency or system component, but they know very little about the operation or behavior of the others on which their decisions may have an impact. The kind of descriptive material included in chapter 4 provides a valuable resource for those concerned with improvement of the operation of the total system. The state criminal justice planning agencies (the SPA's) created under the Safe Streets and Crime Control Act are charged with providing such descriptive information, and a few states have done this extremely effectively.

Ultimately, the key to the development of a capability to perform strategic planning will require valid causal models with good estimates of the parameters in those models. There have been a number of attempts to develop such models, and Falkin's model, summarized in chapter 5, formulated in appendix A, and with parameters estimated in appendix B, is an ambitious attempt in that tradition. Inevitably, such models tend to become complex and elaborate because so many variables affect the behavior of the criminal justice system. Any formulation of such a model requires a choice between a highly simplified model which is reasonably "transparent" (in that the nature of the relationships are clear but highly over-simplified) and much more complex models where the relationships are described in much more elaborate detail (with inevitably limited knowledge of all the relationships that go into such a model), and where the cause and consequences of a change become much more difficult to discern.

In formulating his model, Falkin has brought in a large number of the factors that should be included in such an overall formulation. Thus, his overall model illustrates the ways in which the alternative choices must eventually be addressed. Unfortunately, however, our causal knowledge of the behavior of the criminal justice system, of the constraints on that system, and of the exogenous socioeconomic factors contributing to or inhibiting crime, are known only poorly—we may know theoretically the proper sign of an association, but we are virtually totally ignorant in terms of valid quantitative relationships about the magnitude of the effects. One can estimate those relationships statistically, but the magnitudes of the *causal* coefficients are still largely unknown. Thus, as Falkin properly points out, his model and analyses provide a *structure* within which a wide variety of policy issues can and should be addressed, but the specific forms of the relationships must be regarded at this point as only illustrative. As such, they represent an important agenda for future research into those relationships. For policy makers, they represent the way to think about these strategic planning questions, but they are not yet available for explicitly weighing the tradeoffs involved in virtually all choices within the criminal justice system. In this regard, Falkin has made an important contribution to the development of strategic planning capability. Hopefully, a succession of more narrowly focused research results will accumulate to fill in the matrix, thereby strengthening the overall framework that is needed for rational decisions about crime, the criminal justice system, and social programs in general.

Alfred Blumstein
Carnegie-Mellon University

Preface

If crime in this nation is to be reduced, a strategic crime control plan must be designed. The title of this book reflects the two aspects of strategic criminal justice planning discussed throughout. In the broad sense, the book is concerned with developing a framework for designing strategic plans. The framework was refined in an application to reducing juvenile delinquency in the California juvenile justice system. The book was written for an audience concerned with both the methodology behind strategic planning and its use in criminal justice. This dual topic evolved by combining two areas of research: policy science methodology and strategic criminal justice planning.

The first stage in this research was the development of a general policy science research framework that could be used to assess the impact of government programs on political goals. The framework sets forth a research design, a general procedure for policy science research. Developing the framework involved a study of several policy research methods, such as planning programming budgeting systems (PPBS) and cost-benefit analysis, and a separate, but equally important, study of the use of research in the policy-making process. The focus during this stage of the research was on structuring policy research around the needs of policymakers—and the realities of the political process. Out of this concern came a research framework for evaluating the impact of budgets, programs, and rule changes on political goals, or, more specifically, social indicators of policy goals.

As the policy research framework began to take shape, it became apparent that it could be useful only insofar as it could be applied empirically to specific policy concerns. Consequently, a search for a substantive policy area led to an investigation of the criminal justice system. The field of criminal justice planning offered an opportunity to develop a strategy to ameliorate one of our nation's most serious problems.

Developing the policy research framework and analyzing the criminal justice system were complementary areas of research, and each gained from the other. The overriding objective throughout this research was to use objective, scientific policy research methods to work toward a better understanding of the consequences of criminal justice policies. What follows, then, is the foundation on which to build criminal justice policy research and to design a strategic plan to reduce crime. The conclusion of this book is that proactive policies designed to prevent crime are more cost-effective and more just than reactive criminal justice policies.

The text is organized to combine the two areas of research into a unified topic. Chapter 1 sets the stage by discussing the need for strategic planning in the criminal justice system. Chapter 2 takes a systems view of criminal justice policy, discussing the key theoretical variables in the system. The relationships among the variables are proposed in chapter 3. A policy-relevant synthesis of two "opportunity structure" theories of crime, labeled "relative opportunity," is presented, and several propositions to be analyzed later are spelled out. The decision-making process in the California juvenile justice system is then described in chapter 4. This verbal model of the adjudication and corrections processes is expressed as a mathematical model in appendixes A and B. In chapter 5, the effect of a number of criminal justice policies is analyzed by simulating the behavior of the California juvenile justice system on the computer. The book concludes with a summary of the major points and a discussion of strategic criminal justice planning.

Acknowledgments

Every author is indebted to those who provide assistance, support, intellectual stimulation, criticisms, and encouragement. I am particularly grateful to all who in one way or another helped me during the course of my research.

I would especially like to thank Alfred Blumstein for writing the foreword to this book. His work in the field was inspirational while I was writing the book, and he is uniquely qualified to comment on it.

While at Cornell University, my special committee members, Christopher Babb, Paul Eberts, and Alan Hahn, were most generous with criticism of my work. Since my first orientation week as a graduate student, Chris Babb inspired me by setting an example of intellectual abilities toward which I felt I should strive. Paul Eberts provided the direction by teaching his social science perspective for analyzing public policies. Without his research as a model and without his encouragement, I am certain this book would not have come to be.

Michael Walden, James Zelenski, and William Frisbee, all fellow graduate students, were gracious with their time and contributed significantly to this research effort by acting as a sounding board for ideas.

Since arriving at the U.S. Department of Justice, I have had an opportunity to apply the approach to strategic planning developed in this book to the field of corrections. I am particularly grateful to James F. Hoobler for providing me with this opportunity; as a result, I have been able to clarify a number of issues in this book. In collaborating with Robert J. Comiskey on designing a strategy for federal corrections, numerous discussions have also led to improvements in the book.

This project could not have been completed as efficiently as it was without the typing and editorial assistance of Lorraine Cafini. I am also indebted to Mary Ose for typing the original draft.

Finally, my greatest thanks are extended to my wife, Debbie, who braved more cold Ithaca winters than she preferred so that I could study and write this book.

Crime reflects the character of a people. This is the painful fact we do not want to face. Other premises are easier to accept, other causes easier to control. There is no simple reform for defective character . . . in America we have cultivated crime and hence have reaped a bountiful crop. Crime is the ultimate human degradation. A civilized people have no higher duty than to do everything within their power to seek its reduction. We can prevent nearly all of the crime now suffered in America—if we care. Our character is at stake.

—Ramsey Clark

Reducing Delinquency

A Strategic Planning Approach

be best explained by comparing it to tactical planning.[19] Tactical planning is a form of long-range management control. With a specific set of objectives identified and programs adopted, emphasis is placed on ensuring that resources are available and distributed in the most efficient way for meeting the objectives. Administrators plan ahead for the deployment of the workforce to meet future needs. Resources are allocated to competing programs and components of the process by forecasting future needs from past experience. The central focus of tactical planning is on future budgets.

Strategic planning, on the other hand, looks at all the components in the system and the causes of broad trends. As Daniel Glaser explains, strategic criminal justice planning is concerned with "the explanation, projection and government manipulation of those key variables on which most aspects of crime and delinquency depend."[20] Strategic planning is geared toward clarifying issues so that sound policies may be adopted. In other words, strategic planning is concerned with setting priorities within global systems and developing guidelines to meet the objectives. Robert Anthony has defined *strategic planning* as

> . . . the process of deciding on objectives of the organization, on changes in these objectives, on the resources used to attain these objectives, and on the policies that are to govern the acquisition, use, and disposition of these resources.[21]

Strategic planning is a form of long-range planning in government. As such, its central concern in criminal justice is with determining *how to restructure the system so as to best ensure public safety and enhance justice within the confines of available resources and political considerations.* Strategic planning encompasses the dual processes of policy formulation and policy implementation. In the formulation stage, attention is given to developing a strategy to achieve policy goals. Policymakers decide on goals and priorities, and policy scientists or planners try to find the mix of programs that will reach the goals most economically and equitably. Once a mix of programs is selected, a strategy for implementing them should be devised. In these two phases of strategic planning, policy officials decide what they would like to achieve and how their goals can be reached.

It is essential that there be an ongoing dialogue between policy officials and planners because targets may have to be changed as knowledge about the system's behavior is gained. In other words, as policy scientists learn more about the structural relationships within the system, which place limits on goal attainment, targets may have to be revised. Specifically, tradeoffs may have to be made in light of predictions about the impact of programs on goals. At any rate, the planning function during the policy formulation stage is to design a strategy, that is, to find a combination of rules and budgets for criminal justice programs. Strategic planning can lend some rigor to the policy formulation process. Although policymakers maintain the prerogative for establishing objectives, priorities will be set on the basis of an informed comparison of the relative merits of policy and program option. In the end, targets are more likely to reflect a realistic understanding of the system's limited ability to reduce crime and enhance justice. In short, strategic planning is a method of establishing policy goals and making tradeoffs among them, designing a strategy for achieving the goals, and then revising the goals in light of new information on the feasibility of reaching them.

Although the feasibility of implementing programs must be given careful consideration, strategies for implementation are beyond the scope of this book. However, the important aspects of implementation should be mentioned. Political considerations may enter into the formulation of programs. A program perceived to be just by one group may place hardships on other groups. For example, gun control is advocated as a means of reducing violent crimes but receives strong opposition from lobby groups. In short, programs to reduce crime will have differential effects on the rights of individuals; therefore, the feasibility of implementing these programs depends in part on their impact on justice.

Strategies for implementation comprise three elements: program plans, policy-level intervention, and organizational reform. After policymakers decide which programs should be implemented, they can devise a strategy to ensure that the programs receive adequate funding. This is the program planning dimension. Since programs are not always implemented as conceived, policymakers may have to intervene in the administration of programs. Policy-level intervention can be achieved through informal guidelines or formal policies (that is, rules) for program managers to abide by. Policy intervention is central to strategic planning, and it is discussed throughout the book in terms of rules to guide decisionmakers toward the goals established by policy officials. Some programs cannot be implemented under existing institutional arrangements. Consequently, organizational reforms may have to be considered. Together, these three aspects of implementation can be used to ensure that programs are as successful as anticipated.

The policy science approach to strategic planning is based on four key elements: coordination, comprehensiveness, causal analysis, and cost-effectiveness. Strategic plans must *coordinate* the programs, interactions, and decisions of subsystems. Plans are *comprehensive* when they have considered all possible courses of action for achieving the goals. *Causal analysis* is central to strategic planning because a strategy must be based on some knowledge of how to reach one's goals. Finally, the plan must be *cost-effective*; that is, for any outlay of resources it has the most effective programs for reaching the system's goals.

The criminal justice system comprises many decision-making units or subsystems. The ability of the system to control crime justly depends on the performance of its interdependent subunits. Fundamental to strategic planning, therefore, are policies to coordinate the activities of subsystems. For example, police investigations should be coordinated with prosecutions. Similarly, sentencing decisions can be coordinated within the judiciary through sentencing guidelines. Fragmented decision making can easily result in low levels of goal attainment. If crime and delinquency are to be reduced, then decisions made throughout the system must be coordinated.

In developing a strategic plan, the analyst must study the entire system. If viewing one subsystem in isolation can result in a fragmented policy, then omitting one or more subsystems from a plan will compound the problem. In order to design a strategic plan, the interrelationships among *all* decision-making units that affect the system's ability to reach its goals should be analyzed. The effects of *all* programs on policy goals must be assessed. This is essential if strategic plans are to be comprehensive.

Unlike tactical plans, strategic plans require causal analysis. Strategies are built on theories that explain the relationships among programs and goals. The important aspects of strategic planning are brought together in this book through the policy science research framework. The framework applies two quantitative techniques to model the criminal justice system. Econometrics (or regression analysis) is used to test hypotheses about the system's behavior, specifically the impact of programs on goals. The interrelationships among decision-making units are modeled with systems dynamics, a technique conducive to simulating the behavior of large, complex social systems on the computer. Together, these two modeling techniques can be used to analyze the relative cost-effectiveness of a wide range of programs.

Perhaps the most significant aspect of the policy science framework is that it focuses on both the costs and the effects of programs. Most criminal justice policy studies have emphasized one or the other. In fact, econometric models have dealt primarily with the impact of programs. Strategic plans cannot be developed unless the costs and effects are analyzed together. Thus, a major purpose of this book is to demonstrate how the cost-effectiveness of programs such as preventive detention and juvenile diversion can be analyzed.

This book takes a proactive approach to strategic planning. Proactive policymakers try to anticipate problems and control the system's behavior. Rather than reacting to crises, such as overcrowded prisons, proactive policymakers attempt to anticipate them and take preventive action. Policy choices are made only after considering the consequences of the policy options (for example, build more prisons, increase the use of alternatives to incarceration, reduce the number of commitments). Instead of reacting to sentencing decisions, which increase the prison population, proactive policymakers try to control sentencing outcomes. They try to influence sentencing and correctional programs because that has profound effects on the higher goals of crime reduction and justice.

Strategic planning is but one of several methods of goal attainment in political systems. Alternative approaches range from strategies based on individual decisions to maximizing a social welfare function. Braybrooke and

Lindblom call these two models "disjointed incrementalism" and the "synoptic ideal" (that is, the rational model in political science).[22] Synoptic policy analysis assumes that all society's preferences and all policy alternatives and their consequences are known. The analyst attempts to find the most efficient policies for maximizing the social welfare function. Disjointed incrementalism is a strategy of decision appropriate for "decisions effecting small or incremental change and not guided by a high level of understanding."[23] Braybrooke and Lindblom acknowledge that there are other methods of goal attainment, but they argue that disjointed incrementalism is conducive to the limited intellectual capabilities of human beings and insufficient information for analyzing policies.[24]

Strategic planning is different from synoptic analysis because no assumptions are made about preferences and the effects of policy options. In fact, strategic planning is an analytic process for specifying objectives and program options and clarifying their relationships. In short, it can help policymakers formulate priorities. Unlike synoptic analysis, political feasibility is considered to be an important criterion in designing a strategic plan. Although analyzing the political feasibility of criminal justice policies is outside the scope of this book, no strategy can be implemented unless it is feasible.

Strategic planning is also quite different from disjointed incrementalism. Strategic plans must be developed from whatever data are available, and they work within the limitations of social science methodology. A central aspect of strategic planning is a search for knowledge. Although change may come about incrementally, cost-effective goal attainment demands that a comprehensive restructuring of the system be considered.

Daniel Glaser has suggested that there are four stages to strategic criminal justice planning. Policy scientists must work to

[1] . . . identify the general principles which determine shifts in the definition of crime and the reaction to offenses . . .
[2] determine, as rigorously as possible, the causes of the behavior that society designates as criminal . . .
[3] devise policies for the allocation of resources and responsibilities among various agencies, in and out of the justice system . . .
[4] plan a knowledge-building apparatus, to try to institutionalize research organizations and procedures for evaluating criminal justice practices, and to deliver feedback on effectiveness to key decision makers.[25]

The remainder of this book is devoted to the last three stages. Chapter 3 discusses the causes of crime. Chapter 5 analyzes resource allocations and rules, Glaser's third stage. Finally, the policy science research framework, which is presented in chapter 3, is a method for increasing knowledge about criminal justice policies. A public policy strategy to reduce crime can be based on research designed to predict the impact of government programs on crime reduction targets and indicators of justice. By focusing on one criminal justice system it will be possible to demonstrate an approach for developing a strategic plan to reduce crime and enhance justice.

The California Juvenile Justice System

This analysis focuses on policy making in the California juvenile justice system. The California system was selected for a few reasons. California has the nation's highest crime rate. If the National Advisory Commission's targets are met by 1983, they will indeed have to be met in California. An advantage of isolating one state for analysis is that one can learn some general principles of crime reduction and apply them to other states. Finally, a pragmatic motive for studying California is that it publishes the most complete set of criminal justice data.

Although the criminal justice system is typically thought of as one system, this research is based on a significantly different viewpoint. The criminal justice system may be divided into two analytically distinct systems: an adult criminal justice system and a juvenile criminal justice system. In fact, the President's commission describes a separate juvenile justice system in its chapter on juvenile delinquency.[26] There are several reasons for doing this. First, juveniles and adults may commit the same types of crimes, but they may do so for different reasons. Thus, policies to control crime may have to differ depending on whether the target is adult or juvenile criminals.

Second, the criminal justice system is structured so that juveniles are handled separately and differently from adults. Juveniles are detained in separate facilities, and they are adjudicated in separate courts. Indeed, the philosophies regarding the treatment of juveniles and adults are quite different. Decisions made about juvenile cases are often made by different decisionmakers. Many police departments have special juvenile units. Probation plays a primary role in the juvenile criminal justice system, including the prosecutorial role that the district attorney plays in the adult criminal justice system.

Perhaps the greatest justification for isolating the juvenile justice system as a phenomenon for analysis is that youths under 18 account for a significant portion of the criminal justice system's workload and crime. It is estimated that the juvenile justice system uses about 30 percent of the money spent on the entire criminal justice system. Furthermore, juvenile delinquents may be responsible for as much as 40 percent of predatory crimes committed in California. If juvenile delinquency can be reduced, then, to the extent that juvenile delinquents become adult criminals, adult crime will also be reduced. The National Advisory Commission's first "priority for action" is the reduction of juvenile delinquency:

The highest attention must be given to preventing juvenile delinquency, to minimizing the involvement of young offenders in the juvenile and criminal justice system, and to reintegrating delinquents and young offenders into the community. By 1983 the rate of delinquency cases coming before courts that would be crimes if committed by adults should be cut to half the 1973 rate.[27]

Organization of the Chapters

The chapters in this book are organized around the theme of developing a strategic plan to reduce crime. The approach may be described as the application of quantitative techniques to qualitative criminal justice concepts. The policy science research framework essentially applies general systems theory to criminal justice policy systems by scientifically testing propositions about the system's structure and simulating its behavior. Accordingly, the book is organized in the following parts: (1) a systems view of criminal justice policy, (2) a methodological chapter, (3) a description of the decision-making process in the California juvenile justice system, (4) a stock flow model of the California system's structure, (5) simulations of the system's behavior, and (6) a conclusion.

Chapter 2 is divided into five sections. In the first, criminal justice policy is placed in context as one of many generalized policy systems. The elements of criminal justice policy systems are then described. The elements include public policy inputs, criminal justice agencies as components or throughputs, and the reduction of crime and enhancement of justice as outputs. Various forms of justice are clarified by presenting a typology of justice. Then crime reduction programs and programs that affect justice are described. The chapter concludes with a justification for analyzing criminal justice policy at the state level.

In chapter 3, the policy science research framework used to design strategic plans is described. The framework is developed as follows. First, the relationships among programs and goals that should be considered in any policy analysis are described. Second, a policy-relevant theory (labeled relative opportunity) of the causes and controls of delinquency is proposed. Third, a method of modeling the criminal justice system in order to design a strategic plan is discussed. Fourth, criteria for evaluating public policies are defined. Together, these four features (policy analysis, causal analysis, modeling, and evaluation) compose the framework, which is used in later chapters to analyze criminal justice policies.

The discussion in chapter 4 follows juveniles as they flow through the California juvenile justice system. Each section describes the various decisions that police, probation, courts, and correctional authorities make. Detailed flow charts depict graphically the flow of juveniles through the adjudication and correctional processes. The chapter concludes with a comparison of incarceration programs and noninstitutional corrections.

Chapter 5 analyzes the cost-effectiveness of several policy simulations. To set the stage for the analysis, a nontechnical description of the simulation model of the California juvenile justice system (described in chapter 4) is presented. After reading this section the mathematically-oriented reader should read appendixes A and B. Appendix A presents the mathematical model. The model essentially combines two quantitative techniques, systems dynamics and econometrics. So that the reader can more easily understand the simulation model, it is developed following the order of the adjudications and corrections processes outlined in chapter 4. The method used to estimate the structural parameters for the simulation model is presented in appendix B. The theory of relative opportunity is operationalized and statistically tested; the parameter estimates (for costs, transition probabilities, and time) which will be used in the simulations are discussed in a narrative that accompanies a series of tables.

After reading about the model, the reader should complete chapter 5. First, a preventive detention policy is compared to a juvenile diversion policy. The simulation results show that juvenile diversion is a cost-effective alternative to preventive detention. In order to develop a strategic plan, the relative merits of deterrence and prevention programs must be assessed. A second set of policy simulations leads to the conclusion that reactive policies based on punishment are less cost-effective and less just than proactive policies designed to prevent crime. The chapter concludes by discussing the reliability of these findings. The text ends with a chapter that summarizes the research and discusses some future applications and the role of strategic planning in the political process (chapter 6).

Notes

1. Federal Bureau of Investigation (FBI), *Uniform Crime Reports, 1973* (Washington: Government Printing Office (GPO), 1974), p. 59.

2. Ibid.

3. Calculated from FBI, *Uniform Crime Reports, 1973*, p. 59.

4. The President's Commission on Law Enforcement and Administration of Justice, *The Challenge of Crime in a Free Society*, p. 21.

5. Ibid., p. 49.

6. Michael J. Hindelang et al., *Sourcebook of Criminal Justice Statistics, 1973*, p. 140.

7. Ibid., p. 141.

8. Mark Hoffman, *Criminal Justice Planning*, pp. 7, 8.

9. LEAA, *Sixth Annual Report of LEAA*, p. 4.

10. Ibid.

11. National Advisory Commission on Criminal Justice Standards and Goals, *A National Strategy to Reduce Crime*, p. 7.

12. Eleanor Chelimsky, *High Impact Anti-Crime Program*, p. 425.

13. Ibid., p. 448.

14. James Q. Wilson, *Thinking about Crime*, chap. 3.

15. For an exception see Alfred Blumstein and Richard Larson, "Models of a Total Criminal Justice System," pp. 199-232. Although Blumstein and Larson's model covers the entire system, they fail to include the other two issues in their analysis.

16. For an innovative approach to institutionalizing policy research in federal social agencies, see Walter Williams, *Social Policy Research and Analysis*.

17. Harold Lasswell, "The Policy Orientation," p. 15.

18. Yehezkel Dror, *Ventures in Policy Sciences*, p. 14.

19. This comparison is based on Daniel Glaser, *Strategic Criminal Justice Planning*, chap. 1.

20. Ibid., p. 10.

21. Robert N. Anthony, "Planning and Control Systems: A Framework for Analysis," Harvard University Graduate School of Business Management, 1966, p. 16; cited in Glaser, ibid., p. 4.

22. David Braybrooke and Charles E. Lindblom, *A Strategy of Decision*.

23. Ibid., p. 71.

24. Ibid., p. 61.

25. Glaser, *Strategic Criminal Justice Planning*, pp. 7-9.

26. The President's Commission, *Challenge of Crime in a Free Society*, chap. 3.

27. The National Advisory Commission, *A National Strategy to Reduce Crime*, p. 23.

2 A Systems View of Criminal Justice Policy

This book is based on the premise that criminal justice institutions may be viewed as a system. Observing a lack of coordination and cooperation among criminal justice agencies, often to the extent of hostility, some critics have concluded that U.S. criminal justice is a "nonsystem."[1] In this book problems of coordination and cooperation are considered as reflections of the structure and behavior of the criminal justice system. Accordingly, the design of a strategic plan to solve these problems and reduce crime requires that criminal justice policy be analyzed from a general systems perspective.

The notion that criminal justice may be viewed as a "policy system" is introduced in the next section. After the introduction to policy systems, the various criminal justice elements (inputs, outputs, and components such as the police and courts) are discussed in more detail. Following this, a typology of justice is presented. The typology of justice is perhaps the most important aspect of this chapter because it will be used to clarify the various ways in which crime control policies differentially affect the rights of victims and offenders. Programs for reducing crime and enhancing justice are described in the following section. The chapter concludes with a rationale for analyzing criminal justice policies at the state level. The specific concepts discussed (deterrence, justice, and others) will be, for the most part, familiar to criminal justice scholars and practitioners. The unique aspect of this chapter is that they are systematically brought together so that the cost-effectiveness of criminal justice policies can be assessed.

Criminal Justice as a Policy System

In the past ten years, a number of studies have analyzed the criminal system from a systems perspective.[2] This book departs from previous systems analyses by formalizing criminal justice as a *policy system*. Every government policy can be conceptualized as a generalized policy system. Figure 2-1 depicts the essential elements of a generalized policy system. A policy is a combination of means and ends within a unit of analysis (for example, a state or community). The system's boundary is defined by the goals toward which policymakers wish to have the system strive and every possible course of action that may be taken to meet those objectives. Thus, from a general systems perspective, *government policy* may be defined as an authoritative ranking of objectives combined with an official set of rules to guide decisionmakers and resources to enable them to

13

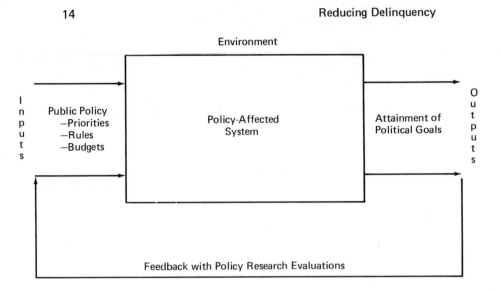

Figure 2-1. A Generalized Policy System.

achieve the objectives. This definition of policy accentuates the two aspects of every policy: the ends and the means.

Figure 2-1 conceives of inputs into a system as the public policy. This includes rules to guide the actions of decisionmakers, budget appropriations, and a ranking of objectives (that is, priorities). Policymakers formulate policy outside the system's boundary, and decisionmakers within the system are responsible for implementing the policy.[3] As figure 2-1 shows, the output of the system is attainment of political goals. In other words, the output is the extent to which implementing a public policy meets its objectives. The purpose of analyzing a policy-affected system, therefore, is to determine how well the combination of rules and budgets adopted by policymakers directs the various decisionmakers in the system toward achieving the policy goals. Any unintended consequences, that is, any external effects or "externalities," are outside the bounds of the policy system being analyzed. For the total polity, externalities may be extremely important. The analyst must, therefore, define the policy system's boundary so that all relevant goals are included. Finally, the bottom line in figure 2-1 indicates that, in addition to other factors, policy research will be considered in the formulation of public policies.

Criminal justice policy systems are a class of generalized policy systems. Figure 2-2 depicts a criminal justice policy system. As previously stated, the system's boundary is defined by the ends and means of the policy. The two goals are crime reduction and justice. The means involve punishment and prevention. The criminal justice system includes police, courts, and corrections. These institutions form a domain of punishment. In other words, the criminal justice

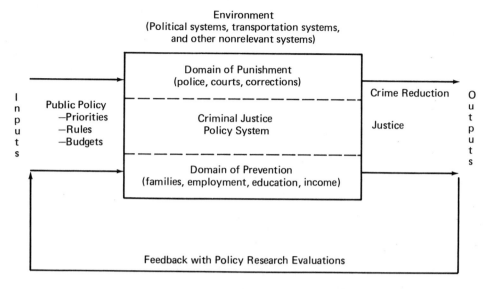

Figure 2-2. A Criminal Justice Policy System.

system, as usually conceived, is an institution of punishment. Other social factors, such as family lifestyles, employment opportunities, education, and income, affect criminal justice outputs. They do not involve punishment, and therefore they are parts of the domain of prevention. All factors that do not affect crime and justice are in the system's environment. As figure 2-2 depicts, the political system is part of the environment. The inputs into the criminal justice system come from policymakers in the political system. The political system does not, however, implement punishment and prevention programs. Thus, even though criminal justice policies are established within the political system, the polity remains outside the system's boundary.

There are several other characteristics of general systems theory not apparent from figure 2-2. They are as follows: purposefulness, structure, process, behavior, and levels of generality.[4] Policy systems are *purposeful* systems in that they serve *social functions* with government policy as an input. (It is government intervention that distinguishes policy systems from other purposeful systems.) The function of criminal law is social control. If the system fails to serve its purpose well, there may be profound and grave consequences. What may result is the victimization of numerous individuals and, more important, a deterioration of the social fabric.

In addition to social control, there are three other basic social functions: production, allocation, and staffing or socialization.[5] That which is produced must be allocated to the population. The allocation function, then, involves distributing all "values," physical and symbolic. In the criminal justice system, the distribution of social goods (criminal justice programs) and social bads (crimes) creates justice or injustice. Thus, the two goals (reducing crime and enhancing justice) are derived from the social functions which the system fulfills.

The components of the system form the system's *structure*. The police, courts, and corrections will have certain patterns of relationships among themselves and with the public and offenders. For example, the degree of respect for the law, the ability of the system to carry out its threat of punishment, and its ability to reform offenders are all structural variables. These structural relationships, or, more properly, the structure of the system, are the causes of the system's *behavior*. A policy system's behavior, therefore, is observed by noting how well its components work together to attain the system's goals. The system's *process* is a set of programs for converting inputs into outputs.[6] This involves flows of information (including technologies), materials, and people. Chapter 4 shows in detail how the process of punishment (that is, adjudication and corrections) works in the California juvenile justice system.

Levels of generality is a central concept in general systems theory. In combination, criminal justice policy systems are a class of generalized policy systems. Policy systems are, in turn, a class of general systems. They form a hierarchy of systems. Within each policy system there are many decision-making units. Each decision unit may be viewed as a system or, within the context of policy systems, a subsystem. Incorporating into the policy system all the decision-making units that convert inputs into outputs defines the boundary of the global system.

There are other dimensions of generality in policy systems. At the highest level the outputs of the system are goals. At a lower level they are objectives. The system may have a number of goals (for example, crime reduction and justice) and numerous objectives (that is, different types of crime and justice) for each goal. Similarly, there are a few programs within the domain of punishment. These general programs (for example, deterrence, restraint) must be implemented through a program structure, that is, a specific set of programs implemented by organizations within the policy system.[7] Most of the discussion in this chapter is conducted at the highest level of generality. When discussing specifics, one is more likely to lose sight of the broad picture, whereas at a higher level of generality all the elements essential to developing comprehensive plans to reduce crime can be discussed clearly.

Elements of the Criminal Justice System

The discussion of generalized policy systems is expanded in this section by presenting a more detailed conceptualization of criminal justice policy systems.

The elements of the criminal justice system are discussed in the following order: inputs, outputs, and components. The components include the police, courts, corrections, and citizens. Figure 2-3 is a diagrammatic representation of the global criminal justice policy system. The discussion that follows is applicable to all criminal justice systems—federal, state, and local.

In systems theory, components convert inputs (resources) into outputs (crime reduction and justice). This is accomplished by implementing programs with the objective of deterring, restraining, or reforming offenders. In policy systems, priorities and rules are established (by policymakers) to guide decisionmakers in allocating resources to programs and in administering the programs. The extent to which program objectives, such as deterrence and rehabilitation, are achieved determines the degree to which policy goals are realized. From a policy perspective, one tries to ensure that outputs are consistent with priorities; that is, the degree of goal attainment actually achieved should meet expectations. If it does not, then either priorities and rules for decisionmakers were inadequate or inappropriate or the activities of the various components (police and courts, for example) were not properly coordinated.

Criminal Justice Inputs

The main input into the criminal justice system is public policy (see figure 2-3). Public policy may be thought of in this regard as guidance for the operation of the criminal justice system. This guidance may be in the form of priorities for allocating scarce resources and rules which place constraints on the system's behavior. Admittedly, priorities are rarely stated explicitly in practice. At best, one might be able to surmise them by inference from the distribution of the budget to the various criminal justice programs. If programs do not receive the amount of resources one might expect from policy statements, then it would seem that policymakers are engaging in political rhetoric. Strategic planning ensures that objectives and their relative importance are stated explicitly. Indeed, one of the main purposes of strategic planning is to help policymakers articulate their objectives and priorities.

Policymakers must determine the level of financing and the distribution of budgets in the criminal justice system. The amount of resources, primarily workforce and capital, that the criminal justice system receives to a very great extent determines how effectively the system reaches its goals. The distribution of the budget (that is, the allocation to the police, courts, and corrections) must reach a proper balance if the system is to operate smoothly. If there is an imbalance in the distribution of resources, in other words, if one of the sectors is overfinanced relative to another sector, then the entire system will operate less effectively.

In addition to allocating resources, policymakers establish pragmatic rules

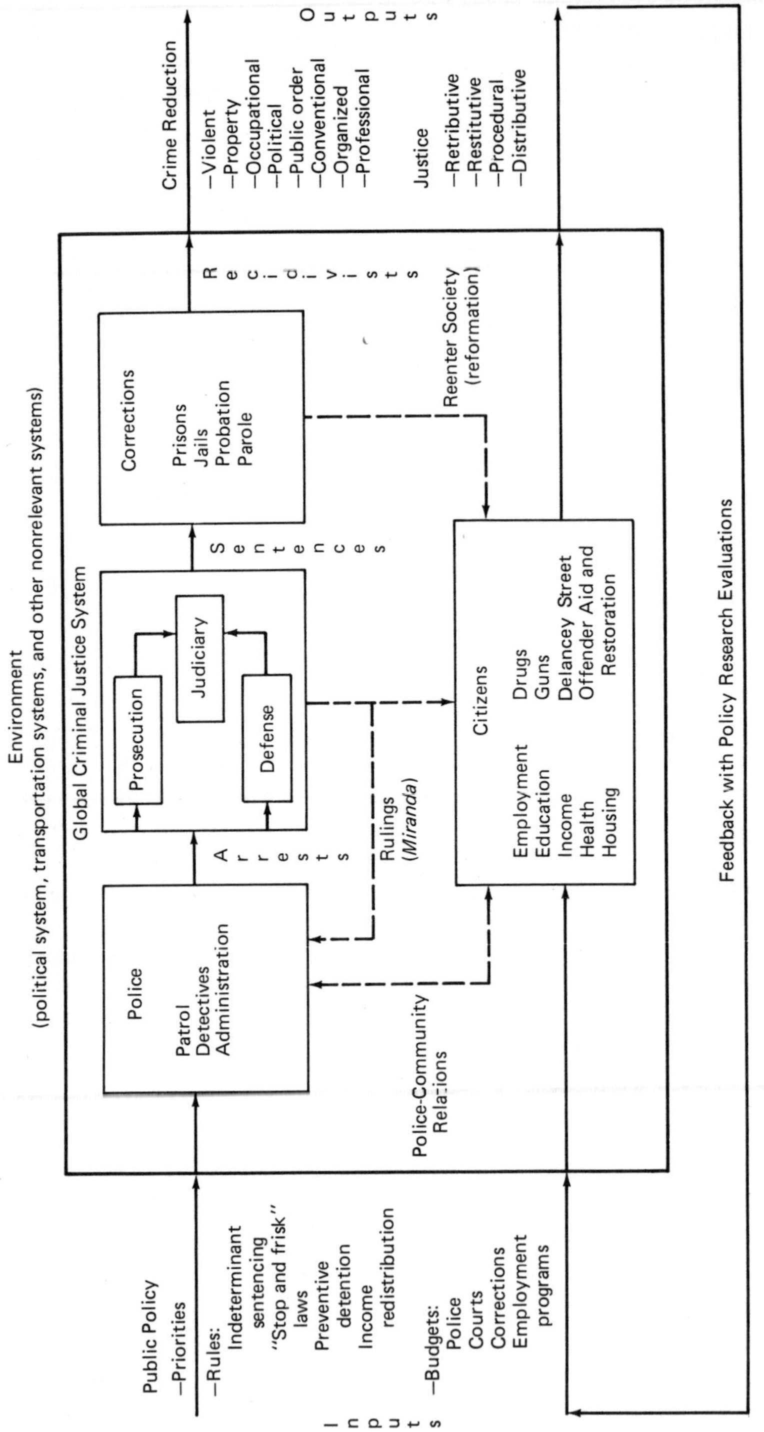

Environment
(political system, transportation systems, and other nonrelevant systems)

Global Criminal Justice System

Public Policy
—Priorities

—Rules:
  Indeterminant
  sentencing
  "Stop and frisk"
  laws
  Preventive
  detention
  Income
  redistribution

—Budgets:
  Police
  Courts
  Corrections
  Employment
  programs

Inputs

Police
  Patrol
  Detectives
  Administration

Arrests

Prosecution

Judiciary

Defense

Sentences

Corrections
  Prisons
  Jails
  Probation
  Parole

Rulings
(Miranda)

Police-Community
Relations

Citizens
  Employment   Drugs
  Education   Guns
  Income   Delancey Street
  Health   Offender Aid and
  Housing   Restoration

Reenter Society
(reformation)

Recidivists

Crime Reduction
  —Violent
  —Property
  —Occupational
  —Political
  —Public order
  —Conventional
  —Organized
  —Professional

Outputs

Justice
  —Retributive
  —Restitutive
  —Procedural
  —Distributive

Feedback with Policy Research Evaluations

Figure 2-3. The Global State Criminal Justice Policy System.

for running the system. Rules are necessary to guide the conduct of agents within the system. For example, the penal code, which in this context may be labeled the "rule of law," guides the public by proscribing certain acts, and it guides judges in sentencing violators. Rules are also extremely important because some decisions made within the policy system work at cross purposes. For example, if a district attorney decides not to prosecute a case, then police resources used in investigating the case are largely wasted. An important part of policy research is to study and suggest rules to coordinate the activities of subunits. Included here are policy rules that guide police investigation and arrest, police-community relations, and the type of treatment accorded offenders.

Criminal Justice Outputs

There are numerous outputs of criminal justice policy systems (see figure 2-3). Each output is associated with certain events occurring in the operation of the system. Instead of considering broad categories of crime, there are a number of reasons for thinking in terms of more narrowly defined behavior, such as the number of crimes committed by embezzlers, prostitutes, or teenage rapists.

First, different crimes are caused by different factors and are more cost-effectively controlled by different programs. Programs designed to reduce organized crime (for example, organized crime strike forces) are inappropriate for reducing juvenile delinquency. Furthermore, programs implemented to reduce a certain type of crime may have side effects on other types of crime. For example, legalizing gambling may turn organized crime toward other more profitable criminal ventures. Strategic planning requires that policymakers establish priorities for reducing specific types of crime. Since different types of crime arise from different social factors, policy scientists may have to develop several theories of crime causality so that a cost-effective mix of programs can be developed.

Second, states differ in their definitions of offenses and their reactions to them. To lump heroin and marijuana into a drug category could produce misleading inferences about a state's treatment of its offenders. All states have harsh penalties for heroin dealers. Some emphasize treatment for addicts instead of punishment. Possession of marijuana has been decriminalized (that is, punishment usually entails small fines) in some states, while others enforce harsh penalties.

Third, a community may have a preference for controlling certain types of crime more than others. Needless to say, all communities prefer as little crime as possible. Scarce resources, however, mean that communities must decide which types of crime to reduce most. Every dollar spent on the reduction of drug offenses, for example, is one less dollar that can be spent on the reduction of robberies, burglaries, and so on.

Because numerous relationships exist between the various types of crimes and their controls, it becomes important to categorize crime. The following list of crimes and their definitions is borrowed from Clinard and Quinney's *Criminal Behavior Systems:*

1. *Violent Personal Crime:* Includes such forms of activity as murder, assault and forcible rape. . . .
2. *Occasional Property Crime:* Includes some auto theft, shoplifting, check forgery, and vandalism. . . .
3. *Occupational Crime:* Includes embezzlement, fraudulent sales, false advertising, price fixing, black market activity, prescription violation, and antitrust violation. . . .
4. *Political Crime:* Includes treason, sedition, espionage, sabotage, military draft violations, war collaboration, radicalism, and the various other forms of protest which may be defined as criminal. . . .
5. *Public Order Crime:* Includes drunkenness, vagrancy, disorderly conduct, prostitution, homosexuality, traffic violation, and drug addiction. . . .
6. *Conventional Crime:* Includes robbery, larceny, burglary, and gang theft. . . .
7. *Organized Crime:* Includes racketeering, organized prostitution, organized gambling, control of narcotics. . . .
8. *Professional Crime:* Includes confidence games, shoplifting, pickpocketing, forgery, and counterfeiting. . . .[8]

In order to develop the framework for strategic planning, this book focuses on juvenile delinquency. Because of data limitations, violent and conventional (property) crimes are aggregated into a category labeled "juvenile victimizations." Admittedly, combining these two variables makes it impossible to analyze tradeoffs between reducing violent and property crimes. Other types of delinquency (drug law violations and minor delinquencies such as truancy, vandalism, and runaways) are also included in the analysis. In addition to juvenile victimizations, measures of justice are developed. They are based on the typology of justice which is presented in the following section.

Components of the System

The criminal justice system is composed of four components (or throughputs): police, courts, corrections, and citizens. Each of these components may be viewed as a decision-making subsystem (see figure 2-3). Each subsystem has its own goals, decision-making subunits, programs, elements, and so on. The purpose of discussing these components individually is to explain how they fit into the larger system. Of particular concern is their function within the global criminal justice system. The relationships among these four components are fundamental to how well the system meets its goals of crime control and justice.

The role or function of police in U.S. society is to maintain order under the rule of law.[9] Each state has a number of different police forces. One force is financed by the state government, and each locality may have its own police force. The police have several responsibilities. James Q. Wilson categorizes these responsibilities as (1) order maintenance, (2) crime control, and (3) social services.[10] This book analyzes only their crime control activities. The effects of arresting, booking, and turning offenders over to the prosecutor or probation are analyzed. Their order maintenance and social service functions are not explicitly incorporated in this book. That is not to say that they are unrelated to crime control.

The courts may be divided into three parts: the prosecution, the judiciary, and the defense (see figure 2-3). The prosecutor has the responsibility of charging a defendant and bringing the case before a judge. In the juvenile system, the probation officer performs certain prosecutorial functions. Accordingly, the term *prosecution* is used to denote the prosecutorial function regardless of whether it is performed by a district attorney. The judiciary has responsibility for operating that phase of the criminal justice system which most closely corresponds to the goal of justice. Judges have responsibility both for seeing that procedural rules are enforced and the rights of the accused are not violated and for sentencing the guilty (retributive justice). The defense plays the vital role of protecting the interests of the accused. The defense may be a privately retained or court-appointed attorney.

Viewed from this perspective, the court is structured as an adversarial institution. Herbert Packer calls this the "due process model" of criminal administration.[11] In practice, however, the courts may be likened to a filtering process which Packer calls the "crime control model." In this conceptualization, plea bargaining is of fundamental importance since resources are insufficient to permit the system to operate on an adversarial basis. Although plea bargaining will not be discussed any further, the crime control model forms the basis for the analysis of the juvenile justice process in chapter 4.

Corrections, as the word implies, has the responsibility, theoretically at least, for inculcating offenders with socially approved values and morals. The correctional subsystem is composed of three major components: probation, institutions, and parole (see figure 2-3). Probation plays a role both before and after offenders are sentenced. Juvenile offenders are referred to probation by the police after they are arrested. The probation department has the dual responsibility of treating these offenders and determining whether they should be adjudicated. Probation also handles juvenile and adult offenders who have been sentenced to probation by the courts. As an alternative to probation, judges may sentence violators to jail (for misdemeanors) or prison (for felonies). Juvenile offenders are usually sent to separate juvenile correctional facilities. After release from an institution, the offender may be placed in a halfway house or on parole supervision.

The fourth component of the criminal justice system is the citizen. Police, courts, and corrections work to control the number of crimes committed by citizens. Virtually all citizens, whether they are ex-offenders or whether they have never violated the law, represent potential offenders. The number of crimes they commit (and the proportion committed by ex-offenders) is a reflection of how well criminal justice policy is formulated and implemented.

Citizens' groups have direct involvement with the crime problem by helping offenders. Offender Aid and Rehabilitation (OAR) provides services and help for offenders in jail. Delancey Street, founded by John Maher, has done much to help keep ex-convicts from recidivating.[12] The citizen component of the criminal justice system is of vital importance to a system that has always suffered from a lack of resources. Citizen action is important for another reason. Self-help groups may be more effective in controlling recidivism than criminal justice authorities, such as parole officers, have been.

A distinction should be made between the role which citizens play in creating and controlling crime and the role they play in shaping policy. Through the political system they affect the public policy input into the policy system. Citizen action has been most influential in a few specialized areas of criminal justice. National associations, such as the National Rifle Association, have lobbied extensively against gun control. This lobby has recently met opposition from the National Gun Control Center. The form and nature of gun control policy in the years to come will be largely influenced by these citizen lobbies. In addition to citizen lobbies, private initiatives influence crime control policies through research (see the feedback loop in figure 2-3).[13]

The interrelationships among these four components are crucial in determining how well the system is able to meet its objectives. Perhaps the greatest problem in U.S. criminal justice has been the failure of these four components to cooordinate their actions. As the police increase their arrest rate and refer more offenders to an already overcrowded court system, there may be a dramatic effect on the crime rate. Many offenders will not be prosecuted because the courts cannot handle the caseload. Most of those convicted will be placed on probation because many judges feel that corrections have failed to rehabilitate or otherwise help offenders.[14] This lack of coordination not only discourages the professionals who work in the criminal justice system, but also causes citizens to lose respect for criminal justice institutions. As stated earlier, when people feel the system is unable to control crime in a just way, they lose respect for the law. When a legal system is not respected by those who must follow its code, incentives to abide by the law are dissipated. A natural consequence is that the law will be violated. In conclusion, coordinating the activities of the interdependent subsystems is an essential part of strategic planning.

A Typology of Criminal Justice

Popular notions of criminal justice are often based on the idea of "rendering that which is due." In this book, criminal *justice* is defined as the distribution of the monetary and psychological benefits and costs that result from controlling crime. Criminal justice is typically conceived as such matters as the right to a speedy trial or giving a guilty person his "just deserts." Underlying all conceptions of criminal justice is some notion of a distribution of costs. The social costs of crime fall on victims. They suffer the direct loss of property, injury from violence, and fear and intimidation in areas where it is unsafe to walk alone at night. The accused may be unjustly deprived of liberty while awaiting trial. This deprivation may occur because of a false arrest or because the defendant was denied bail. In either case, the accused suffers the indignities of jail, the stigma associated with an accusation, the monetary costs resulting from loss of work, and perhaps the payment of a defense. The only difference between depriving an innocent person of liberty and depriving a guilty offender is that the former offends public sensibilities while the latter often seems justifiable. Finally, the guilty may be punished. The guilty suffer the psychological "costs" of punishment while the taxpayer pays for the punishment. How these costs are distributed between the guilty and the innocent reflects on the integrity of the criminal justice system.

In this section, a typology of criminal justice is constructed. It is essential that the various aspects of justice in the criminal system be kept distinct, for no matter how well the system controls crime, the rights of various groups are affected differentially. Tradeoffs are made—often unknowingly—among the rights of victims and offenders. In developing a strategic plan, these tradeoffs should be made explicit. Furthermore, by clarifying the various forms of justice, indicators can be developed so that programs can be assessed for their impact on both crime reduction and justice.

It is useful to classify criminal justice according to four types of justice that relate to the criminal system. Retributive justice, restitutive justice, procedural justice, and protective justice are four distinct goals of criminal justice. As figure 2-4 indicates, these four forms of justice are deduced from the following two factors: how rights are guaranteed and how costs and benefits are distributed. Rights may be guaranteed by protecting the rights of victims and offenders from abuse or by restoring a balance between rights. Each type of justice also relates to who bears the burden of the costs and who benefits—victims or offenders.

The first dimension of the typology deals with protecting the rights of victims and offenders. With regard to victims, the distribution of the social costs of crime is labeled *protective justice.* As for offenders, protecting the rights of the accused and the sentenced is called *procedural justice.* In the second dimension of the typology, the rights of victims are restored either by penalizing offenders or by compensating victims. *Retributive justice* is determined by the degree to which punishments are equitable and fitted to crimes. *Restitutive justice* establishes a victim's right to compensation. In practice, criminal justice policies affect various groups differentially through a mix of these four forms of justice.

This typology of criminal justice is based on the concept of distributive justice. *Distributive justice* may be defined as the distribution of all costs and

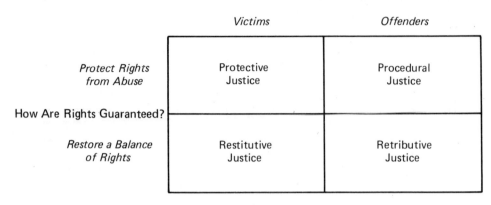

Figure 2-4. A Typology of Criminal Justice.

benefits in a society, in particular the distribution of money, wealth, power, and prestige. This means that protective, procedural, retributive, and restitutive justice are special cases of distributive justice. People have different conceptions of justice. As John Rawls states, "What is just and unjust is usually in dispute."[15] As mentioned earlier, people may place greater importance on one form of justice than on another. Indeed, the courts have emphasized procedural justice, and they have largely neglected restitutive justice in favor of retributive justice. Furthermore, a policy may benefit one group and harm another. For example, concentrating resources in one area to combat crime may shift the incidence of crime (costs) to another area.[16] Thus, distributive justice is a relative concept. It is a variable, and it takes on different values according to the principles used to distribute social benefits and costs.[17]

Protective Justice

Distributive justice is a goal of every policy system. John Rawls has written that "justice is the first virtue of social institutions."[18] This is particularly true of crime control systems. If the criminal justice system fails to control crime, direct costs are placed on citizens. Everyone may suffer a fear of being victimized. Some people will actually suffer a loss of property or an injury. In U.S. society the direct costs of predatory crime fall heaviest on the poor, for predatory crime is primarily a lower-class phenomenon. On the other hand, the social costs of white-collar crime are reflected primarily in higher prices and are, therefore, more evenly distributed among income classes. The distribution of social costs of crime, that is, protective justice, is a part of the distribution of all social costs. Thus, crime control policies and priorities have tremendous implications for social justice.

As in all policy systems, costs are incurred from implementing policies. In the case of crime reduction policies, the costs include program costs as well as other social costs (for example, hospital costs, loss of income). The benefits of a policy would be measured as the reduction in the social costs of crime for a particular group. The costs associated with operating the criminal justice system are hidden or indirect costs. The degree of justice is reflected in part by who bears the burden of taxpayer costs for operating the institution of punishment. Under a proportional tax structure, the burden of paying for police, courts, and corrections falls heaviest on the lower and middle classes. Not only are they most likely to be victimized, but they also pay a disproportionate share of crime control costs. A major contention of this research is that a just society is a society with less crime than an unjust society. As the distribution of costs and benefits in a society (particularly those associated with crime control) become equalized among the various classes, crime is reduced. Thus, the goal of distributive justice is complementary to (in causal theory, a determinant of) the goal of crime reduction. The converse may not necessarily be true. Depending on criminal justice policies and priorities and the success in reducing particular types of crime, it is possible that the benefits of programs will not be shared equally among all segments of society.

Procedural Justice

Procedural justice has been the hallmark of U.S. jurisprudence, perhaps to the neglect of other forms of justice. Procedural justice deals largely with the rights of the accused. The objective of procedural justice, or, more specifically, procedural rules of law to ensure justice, is that the innocent not suffer at the hands of the state. The state may institute a criminal proceeding at any time against any individual when there is reasonable cause to believe that he has committed a crime. In fact, it is the duty of the prosecutor to do so. Any individual may, however, become subject to erroneous or arbitrary prosecution. Accordingly, certain procedural safeguards have been instituted to protect the accused. This protection may be viewed essentially as a means of minimizing the costs imposed on the wrongly accused.

As for sentenced offenders, humane punishment is an important part of procedural justice. Indeed, the courts have ruled that, except for their physical isolation, inmates maintain their constitutional rights while in prison. Thus, procedural justice can be realized in part by providing a safe and healthy correctional environment for offenders. Violence and disease among inmates would indicate that these goals are not being achieved. These goals can, therefore, be objectively measured in accordance with the incidence of inmate violence and their mental and physical well-being.

Procedural justice protects the guilty as well as the innocent. This has created much confusion about and discontent with procedural rules of criminal law. There is a great feeling of outrage when a guilty offender goes free because of a legal technicality designed to protect the innocent. One must realize, however, that this is a tradeoff between retributive justice and procedural justice. An important value judgment must be made about whether the rights of the wrongly accused are more important than seeing that the guilty get punished. The fundamental question is, How many innocent people should be unjustifiably punished so that a guilty person does not go unpunished?

To answer this question, one must examine another dimension of the tradeoff between retributive and procedural justice. The issue essentially relates to determining a proper or fair penalty for a crime. The usual argument is that the punishment should fit the crime. However, this issue of retributive justice is related to procedural justice. When should the punishment begin? Should a guilty offender be punished before he is adjudicated? Clearly, the cornerstone of Anglo-American jurisprudence is that he should not. If it were otherwise, an innocent person might be punished. Thus, procedural justice may legitimately protect the guilty until they are convicted. At that time, a judge makes a subjective determination as to the proper penalty. The purpose of this discussion is to raise as an issue the relationship between retributive justice and procedural justice. It is studied in detail in chapter 5.

Retributive Justice

Retributive justice (or "just deserts") is the imposition of a penalty on an offender for previously depriving another of his life, liberty, or property. Retributive justice may be thought of as vengeance carried out in the name of the state. Unlike vengeance, as in a personal vendetta, the courts may impose retribution by penalizing an offender for his wrongdoings.[19] Retributive justice has been used in philosophical arguments as a justification for punishment.[20] If an individual deprives another of his rights, the balance of rights must be restored by punishing the offender.

Retributive justice plays an important role in establishing the integrity of the criminal justice system. If people feel that criminals do not get their due, then people will feel that the system is unjust. There is a feeling that the guilty go free while the innocent suffer. In this sense, retributive justice plays a very important role in the process of maintaining an orderly society. If people feel that justice is not done, there is a lack of incentive for them to behave the way society defines as moral, that is, noncriminal. The validity of this argument exists wholly apart from the deterrent effects which may arise from punishments. People may be careful not to break the law because they are afraid they will be punished or because they believe that to do so would be morally reprehensible. On the other hand, people allow the law in a retributively just system specifically because they perceive the system is just. This point holds true for the four types of criminal justice. If people feel that the system is just, they will be less inclined to create an injustice. They will want to keep the system just.

Perhaps the most important thing that can be said about retributive justice is that it penalizes the offender without providing any major direct benefit to his victim. The offender is punished, he suffers a deprivation, but the only benefit to the victim is the psychological comfort of knowing that his perpetrator has been punished. Retributive justice places a cost on the offender for violating the state's penal code. It is not carried out for the purpose of benefiting his victim, another important goal in the criminal justice system.

Restitutive Justice

Restitutive justice may be defined as restoring the balance of costs and benefits between the victim and offender by compensating the victim. Whereas retributive justice places a negative sanction or cost on the offender, restitutive justice places a positive reward or benefit on the victim. Restitutive justice and retributive justice are not mutually exclusive. There is no reason that an offender cannot be punished while his victim is recompensed. Needless to say, restitution is more amenable to certain types of crimes, such as property crimes, than other types of crimes, primarily violent crimes.

There may be beneficial effects from a system of criminal justice that requires the offender to directly compensate his victim. An offender may come away with a more moral outlook and greater respect for another's property and liberty. He will have contact with his victim and, perhaps, gain a better understanding of the suffering he caused. In this way he may be more likely to reform than if he is punished by an abstract, seemingly arbitrary state.

Programs for Reducing Crime and Enhancing Justice

Just as criminal justice policy systems have two goals, they have two sets of programs. First, crime is controlled through the institutionalization of punishment and by changing certain social conditions which are usually considered to be outside the criminal justice system. The latter includes such factors as the opportunity structure, health, education, and welfare. The second set of programs is aimed at enhancing justice. Policymakers establish policy initiatives, and program managers and administrators implement supporting programs.

Programs to Reduce Crime

The crime control program structure may be divided into four general programs: restraint, deterrence, reformation, and prevention. The level and mix of these programs are assumed to explain the actual number of crimes committed during any time period.

Restraint. *Restraint* is defined as the physical isolation of an offender from the law-abiding community. He may be restrained in a number of ways. In the United States most offenders are restrained by being placed in jails, prisons, or youth detention centers. Alternative methods of restraint exist but are rarely used. Banishment or exile, as Ernest van den Haag points out, could be used as an alternative to imprisonment.[21] Restraint is designed to prohibit an offender from committing another crime. The effect of restraint, however, lasts only while the offender is in an institution or banished. It must be pointed out, however, that many crimes are committed while incarcerated and that banishment does not prohibit a person from committing a crime in another area.

The type of confinement and the treatment that an offender receives while incarcerated will, in part, determine whether he commits crimes after being released. But recidivism and restraint are separate issues. Furthermore, restraint is offender-specific in that the offender is the only one who cannot commit a crime. Whether other people commit crimes because he is restrained or whether he commits another crime when he is released is a wholly separate issue.

Deterrence. An individual is *deterred* from crime when he refrains from committing a crime because he fears the threat of punishment.[22] Deterrence is a utilitarian justification for punishment. The argument is that punishment, or more specifically the threat of punishment, is a necessary—perhaps effective—means of controlling crime. Naturally, punishment controls crime by restraining offenders. But their punishment deters others from committing crimes and may deter them when their punishment is completed. Thus, there are two facets of criminal deterrence. *General deterrence* means that some people will refrain from crime if they feel that they may be punished. The threat of punishment for "persons who have not been punished," as Zimring writes, "and the example of the punishment of others, must influence behavior independent of any personal experience with the threatened consequence."[23] It is important to distinguish between general and *special deterrence*. The latter denotes that an individual is deterred from crime specifically because of the previous punishment he received for a prior crime.[24] In either case, whether previously punished or not, an individual is said to be deterred if he refrains from crime because of the threat of a future punishment.

In addition to acting as a threat to criminal behavior, punishment also works subtly to produce conformity. Most important, punishment instills law-abiding values in people. The thesis of Ernest van den Haag's *Punishing Criminals* is that punishment is essential to the process of socialization whereby people learn to distinguish between right and wrong. When people see certain behavior being punished, by a process of association they come to view that behavior as wrong.[25] Even for those who feel stealing is wrong, temptation may at times draw one close to violating the law. In such cases the threat of punishment may be, as Zimring and Hawkins suggest, "a rationale for conformity."[26] These authors explain that the deterrent process may work as a "habit builder." In other words, "The threat of punishment may produce a number of separate habits of compliance which in turn result in a more generalized habit of obeying the law."[27]

Reformation. After a person has committed a crime, the criminal justice system may keep him from committing another in one of three ways: restraint, special deterrence, or reformation. *Reformation* is a process whereby the individual's values are changed to conform with societal values. Restraint and special deterrence can work only through punishment. Reforming criminals may be done in conjunction with or separate from the institution of punishment.

To avoid confusion, in this book the term *rehabilitation* is used whenever values are inculcated in conjunction with a deprivation of liberty. Programs designed to reform offenders without depriving them of their liberty are labeled *reintegration.* Thus vocational and educational programs in prisons, halfway houses, and work release are rehabilitation programs. Juvenile diversion (that is, providing treatment without adjudication), probation, and parole are reintegrative programs. Certainly, one may argue that parole deprives the parolee of a small degree of liberty. He must report to the parole agent once a month, he cannot leave the state, and he may be returned to prison if he violates the terms of his parole. Relative to imprisonment, however, this is certainly a small deprivation. The important difference is that there is no physical isolation as part of his punishment. Thus, in practice, rehabilitation includes some degree of restraint; while reintegration is less restraining, it is community-based.

Reformation programs, like deterrence and restraint, have come under critical examination in a number of studies. In an article entitled, "What Works? Questions and Answers about Prison Reform," Robert Martinson concluded that "with few and isolated exceptions, the rehabilitative efforts that have been reported so far have had no appreciable effect on recidivism."[28] This has led many others to the conclusion that rehabilitation does not and cannot work. In a rebuttal to Martinson's article, Ted Palmer reevaluated Martinson's findings.[29] Palmer found that several programs reviewed by Martinson were of "differential value" and that the programs varied in their "degree of effectiveness." In other words, some offenders ("middle risk," "higher maturity" offenders) are more likely to be reformed than others, and some programs (community-based, counseling, reintegrative programs) are generally more effective in reducing recidivism than others. As Palmer concludes,

Rather than ask, "What works—for offenders as a whole?" we must increasingly ask, "Which methods work best for *which* offenders, and under *what* conditions or in what types of settings?"[30]

Prevention. Crime may be controlled by punishing criminals, as explained in the discussion of restraint, and deterrence. After an offender commits a crime, he may be reformed. His values may be changed through rehabilitation, which includes punishment, or he may be reintegrated into the community. In either case, a future crime is averted by a program which acts on, or, more appropriately, reacts to, a past crime. In contrast, crime *prevention* emphasizes incentives for legitimate conduct, such as job opportunities, rather than sanctions or reform of criminals. In this sense, crime prevention is the criminal justice system's only truly proactive policy.

Crime prevention, strictly construed, means that crime is controlled without any threat of punishment. There are a few areas where this distinction is not always clear. For example, burglaries may be reduced by installing burglar alarms (possibly with direct lines to the police department). People commonly say that burglary alarms prevent crime. According to the conceptualization presented here, burglary alarms deter crime. They deter crime because burglars feel that their chances of getting caught are increased, and they fear the consequent penalties. Another area that is even less clear is restructuring the urban environment (for example, brighter street lighting), as proposed in Newman's *Defensible Space.*[31] Again, although one may be inclined to call this a crime prevention program, it really works to deter crime. The potential offender is less likely to commit a crime if he feels he is more likely to be caught. The distinction between crime prevention and deterrence is extremely important if criminal justice policy research is to be precise.

Naturally, if one were to ask why an individual refrained from committing a particular crime that he contemplated, the answer would usually imply that the crime was both prevented and deterred. Elements of both these programs exist coterminously. Policy research, however, deals with manipulating policy inputs at higher levels of abstraction (community, state, nation) to influence the individual's behavior. Accordingly, the effects of prevention and deterrence must be analyzed separately.

The central issue in criminal justice policy research is finding a cost effective mix of the four programs previously discussed. How many resources should be devoted to abating recidivism? How much should be spent on prevention programs? What rules should be adopted? As Ernest van den Haag writes,

> The alternatives "improve social conditions" and "increase punishment" are not mutually exclusive. They are cumulative. The question is which combination promises the greatest benefit at least cost.[32]

Programs to Enhance Justice

As there are programs to reduce crime, there are programs to enhance justice. Following the discussion of four types of justice, this section presents four general programs for justice: redistribution, procedural safeguards, punishment, and compensation. These four programs are the means to protective, procedural, retributive, and restitutive justice, respectively.

Redistribution. The distributions of penalties and rewards, poverty and wealth, powerlessness and power are changed through redistribution programs. The nature of redistribution programs depends on the type of costs and benefits being allocated. In criminal justice, reallocating police patrols from one area to another redistributes the benefits of crime reduction programs. Similarly, making the reduction of juvenile assaults a greater priority than the reduction of prostitution benefits both prostitutes and the elderly by reducing the costs of crime for each. As far as the taxpayer cost associated with the criminal justice system is concerned, a progressive tax structure places a smaller burden on lower-income families. But, this says nothing of the benefits which, depending on how tax revenues are spent, may disproportionately benefit upper-income families. Public service jobs, hiring programs for the disadvantaged, and minimum wages restructure job opportunities. These programs are cumulative, for increasing income and job opportunities also increase power and prestige. In chapter 5 the effect of income redistribution programs on crime and justice is analyzed.

Procedural Safeguards. Certain constitutional rights have been guaranteed to enhance procedural justice. The Bill of Rights protects "against unreasonable searches and seizures," double jeopardy, self-incrimination, unjustifiable charges, unfair trials, excessive bail, and cruel and unusual punishment. Based on the Bill of Rights, common and statutory laws have provided procedural safeguards to ensure that rights are not violated. For example, an individual is likely to receive a fair trial if it is " a speedy and public trial, by an impartial jury," if he is informed "of the nature and causes of the accusation," and if he can have witnesses and counsel for his defense.[33] Due process, habeas corpus, and appeal of conviction are other procedural safeguards. In corrections, standards are established for acceptable levels of crowding, health care, recreation, sanitation, rehabilitation, and other programs. As a set of programs, procedural safeguards are essentially rules or principles of law which agents in the criminal justice system must follow if the accused and sentenced are to be treated justly.

Punishment. As previously defined, retributive justice places a penalty on an offender in the name of the state. The penalty may be an extreme deprivation of liberty, such as incarceration or death, or it may be a fine. In the aggregate, retributive justice implies that offenders are punished; in other words, retribution can be measured as the average severity of punishment for each type of crime weighted by the probability that an offender will indeed receive the punishment. Depending on societal definitions of what is due an offender, retribution and crime reduction may be complementary goals. In other words, if anyone convicted of a capital offense receives the death penalty, then members of society may feel that retribution has been carried out and, at the same time, murderers may also be deterred. On the other hand, if the death penalty is not an effective deterrent to murder (or if it is and for some unknown reason other crimes increase as a result), then enhancing retributive justice may cause an increase in certain crimes.

Compensation. There are two compensatory programs for restitution. *Direct compensation* implies that the offender repays his victim. The offender may be fined, and his victim receives the proceeds. The victim may also be *indirectly compensated* by the government. The U.S. Department of Housing and Urban Development sponsors the Federal Crime Insurance Program. The program offers insurance against property crimes (at reduced rates) in states which do not have programs to solve their "critical crime insurance availability problems."[34] A number of states, such as New York, now have victim compensation boards for persons violently assaulted. It should be noted that direct compensation programs have seldom been institutionalized, and one can only posit that this is primarily because punishment has been.

Conclusion: Analyzing the Criminal Justice Policy System at the State Level

In the preceding sections, the elements of criminal justice policy systems, four forms of justice, and a number of programs were presented without specifying a particular system. This chapter concludes by discussing some of the reasons for and implications of analyzing policy and planning at the state level. Determining the appropriate unit of analysis is particularly difficult for the following reasons. First, there are many different criminal justice systems. Second, within each system there are many decision-making units with influence in the policy-making process. Third, theories of crime have not been developed for the state, which is the primary unit responsible for controlling criminal behavior. As shall be explained, state policy making encompasses most decision-making units and has the most far-reaching control over crime.

The U.S. criminal justice system is composed of a multiplicity of relatively independent legal systems. There exist a federal system of criminal justice and fifty state systems. Each of these fifty-one systems has its own police, courts, corrections, and numerous local criminal justice systems. These distinct legal systems may be viewed as separate analytical entities, having their own criminal code and legal procedure. Although an important subject of inquiry, the various federal, state, and local criminal justice system linkages (for example, U.S. Supreme Court rulings on the constitutionality of a state's criminal law) are not explicitly considered in this book. The approach adopted here is to analyze in detail one criminal justice system (California) so that generalizations may be made to other systems.

Perhaps the most important consideration in selecting a specific system to analyze is clarifying the policymakers and distinguishing them from the lower-level decisionmakers. In general, policymakers determine the goals and decisionmakers implement programs to achieve them. In theory, then, the boundary of the system is determined by placing policymakers outside the policy system and by incorporating all decisionmakers who convert inputs into outputs within the system. This is not always a simple matter, for there are often factors which make it difficult to distinguish between policymakers and decisionmakers. Furthermore, many decisions are not easily controlled from the policy level. These difficulties in clarifying the policymakers complicate the selection of a particular system to analyze.

As a guide to defining the system's boundary, a distinction should be made between decisions that affect the system's goals and rules that guide those decisions. For example, a police officer's decision to arrest a suspect would not be a policy input, but laws regulating "stop and frisk" and police interrogations would be. Similarly, a court may require correctional administrators to ensure that the treatment which inmates receive complies with certain standards. In this case, the standards would be a policy input into the correctional subsystem, even though judges are decisionmakers within the system. Like the judiciary, the attorney general may play a dual role. The U.S. Attorney General, for example, has been called the nation's "chief law enforcement officer." As a cabinet member, however, he also acts as a policy official for the entire federal justice system.

In this book the state legislature is considered to be the primary policy-making body for several reasons. First, state legislators have authority for defining criminality. Second, they can set priorities and pass laws to guide the operation of the criminal justice system. The state is an appropriate unit of analysis for a number of other reasons. United States government has a long legal tradition of viewing crime control as a state and local, rather than federal, matter. Overall plans for the criminal justice system are supposed to be developed in state planning agencies (SPAs). They can serve as an input into the policy-making process.[35] In addition to judging criminal cases, that is, administering the law, state appellate courts often rule on the constitutionality of the criminal law. Prisons are financed by states and operated at the state level by a department of corrections.

At the local level also, where crime is of primary concern, there are many influential actors in the policy process. Police departments have an effective lobby for acquiring budgets from community governments. The very fact that local governments finance a large proportion of the total criminal justice system means that they play an important role in the operation of the system and in the policy-making process. Citizens' lobbies in both state and local government influence the policy process. In order to incorporate the influence of local and state decision-making units into a strategic plan, the larger unit—the state—is analyzed.

Another problem which arises in determining the appropriate unit of analysis relates to the formulation of theories of criminality. The causes of crime, in most theories, are rooted either in concepts of community or in personality. The state is usually conceptualized as a government unit, and there are few, if any, sociological theories of human behavior at the state level. Still, as previously argued, the nature of crime (that is, legal definitions of crime) and the controls of crime are matters that must be analyzed at the state level. Theories of crime causation must, therefore, be developed within that unit of analysis. Accordingly, the theory presented in the next chapter is formulated at the state level.

In conclusion, the public policy inputs in this book encompass all budgets and rules that can be implemented or influenced by state policymakers and policy planners. Although much of the criminal justice enterprise is financed by local governments, it will be assumed that state officials can influence these inputs. This is essential if there is to be a balance in the distribution of resources in the system. Thus, budget appropriations to the police, which are made primarily by local governments, come within the realm of inputs in this study. Similarly, in an effort to develop a comprehensive plan, it is assumed that state officials can directly influence or indirectly guide a number of local decisions. For example, it is assumed that state policymakers and policy planners can influence preventive detention in juvenile halls and the severity of sentence in correctional facilities. They can also influence probation and parole decisions by reducing budgets and proscribing certain aspects of their conduct through legislation. There are, however, many decisions that state policymakers and policy planners cannot control. As figure 2-3 shows, a U.S. Supreme Court decision such as the *Miranda* ruling is outside the control of state policymakers. Many decisions made (primarily in day-to-day operations) by police, court, and correctional officials are, as a practical matter, also outside their control. Just the same, by placing state policymakers outside and decisionmakers within the system's boundary, all possible courses of action for reducing crime and enhancing justice can be analyzed.

Notes

1. See Daniel J. Freed, "The Nonsystem of Criminal Justice," in eds. James S. Campbell, Joseph R. Sahid, and David P. Stang, *Law and Order*

Reconsidered (New York: Praeger Publishers, 1970), as cited in Yong Hyo Cho, *Public Policy and Urban Crime*, pp. 66, 67.

2. Perhaps the first official body to view criminal justice as a system was the President's Commission on Law Enforcement and Administration of Justice, *The Challenge of Crime in a Free Society*. For a technical systems view of criminal justice, see John P. van Gigch, *Applied General Systems Theory*.

3. This conceptualization of policy making and implementation should be compared to Theodore Lowi, "Decision-Making vs. Policy Making: Toward an Antidote of Technocracity," pp. 314-325.

4. The first four are discussed in van Gigch, *Applied General Systems Theory*, pp. 13-15.

5. Paul R. Eberts, "Consequences of Changing Social Organization in the Northeast," p. 30.

6. The conversion process may be distinguished from a morphogenic process. The latter refers to changes in the system's structure over time. See Walter Buckley, *Sociology and Modern Systems Theory*, p. 58.

7. Cf. van Gigch, *Applied General Systems Theory*, p. 20.

8. Marshall B. Clinard and Richard Quinney, *Criminal Behavior Systems*, pp. 15-18. Clinard and Quinney's typology was developed from the following four factors: (1) the offender's criminal career, (2) the degree to which his/her behavior has group support, (3) the relationship between legitimate and illegitimate behavior patterns, and (4) social reaction (p. 14). As they suggest, a general theory of crime may be constructed after lower-level theories have been formulated for specific types of crimes (p. 3). Their typology offers policy scientists a systematic conceptualization from which to begin the lower-level theory of crime control.

9. Jerome Skolnick, *Justice without Trial*, p. 6.

10. James Q. Wilson, *Varieties of Police Behavior*, p. 16.

11. Herbert Packer, "Two Models of the Criminal Process."

12. Sales Grover, *John Maher of Delancey Street* (New York: Norton Publishing Co., 1976).

13. See, for example, Peter Greenwood et al., *Prosecution of Adult Felony Offenders*; Rutherford et al., *Prison Population and Policy Choices* (Washington: National Institute of Law Enforcement and Criminal Justice, 1977).

14. George F. Cole, *Politics and the Administration of Justice*.

15. John Rawls, *A Theory of Justice*, p. 5.

16. For a theoretical discussion of this issue, see Lester C. Thurow, "Equity versus Efficiency in Law Enforcement," *Public Policy* 18, no. 4 (Summer 1970):451-462.

17. For two logically deduced principles, see Rawls, *A Theory of Justice*, p. 302.

18. Ibid., p. 3.

19. Ernest van den Haag, *Punishing Criminals*, p. 11.

20. Andrew von Hirsch, *Doing Justice*, pp. 45-55.

21. van den Haag, *Punishing Criminals*, p. 256.

22. Franklin E. Zimring and Gordon J. Hawkins, *Deterrence,* p. 71.

23. Franklin E. Zimring, *Perspectives on Deterrence*, p. 2.

24. Ibid., p. 2.

25. van den Haag claims that this is the main purpose of retributive justice. From the previous discussion of retributive justice it becomes apparent that retributive justice denotes a redistribution of the costs of criminality onto the criminal. Although retributive justice may have the beneficial "by-product" of internalizing morality, this latter process is specifically one of deterrence. To clarify this conceptualization, one must realize that it is plausible that punishment could deter crime even if it was not retributively just. An extreme example of this occurs in totalitarian regimes when enemies of the state are punished indiscriminately; that is, some may never have committed crimes against the state. It is not clear whether under such injustice people refrain from crime because they view it as immoral (that is, they have been socialized by the state) or they fear the state.

26. Zimring and Hawkins, *Deterrence*, p. 88.

27. Ibid., p. 87. Zimring and Hawkins claim that deterrence is a mechanism for building respect for the law. On this point, van den Haag's conceptualization seems more accurate. It is not the fear of punishment that builds respect for the law, but rather retributive justice. The power of the law to control conduct is vitiated when criminals go unpunished [paraphrase Zimring].

28. Robert Martinson, "What Works?—Questions and Answers about Prison Reform," p. 25.

29. Ted Palmer, "Martinson Revisited."

30. Ibid., p. 150.

31. Oscar Newman, *Defensible Space.*

32. van den Haag, *Punishing Criminals*, p. 104.

33. U.S. Constitution, Amendment VI.

34. U.S. Department of Housing and Urban Development, "HUD News," October 10, 1974.

35. Under the Omnibus Crime Control and Safe Streets Act (1968), states were encouraged to "prepare and adopt comprehensive plans . . . of law enforcement." SPAs have responsibility for developing these plans and distributing funds accordingly, under a program administered by the Law Enforcement Assistance Administration. See Mark Hoffman, *Criminal Justice Planning,* pp. 7-10.

3 A Framework for Strategic Criminal Justice Planning

The purpose of this chapter is to explain the policy science framework for designing a strategic plan for criminal justice. In chapter 2 elements of the criminal justice system were discussed individually. The fundamental concern in this chapter is with developing a framework to analyze the interrelationships among criminal justice programs and their impact on policy goals. The framework is based on the premise that social science theory and methods can be used to clarify and analyze policy and program options.

The policy science research framework evolved from an interdisciplinary perspective. Policy science is political science, in trying to improve the formulation of public policies by analyzing their outcomes; sociology, in developing causal theories of the behavior of social systems; systems analysis, in expressing theoretical properties in quantifiable terms so that certain aspects of reality may be simulated on a computer; economics, in seeking cost-effective allocations of scarce resources; and (in this book) jurisprudence, in describing the structure underlying the criminal justice process. The chapter sets forth the policy science research framework by discussing the various aspects of its interdisciplinary methodology as follows. First, policy analysis is structured by describing the various relationships among programs and goals that may be found in any policy-affected system. Second, causal analysis in criminal justice is discussed by proposing a policy-relevant theory of crime reduction. Third, criminal justice models are critiqued in order to develop a strategic planning model of the criminal justice system. Fourth, cost-effectiveness and several other criteria for evaluating public policies are defined. Finally, the policy science framework is placed in perspective by discussing its relationship to another planning framework which contributed significantly to its development.

Structuring Policy Analysis

Policy analysts may have one of two concerns about public policy. They may be concerned about *how* public policies are formulated and implemented. In *A Systems Analysis of Political Life*, David Easton described the formation of public policy within the "political system."[1] People place demands on and lend support to the political system. This general conceptualization includes demands made by elites, special interest groups, government officials, and bureaucrats. As a response to the demands placed on it, the system creates public policies. David

Easton defines this output of political systems as an "authoritative allocation of values."[2]

Analysts may be concerned, on the other hand, with the *effects* of public policies. Government actions are assessed by analyzing their outcomes on public and private institutions (that is, the social system) and their impact on political goals.[3] This is the subject matter of the present research effort. Social science theory and methods are linked to the pragmatic concerns of criminal justice policymakers and policy planners. Out of this concern comes a policy science research framework for analyzing the impact of government programs on political goals. The framework is presented by discussing the following four features, which are applicable to any analysis of policy: policy science variables, ranking objectives, implementing programs, and structural interrelationships. In combination, these four items can be used to structure the process of designing strategic plans.

Policy Science Variables

Before the details of the framework are presented, its basic feature should be explained. The methodology involves quantifying concepts so that qualitative hypotheses can be tested and the system's behavior simulated. Thus, the high level of generality appropriate for describing a system's theoretical variables (such as in chapter 2) is no longer adequate. Relationships should be expressed in terms of specific variables or indices. For example, the number of robberies depends on the subsystem's budgets and structural variables such as the probability of arrest, the court caseload, and the unemployment rate. A generalized policy system may be viewed as the targets (quantified goals) toward which the system strives, the instruments (quantified rules and budgets) which are implemented to achieve the targets, and the structural variables (quantified patterned relationships among decisionmakers) on which all depends. Figure 3-1 is a visual representation of the basic idea behind the framework.

One of the main purposes of the policy science framework is to analyze the effects of program options. There are several types of effects (see figure 3-2). If a change in a variable causes a target to change, it has a *direct effect* or *impact* on the target. Figure 3-2*a* shows three examples of direct effects (arrows show the direction of the effect). Instrument variables, structural variables, and targets can have an impact on the system's objectives. Bank robberies may be directly reduced as a result of any of the following: imposing a mandatory minimum sentence (a rule as an instrument) for committing a robbery with a gun; increasing the certainty of arrest (deterrence as a structural variable); changing the distribution of income (a target for distributive justice). An *indirect effect* implies that a variable changes a target through a change in an intervening variable. In figure 3-2*b* bank robberies, for example, are indirectly reduced by

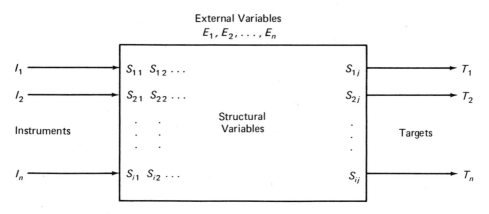

Figure 3-1. Policy Science Variables.

increasing the police budget (I_1) which improves investigation techniques (S_1) and leads to an increase in the certainty of arrest (S_2). Figure 3-2c shows that a *side effect* of increasing the number of arrests (S_1) is that the probability of conviction (S_2) declines (because of overloading the court's resources). Finally, an increase in the number of assaults (T_1) has *external effects* on hospital (E_2) systems (because more victims require medical attention). The analysis of the juvenile justice system (chapter 5) makes explicit these relationships as they exist in reducing delinquency.

Ranking Objectives

The focus of policy research must be on the goals of the system. Politicians—and ultimately the electorate—decide on the goals. The researcher must clarify the objectives that must be realized in seeking the goals. Every system has multiple objectives. There are three types of objectives: compatible, complementary, and competing objectives (see figure 3-3). In figure 3-3a teenage employment program (I_1) reduces burglaries (T_1) and grand larcenies (T_2). These objectives are, therefore, *compatible*. Some objectives are *complementary* because meeting one objective is the means to realizing another. A central hypothesis in this book is that reducing inequality $(T_1$ in figure 3-3b) will *cause* another objective, crime reduction (T_2), to be met.

Finally, some objectives are in *competition* with one another (figure 3-3c). For example, controlling felonies and controlling misdemeanors are competing objectives. Every tax dollar spent on the arrest and prosecution of a misdemeanor is one less dollar that can be spent to control felonies. Competing objectives are particularly important in policy research because they imply that

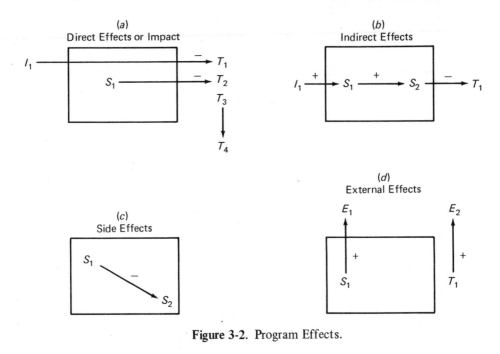

Figure 3-2. Program Effects.

the public must make tradeoffs among the goals it seeks. How many resources does the public care to devote to the enforcement of misdemeanors as compared to felonies? Furthermore, political reality dictates that many objectives will compete, for many interest groups do not share the same objectives. A major function of policy research is to clarify and analyze the relationships among objectives—those that are complementary or compatible and those that are competing—so that objectives can be ranked. In this way, priorities can be set objectively.

Implementing Programs

In order to achieve objectives, policymakers must be able to implement the necessary programs. This means that a program structure must be constructed. The program structure comprises the agencies that must implement the programs and the values of the necessary instrument variables. The instrument variables are those variables that can be *directly manipulated* by policymakers. As stated earlier, these include rules and budgets. A major difference between the two, as far as the analyst is concerned, is that the cost of rules (for examples, mandatory minimum sentences) is not always clear. Policy research can bring out these costs. This is particularly important because a major concern in the policy formulation stage is the cost-effectiveness of alternative program structures.

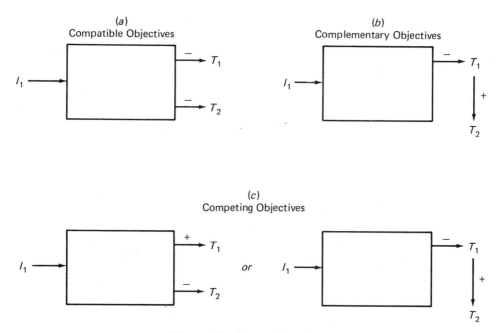

Figure 3-3. System Objectives.

This research focuses on two types of programs: program complements and program substitutes. As in the case of objectives, some programs may be *complements*. For example, if youth employment programs are implemented along with income redistribution and juvenile delinquency declines, then the two programs are complementary. Other programs may be categorized as *program substitutes*. For example, if resources for juvenile detention are reallocated to juvenile diversion programs and delinquency declines, then the two programs are substitutes. Policy research must focus on the interrelationships among programs and their relationships with objectives.

Structural Interrelationships

Implementing cost-effective programs would be a simple task were it not for the fact that policy systems have highly complex structural interrelationships. There are four important aspects to the interrelationships among subunits. First, *interaction* among decision-making units is a key determinant of how well a policy is implemented. Deterrence, for example, could be increased by coordinating police and prosecution efforts. The police often view the courts as a "revolving door." Many police feel that defendants who should be prosecuted are often not prosecuted, and that if they are prosecuted, they receive lenient sentences because of plea bargaining. Yet prosecutors often allow bargains or otherwise do not press charges because they feel the police did not provide them with sufficient evidence to get a conviction. Strategic planning is planning that seeks to coordinate subsystem interactions.

Second, some government programs have numerous *side effects* (see figure 3-2c). The side effects may, perhaps through a very indirect process, have an impact on the system's objectives. For example, a law enforcement campaign implemented to confiscate drugs will reduce the supply of drugs and hence raise drug prices. A side effect of controlling drug crimes is that drug-related crimes such as robbery may increase because the cost of maintaining an addict's habit increases. As another example of a side effect, victim compensation programs, instituted to improve restitutive justice, may decrease social justice. A side effect of these programs is that as a result of some people presenting false claims, money is redistributed illegitimately. Side effects are not always detrimental; they may be beneficial depending on the circumstances. As these examples demonstrate, side effects occur when one objective is affected by the programs and decisions related to another objective.

Third, the actions of each decision-making unit are *constrained* by other decision-making units. When prisons are overcrowded, judges are not inclined to sentence as many defendants to prison as they would if prisons were not crowded. If the parole board does not release enough inmates, the number of offenders sentenced and hence the certainty of punishment may decline. Constraints such as prison capacity influence decisions and limit the system's ability to reach its targets.

Finally, formulating and implementing programs in one part of the system without considering the effects on other parts can lead to *suboptimal* results. Suboptimization can be caused by budgets or rules that create an imbalance of work and activities in the system. For example, allocating a disproportionate budget to the police relative to the courts and prosecutors may undermine the very objectives that these resources are used to achieve. If the prosecutor must reject many cases and plea bargain most others because his office is understaffed and the court calendar is overcrowded, the certainty of punishment may decrease. This will increase the crime rate, and as a result, the police workload becomes greater. Kenneth Boulding has defined suboptimization cleverly as

> finding the best way of doing something which should not be done at all, or more generally, finding the best way of doing something in particular without taking account of the costs which this solution imposes on other segments of the system.[4]

Policy analysts often try to improve the function of a subsystem without fully taking into account the consequences for the system as a whole. In the belief that police are not performing at a social optimum, an analyst may recommend increasing their resources. This may create an imbalance in the distribution of resources throughout the system. From a societal viewpoint, the system cannot reach its goals adequately because it has been suboptimized. A fundamental premise of the policy science framework is that suboptimization can be prevented only by analyzing the global system. The structural interrelationships (interactions, side effects, and constraints) within a system must be analyzed fully, for depending on their configuration they can produce suboptimal results. The policy science framework avoids suboptimization by analyzing the significant interrelationships within the entire system. In this manner, a comprehensive plan can be developed.

Causal Theories of Crime and Delinquency

The policy science research framework sets forth the various relationships that can exist within any policy system. In applying the framework to a particular system, relationships among specific programs and objectives are hypothesized and tested scientifically. The analyst, therefore, devises a strategic plan to reduce crime and delinquency by first explaining the causes and controls of crime. Accordingly, a policy-relevant theory of crime control is presented in this section. Since this theory (labeled "relative opportunity") is derived by synthesizing two opportunity structure theories of crime, the opportunity structure theories are summarized first. The section ends by listing several propositions to guide the analysis in later chapters.

Opportunity Structure Theories

From different theoretical perspectives, both economists and sociologists have formulated opportunity structure theories of crime. The economic theory of crime is of particular relevance to policy science research on crime. It emphasizes both a microcausal explanation of crime deterrence and prevention and an empirical verification of the theory. The sociological theory of differential opportunity provides an inductively reasoned complement to the economic approach to crime. It explains, in detail, the system's procedure for creating delinquency. Both theories are based on the premise that illegitimate activities are an alternative to legitimate ones. They have in common a number of explanatory variables and similar hypotheses.

In the recent past, economists have brought to the field of criminal justice a new methodological perspective. The modern economic theory of crime dates to the mid-nineteenth century. Following Jeremy Bentham's utilitarianism, criminals are conceived as rational human beings. They seek to maximize their pleasure and minimize their suffering. They conduct an intuitive benefit-cost calculus and follow that course of action, legal or criminal, which yields the greatest benefits over costs. People follow the path to a criminal career because it "pays" better than legitimate behavior.

This economic theory of crime may be labeled an "opportunity cost" theory of crime. The opportunity cost of acquiring something is whatever else cannot be had. People who follow the law forgo any pleasure and pain they would acquire through illegal behavior. In contrast, criminals sacrifice legal earnings and satisfaction for the illicit. They commit crimes, according to the economic theory, because they feel criminal conduct will net them more, and they are willing to take the chance of being punished. People participate to various degrees in both criminal and noncriminal activities, depending on their assessment of the costs and benefits of illicit activity relative to legitimate alternatives.

The economic theory is a set of hypotheses deduced from the assumption that individuals, including criminals, act rationally. Economists have hypothesized that crime is caused by the following several factors: (1) insufficient penalties for those who might participate in illegitimate activities; (2) opportunities for illegitimate activities (as indicated perhaps by transferable assets); and (3) greater monetary and psychic rewards for participation in illegitimate activities than legitimate activities.

Cloward and Ohlin, in their treatise *Delinquency and Opportunity*, provide the sociological counterpart to the economic opportunity cost theory.[5] They theorize that delinquency is an adaptive response to social pressures. They point out, as the data indicate, that delinquency is most prevalent among lower-class adolescent males in cities. This forces them to raise the question as to what social pressures cause delinquency among the young. Their answer is that "pressures toward the formation of delinquent subcultures originate in marked discrepancies between culturally induced aspirations [that is, monetary success] among lower-class youth and the possibilities of achieving them by legitimate means."[6]

When youths become alienated from conventional norms, delinquent norms may develop. Youths become alienated if they have high expectations for success (and feel that others hold these expectations for them) but fail to meet these expectations. In addition to an incongruity between expectations and achievements, which results in a feeling of unjust deprivation, some youths may feel that they have been discriminated against. Youths who blame the system for their failure, Cloward and Ohlin hypothesize, are likely to become delinquents. In short, barriers to legitimate opportunities create pressures toward delinquency, and behavior patterns may become "buttressed by delinquent norms" when the system is blamed as the source of failure.

Three distinct delinquent subcultures may emerge under different social conditions. Delinquent subcultures take on distinct behavior patterns because, in addition to facing barriers to legitimate opportunities, some youths face obstacles to participation in illegitimate activities. Delinquent subcultures that specialize in property crimes such as burglaries, confidence swindles, and extortion (which has an element of violence) are labeled *criminal* subcultures by Cloward and Ohlin. Criminal subcultures arise if youths can learn criminal values and techniques from older criminals and if there are stable relationships between criminals and members of the legal system (for example, police to take graft, citizens to buy criminals' services). If these conditions do not exist, then a *conflict* subculture, emphasizing violence as a means of alleviating socially induced frustrations, will emerge. Finally, *retreatist* or drug subcultures are formed by youths who cannot succeed in either legitimate or illegitimate cultures. These various subcultures are created, therefore, as a result of differential opportunities within illegitimate subcultures.

Both the economic opportunity cost theory and Cloward and Ohlin's theory of differential opportunity have provided important hypotheses in criminal justice. Yet neither theory alone is adequate for designing a strategic plan to reduce crime and delinquency. Before these two theories are synthesized, the differences between the economic approach to crime and the sociological perspective and the areas where they complement each other should be pointed out. Whereas economic theorists assume that criminals are rational, criminologists assume that criminal behavior is the result of sentiments that do not attribute legitimacy to official norms. Sociologists are concerned with how and why a social structure produces conformity to legal norms among some people and conformity to delinquent or deviant norms among others. The underlying assumption is that delinquent subcultures will arise in a society where the legitimacy of established rules of conduct (that is, criminal laws) is not shared by all members.

The opportunity cost theory, as empirically tested, offers a logical explanation for the causes and controls of property crimes. The same cannot be said about crimes of violence. In general, the theory may be true that as the cost of committing violent crimes increases, the number of violent crimes decreases. But there is no reason to assume, as many economists do, that increasing legitimate monetary opportunities (for example, employment, income equality) should also reduce violent crimes. Cloward and Ohlin's theory of differential opportunity provides the justification for believing that improving monetary opportunities will control violent crime. As they explain, violent subcultures emerge from the same social pressures as criminal (property) subcultures. They take on violent behavior patterns because of barriers to illegitimate (property crime) opportunities.

Economists have given no indication why some youths commit crimes while others do not, other than to say that individuals perceive and weight costs and benefits differently. Cloward and Ohlin offer some insights into this process. Their theory suggests that the greatest cause of delinquency is a youth's perception that there are social barriers to achieving the money and prestige to which he aspires. They hypothesize that discrimination tends to make a youth blame the system as the source of his failure. Cloward and Ohlin also suggest that youths who find support among their peers adopt delinquent norms and that being singled out for punishment strengthens their allegiance to these norms. Although Cloward and Ohlin are able to explain why delinquency is more prevalent among low-income minorities, they do not explain why delinquent adaptations vary within social groups. Some youths do not commit predatory crimes because punishment teaches the difference between right and wrong. In addition, morality is instilled through religion, examples of public morality, and parental affection. These three factors are methods of crime prevention. Furthermore, some youths are psychologically incapable of violently assaulting others. They know that guilt feelings will result and produce an unbearable emotional strain. Thus, development of conscience is a key to crime prevention.

Cloward and Ohlin are able to bolster the economic theory by explaining the process that creates delinquency. Other than suggesting that discrimination ought to be reduced and education improved, they do not provide policy analysts with variables that can be controlled readily by policymakers to reduce crime. Economists have made significant inroads along these lines. They suggest that punishment deters and restrains criminal activity. Cloward and Ohlin failed to mention the importance of negative sanctions in their book. Although their thesis implies that opportunities for goal attainment should be improved, one cannot infer that direct goal gratification would reduce delinquency. Economists have provided a rationale for advocating an income redistribution policy as a means of reducing delinquency. Danziger and Wheeler postulate that each person's feeling of well-being depends on his absolute income, his income relative to his reference group, and his "taste" for equality.[7] In conclusion, it would seem that by combining and refining these two theories one could develop a policy-relevant theory of the causes and controls of juvenile delinquency.

A Policy-Relevant Theory of Crime Reduction

This section presents a synthesis of the two opportunity structure theories discussed previously. The synthesis is labeled relative opportunity—to be consistent with the terminology. It is conducive to developing a strategic plan to reduce delinquency. There are three main aspects to this synthesis: the opportunity cost of crime, relative deprivation, and the cost-effectiveness of program options. The first is concerned with the comparison individuals make between rewards and penalties from illegitimate careers with those from legitimate careers. Relative deprivation is concerned with the comparison individuals make between their position in society and the position of other groups. Finally, policymakers compare policy options to determine their relative merits.

The theory of relative opportunity is compared to the opportunity cost and differential opportunity theories in table 3-1. The assumptions about individual behavior include an economic and a sociological assumption. The theory of relative opportunity is based on the assumption that criminal proclivities vary among people and are affected by positive and negative sanctions (compare economic assumptions). That is, penalties can deter an individual, and rewards can prevent him from committing a crime. Relative opportunity also assumes

Table 3-1
Comparison of Three Opportunity Structure Theories of Crime

Theory	Opportunity Cost	Differential Opportunity	Relative Opportunity
Paradigm	Economics	Sociology: Structural-functionalism	Policy science
Dependent variable	Social cost of crime	Delinquent subcultures	Number of violent and property crimes
Unit of analysis	Individual	Neighborhood	State
Behavioral assumptions	(1) Criminals are rational. (The decision to commit a crime results when monetary and psychological benefits are greater than costs.) (2) Individuals respond to incentives (i.e., sanctions).	Criminal behavior is the result of sentiments that do not attribute legitimacy to official norms.	Criminal proclivities vary among people and are affected by both sanctions (punishment and rewards) and variables that affect sentiments about official norms.
Thesis	Raising the cost of committing a crime (i.e., increasing punishment and opportunities for legitimate income) will reduce the social cost of crime.	If a lower-class youth wants to improve his economic position, barriers to legitimate opportunities will frustrate his aspirations. If delinquent subcultural norms are legitimized and differential opportunities exist in these subcultures, then different patterns of delinquent behavior arise.	(1) The relative cost-effectiveness of deterrence, restraint, reformation, and prevention programs must be assessed. (2) As opportunities and rewards for participating in legitimate activities are increased and as relative deprivation is decreased, crime and delinquency are reduced.

that sentiments about official norms can be changed (compare sociological assumptions). Unlike the economic methodology, which takes tastes and preferences as given, the policy science approach is concerned with changing individual attitudes and values.

Criminal proclivities can be reduced by changing offenders and by changing the system. The former emphasizes reforming offenders through treatment. The latter focuses on internalizing legal norms by increasing the integrity of the "system." This can be accomplished in two ways. By making punishment swifter, fairer, and more certain, people are more likely to learn the difference between right and wrong. They refrain from crime not only because they fear the consequences (that is, the economic rationale for punishment) but also because they believe it is wrong. In addition, alienation can be reduced by increasing opportunities and rewards for following legitimate norms.

The costs and benefits of legitimate opportunities relative to illegitimate ones are key structural variables in the crime control system. Both the opportunity cost theory and the theory of differential opportunity suggest that barriers to legitimate opportunity make criminal careers more attractive, in fact, necessary. Yet, even Cloward and Ohlin have very little to say about the nature of those barriers. They claim that social advancement is based on education.[8] They explain that education is inhibited by cultural barriers. For example, certain ethnic groups devalue the importance of education. In addition, the poor face structural barriers to education. Youths working to help support their families have little time for education. Studies such as Jenck's *Inequality*—published since Cloward and Ohlin's treatise—have shown that educational success is less likely for the financially disadvantaged than for the economically advantaged.[9] Indeed, lack of education may be a severe barrier to social advancement. But this barrier is largely the result of cultural and structural factors specifically related to the disadvantaged. These factors may be significantly more difficult to change through public policy than structural barriers outside the control of social groups.

Whether by oversight or deliberate exclusion, Cloward and Ohlin omit a major barrier to opportunity. In this refined version of their theory it is argued that the employment structure is more of a barrier to legitimate opportunities for the lower class than lack of education. Entrance into middle-class and upper-class professions requires considerable education. These occupations are largely closed to the lower class, as Cloward and Ohlin point out, because of barriers to education. Their theory proposes, however, that delinquency occurs primarily among those who desire more money, not middle-class status. Many occupations attainable by members of the lower class do not require significant education. Some of them pay quite well. Dock work and factory work do not have any formal education requirements for entrance (although job training may be necessary). They pay well because of union influence in the collective-bargaining process. Thus, for many lower-class youths lack of education may not be

general to analyze specific policy options. Indeed, virtually all econometric criminal justice models combine adult and juvenile offenses in measuring the dependent variable and exclude the goal of justice. Since juveniles and adults may respond differently to incentives and treatments; and since decisions about the two are made by different decisionmakers, lumping the two together inhibits the researcher's ability to find cost-effective programs. In this book, therefore, juvenile offenses are separated from adult offenses in measuring the dependent (crime rate) variable.[14] In addition, indicators of justice (for example, the number of inmates in jail pending trial as a measure of procedural justice) are used to evaluate the impact of crime reduction programs on justice.

Economic models represent a hypothesized set of relationships among variables. The structure of these models must be assessed from a policy science perspective. Some econometric models incorporate a simultaneous system of equations. For example, Ehrlich's model included three equations: (1) a "supply-of-offenses" or crime equation; (2) a police production function (that is, an equation predicting the probability of imprisonment); and (3) a "demand function for (expenditure on) law enforcement activity."[15] The assumption behind Ehrlich's model (and other similar models) is that the crime rate, probability of imprisonment, and police budget are determined simultaneously.

Even these simultaneous econometric models, although capable of providing certain general findings, abstract to such an extent from a complex criminal justice system as to be inadequate for policymakers. As later chapters show, the system is extremely complex in that numerous relationships among the elements in the system (and ultimately their effect on crime) must be analyzed. Not to do so would be to exclude from consideration some potentially effective programs for reducing delinquency. For example, a number of studies have found that job programs for parolees effectively reduce recidivism.[16] In addition, juvenile counseling (a specific reintegration program), preventive detention in juvenile halls (a specific restraint program), and other specific programs must be included in criminal justice policy research. Econometric models are limited in their capacity to incorporate the necessarily fine details of program options in complex social systems. Furthermore, since these models usually include only a limited number of (program) variables, they are likely to produce suboptimal results. Only by including all relevant programs and developing a comprehensive model can the analyst avoid suboptimizing the system.

James Q. Wilson has suggested that the failure of criminology—or, more generally, social science studies of crime—"lies in confusing causal analysis with policy analysis."[17] Economists and other social scientists have operationalized crime prevention in terms of socioeconomic variables such as percentage nonwhite, percentage male, percentage unemployed, percentage teenagers, percentage of families below one-half of median family income, and other control variables. The issue is whether these variables adequately reflect the structural causes of crime. This matter must be kept separate from whether they are relevant to policy research, that is, whether they can be controlled by policymakers easily.

Wilson argues that "...ultimate causes cannot be the object of policy efforts precisely because, being ultimate, they cannot be changed."[18] As he points out, the fact that "men commit more crimes than women ... means little for policy makers concerned with crime prevention, since men cannot be changed into women...."[19] But this is a misinterpretation on the part of Wilson (and a number of other social scientists). The question should be, What causes men or nonwhites to commit crimes more often than women or whites? Aggregate variables such as percentage male or percentage nonwhite are *not* causal variables—"ultimate causes," as Wilson writes.

Structural variables, such as unemployment (which reflects a lack of access to legitimate opportunities) and income inequality (which indicates that relative deprivation exists), can *cause* people to turn to crime. Structural conditions cause certain social categories (males, nonwhites, teenagers) to comprise a greater proportion of criminals than other categories (women, whites, adults). Since sex roles in this society have traditionally dictated that males must be providers, a lack of legitimate opportunities puts greater pressures on males than on females. Since nonwhites face more barriers to opportunity than whites, nonwhites are more likely to turn to crime. Structural variables (which represent patterns of relationships) are causal variables. In general, structural variables cause aggregate variables to take on certain values.[20] Accordingly, policy research must focus on structural variables. Then, Wilson and others can fairly address the issue of whether causal analysis is relevant to the concerns of policymakers.

The economic approach to crime offers a very powerful method in its manipulation of objective factors that affect crime rates. The economist takes as given individual "tastes and preferences" (that is, societal values) and seeks to determine the objective conditions that influence behavior. Edward Banfield has suggested that policymakers must take cultural and psychological factors as given. Inducements or situational factors (for example, police presence) have to be manipulated by policymakers because the propensity (for example, cultural and personality factors) toward crime cannot be. According to Banfield, subjective factors such as alienation cannot "be defined and related to crime with much precision."[21] If Banfield's assessment of the limits of policy making is correct—and it is certainly consistent with the policy science framework—then the economists' approach to manipulating the objective conditions that affect crime would seem to offer a very useful methodology for policy scientists. Policy scientists, however, should address two issues. First, what are the inducements or situational factors that must be modeled? Second, how do these objective factors relate to subjective factors such as cultural and personality factors?

Although individuals may be deterred by the certainty and severity of punishment, objective factors such as these, which have been central to econometric models, are not always easily controlled by policymakers. Since budgets and rules are essentially the only variables that can be manipulated *directly* by policy officials, the important question is whether these variables have been or could be modeled appropriately using econometrics. Econometric models have yet to include all budgets in the criminal justice system. Ehrlich includes police expenditures but omits expenditures on courts and corrections. This may have profound effects on one's results. Increasing law enforcement expenditures, as Ehrlich advocates, may have little or no effect unless other budgets are increased commensurately.[22] It is plausible that econometric models could be developed to include budgets other than that of the police. It is not clear, however, that all budgets could be appropriately modeled. It is difficult to incorporate budgets in the corrections sector, for example, because they act as capacity constraints and because correctional outputs (for example, recidivism) cannot easily be measured and related to resource allocations.

A careful review of econometric studies will not produce any indication that economists have considered the importance of rules.[23] The severity of punishment has to be changed through a rule-making process. Yet, even under determinant sentencing, where the effective sentence length depends on legislatively fixed sentences, prosecutors and judges can influence the average length of sentence through plea bargaining. In order to change the length of sentences, therefore, legislators must develop guidelines for prosecution and adjudication. Similarly, changing the certainty of punishment may require certain rules to guide decisionmakers throughout the system and to coordinate their activities. Procedural rules cannot easily be incorporated into econometric models. It is important to develop models capable of analyzing rules because rules have budgetary implications (as well as indirect effects on crime). For example, a preventive detention policy requires an expenditure and may create additional costs in other parts of the system. In general, rule making is difficult to operationalize, measure, and hence test in an econometric framework. In short, although econometric models allow researchers to ascertain the effects of changing certain objective conditions, not all policy manipulatable variables have been (nor are they likely to be) incorporated into these models.

The previous remarks may seem to indicate that Banfield's argument for modeling inducements—an ideal toward which policy researchers should strive— should focus primarily on directly controllable variables. A major oversight, however, can result from such a perspective. Banfield's statement that alienation and other subjective factors "cannot be defined and related to crime with much precision" is simply without merit. Cloward and Ohlin's theory of differential opportunity demonstrates that alienation is an important causal factor of delinquency. Although alienation can be neither directly measured nor directly manipulated, the concept is a necessary part of the relative opportunity theory of delinquency. By deemphasizing subjective causal factors (or explicitly suggesting that societal values should not be modeled, as economists do) many of the important concerns of policymakers go unanswered. Empirically oriented policy researchers must be able to spell out the relationships between incentives and subjective factors such as alienation. In other words, the chain of impact from directly manipulatable budgets and rules to deterrence variables (police presence) and prevention variables (employment opportunities) must be modeled if the effect of these objective or subjective factors on crime is to be analyzed.

There is another important dimension to modeling subjective factors. Values a society places on life and property affect the amount of crime it has. Societal values also act as constraints on policy making. Justice and social order are the two central values to criminal justice. No crime policy is ever implemented without first considering both these values in some way. For this reason, policy researchers have an obligation to quantify subjective factors in their studies. The point is not that the researcher must make his own values explicit. Rather, the researcher must make the values in the policy system explicit and determine how emphasizing societal values differentially constrains the policies that may be adopted.

Although econometric models are well suited for finding the marginal effects of programs, they are generally inadequate for finding cost-effective programs. Econometric models usually do not include budget constraints, and interdependencies among variables are often relegated to the assumption that most independent variables are held constant. Ehrlich estimated that "a one percent increase in expenditure on direct law enforcement would result in about a three percent decrease in all felony offenses."[24] Yet this assumes that the system's response to the "optimal" increase in police expenditures would be stable.[25] It is plausible that there could be destabilizing tendencies in that the courts and prisons could not handle the increased workload efficiently. Thus, the probability of imprisonment could decrease if court and prison expenditures (which were excluded from Ehrlich's analysis) are not increased commensurately. In addition, certain changes in attitudes toward the police (for example, loss of respect for law enforcement) and courts (for example, anger over increased plea bargaining) could occur. The combination of these factors could offset the effect of increasing police expenditures. In short, it is difficult to make a choice among program options on the basis of coefficients estimated from regression analysis because many of the costs and benefits are hidden.

Economic studies can give policy scientists an indication of the direction and magnitude of the effect of general independent variables on crime. Some of the studies, however, have produced conflicting results which leave the issue of the effect of the programs as yet unresolved. Brian Forst did an empirical analysis similar to Ehrlich's. Forst developed a simultaneous equation model using 1970 data, whereas Ehrlich used 1940, 1950, and 1960 data. Forst found "the crime rate to be virtually insensitive to cross-state variation in either the probability or length of incarceration."[26] In fact, Forst found a positive relationship between the average sentence and crime. Since Forst's and Ehrlich's models are somewhat different (and they measure some variables differently), it would be wrong to assume that their findings should be identical. But the extreme difference—in particular, the change of sign for the average time in prison—points to the fact that the results are inconclusive. Advocating a crime reduction strategy based on the certainty and severity of punishment as cost-effective crime deterrents cannot be substantiated on the basis of econometric studies.

Empirical findings on the relationship between income inequality and crime have been more consistent. Ehrlich found a significant, positive relationship between inequality and property crime.[27] Inequality had a smaller effect on crimes of violence and was less statistically significant.[28] Forst found that a 1 percent change in income dispersion would produce a 0.4 percent change in the crime index.[29] In a study by Danziger and Wheeler, they found that a 1 percent reduction in inequality has a greater effect in reducing crime than a 1 percent increase in deterrence.[30]

Criminal Justice Simulation Models

A number of simulation techniques have been used to analyze the criminal justice system. They fall into two broad categories: operation research models and systems dynamics models. Criminal justice simulation models can be categorized according to the subsystems incorporated into the model. There are four categories: police, court, corrections, and total subsystem models.[31] The last of these includes the police, courts, and corrections but is not a global model because it omits relevant social substructures. Thus, from the point of view of strategic planning, none of these models are comprehensive.

Police models are primarily concerned with resource allocation in patrol divisions. Some aspects of law enforcement resource allocations incorporated into models are as follows: (1) allocation of patrol cars to geographical areas at different times of the day, (2) deployment of patrol forces to different police functions (including "communications systems for handling calls for service"), and (3) scheduling workforce needs.[32] The objective of these models is to aid the police in meeting the demand for their services.

The main thrust of court models is to decrease delay. Court queuing models follow the flow of defendants through the court system. Some methods of reducing delay are to revise procedural rules, increase resources available to the courts, and improve scheduling of cases. These models aid court administrators in managing the caseloads more efficiently.[33] Other issues such as the effect of granting bail, indigent defense, and sentencing on recidivism have received virtually no attention in these court subsystem models.[34]

Corrections has been the most neglected area of the criminal justice system largely because it is not easily amenable to modeling.[35] Recidivism data are inadequate because of difficulties in both operationalizing the concept (that is, rearrest or reconviction) and measuring it. A model of the Washington, D.C., correctional system designed by Stephen Stollmack predicts prison and parole populations.[36] This system's dynamic model can be used by correctional authorities and criminal justice planners to anticipate the demand for correctional services (say, rehabilitation programs). As with other subsystem models, the dependent variable (prison inmate populations) is outside the decision-maker's control. In other words, given a certain arrest rate and certain probabilities for indictment, conviction, and sentencing, the prison and parole population is deterministic. Crime causal variables (for example, prevention, deterrence) are excluded from the model. Thus, its predictive reliability is accurate only for short-range (two- to three-year) projections.[37]

The fourth approach to modeling the criminal justice system is to include the three main subsystems in a total model. Blumstein and Larson developed a model which can be used to evaluate changes in the system's resource costs, workforce requirements, and criminal population for several types of crime at each stage of the criminal justice process.[38] Other models, such as JUSSIM, follow the flow of offenders through the system and their effect on the system.[39] As Blumstein admits, these models do not assess the effect of organizations outside the criminal justice system on crime control; nor do they, for that matter, attempt to determine the deterrent effect of the criminal justice system.[40]

Total criminal justice system models are really subsystem models. They include the three major subsystems but omit certain aspects of the social structure (for example, the opportunity structure) that can have a great effect on the crime rate and hence the criminal justice system's workload. As Blumstein has been able to demonstrate, total system models can be extremely useful devices for tactical planning. But the fact that they are not global models (that is, they omit some relevant subsystems) and that they are noncausal limits their usefulness as strategic planning tools.

Policy Science Simulation

By combining econometrics with systems dynamics, policy scientists can build models for strategic planning. Systems dynamics, a simulation technique developed by Jay Forrester, is capable of modeling large, complex social systems.[41] Econometrics can be used for predicting the crime rate from variables within the system. The combination of these techniques allows the researcher to resolve questions about the structural interrelationships among subsystems and test the effect of alternative programs on hypotheses about the system's behavior. The combination allows for policy science simulations.

There are three important policy research objectives which neither of the two simulation techniques alone can achieve. First, by merging these two techniques the model can ascertain the cost-effectiveness of a wide range of alternative policies. The distribution of budgets among the subsystems can be balanced. Second, the limits to program options can be found. For example, it may not pay to increase a budget over a certain amount (without also increasing the budget of some other program) because the marginal effect may be zero. On the other hand, a budget under a certain level may create an astronomical rise in the crime rate. By incorporating resource constraints into policy simulation models, budget limits can be found. Finally, the entire system can be modeled. In this way, comprehensive planning can prevent suboptimal solutions.

Systems dynamics concepts (stocks, flows, and delays) are conducive to describing the criminal justice process. The main advantage in using this simulation technique for analyzing the criminal justice system is that interrelationships among subsystems can be analyzed without a great loss of detail. In other words, the indirect effects of programs are clear and measurable. Furthermore, budget constraints can be built into the police, court, and corrections subsystems. This prevents any subsystem from taking on an unrealistic workload. The police, probation, and court determinations can be expressed (as they are in this book) in terms of their probabilities, or they can be predicted from behavioral equations. Policy instruments and parameters, which are directly manipulatable by policymakers, can easily be included in these models.

In systems dynamics, the analyst inductively makes a number of assumptions about the system's behavior and designs the model on the basis of the assumed structure. The model must be evaluated on the validity of the assumptions. Thus, assumptions do not detract from the model's usefulness; rather, they focus the debate on important aspects of the system's structure and behavior. An assumption that proves invalid requires that the model be revised. The revised version will, therefore, be a more accurate representation of the real-world system. In the next chapter, the adjudication and correctional processes are described verbally and depicted graphically. The framework for policy science research is then used to model the California juvenile justice system in the appendixes so that the effect of crime reduction programs can be analyzed (chapter 5).

Criteria for Evaluating Public Policies

Criminal justice programs should be evaluated for their impact on both crime and justice. Accordingly, criteria from the social sciences and ethics need to be applied. In designing a strategic plan, the analyst must determine how well the programs perform, that is, how efficiently they reduce crime. Cost-effectiveness is the criterion that will be used in the policy formulation stage. After a policy is found to be cost-effective, the feasibility of implementing it should be assessed.

A policy will be feasible to the extent that the following four factors exist: (1) community and political support for the policy and supporting programs, (2) legal authority to implement the policy, (3) availability of resources and technological expertise, and (4) institutional structure and qualified people to manage the programs. Feasibility is not discussed further, however, because this book focuses on the formulation of strategic plans rather than on their implementation. Since policies change the distribution of social costs and benefits, they should also be evaluated in terms of equity. Principles of justice are, therefore, needed to evaluate criminal justice policies.

Cost-Effectiveness

Cost-effectiveness is an ideal criterion for policy research because it emphasizes both the cost of allocating resources to programs and the subsequent impact on policy goals. The least costly policy option among those that provide equal degrees of goal attainment should be preferred. For equal expenditures the most effective option would be preferred. In some instances, policymakers may choose to spend more because they seek a higher level of goal attainment; or, conversely, they may set their goals lower because they wish to keep costs down.

Economists generally use efficiency, which is a different criterion, in analyzing resource allocations. Economic efficiency is said to exist when the marginal benefits of any action equal (or exceed) its marginal costs. The activity with the greatest difference (or ratio) between benefits and costs is considered the most efficient one. There are a few reasons, however, why cost-effectiveness is preferred over efficiency in analyzing public policies.

Cost-benefit analysis, a technique used for finding efficient policies, requires that all variables be measured in dollars. At best, income benefits can be maximized (and costs minimized) for a group and distributed among various groups. In social policy other goals are very important. Many of them, such as reducing fear of crime, cannot be meaningfully expressed for policymakers in dollar terms. Cost-effectiveness allows the analyst to measure the impact of policy instruments on targets while reserving the prerogative of making value judgments for policymakers.

Efficiency is not a value-free criterion. Economists, however, usually assume that efficiency is the most important value in any system. Indeed, Gary Becker, the father of the modern economic approach to crime, has stated that deterrence, rehabilitation, and compensation can all be subsumed under the criterion of minimizing the social cost of crime (that is, efficiency).[42] Some programs are adopted, however, because of expediency, with little regard for their efficiency. Furthermore, ethical criteria enter into the formulation of policy. For example, if two (or more) policies combining reactive (deterrence) and proactive (prevention) programs are equally cost-effective in reducing homicide, one will be implemented because it may be deemed morally preferable. In other words, retributive justice may be an implicit goal of punishment, whereas protective justice may be an implicit goal of prevention. Similarly, some policymakers may prefer a less cost-effective reactive policy because it is more retributively just. Others might prefer a less cost-effective proactive policy because (for a given budget) fewer offenders are given life (or death) sentences. In short, principles of justice (equity, in economic jargon) may be as important as efficiency in selecting a policy. Cost-effectiveness can be used as a criterion to evaluate the effect of programs on various forms of justice.

Another difference between efficiency and cost-effectiveness is that efficiency is generally used as a criterion for determining optimal resource allocations, but a cost-effective policy is not necessarily an optimal one. Optimization is often neither politically nor economically feasible. On some issues policymakers agree about the targets that should be sought. Policy scientists can find the budgets and rules that balance the distribution of work and activities in the system. That is to say, they can find a cost-effective program structure. Political reality, however, dictates that tradeoffs will be made among objectives. In this case, policy scientists can demonstrate the effect of different program structures on the various targets. Policymakers can then select a program structure on the basis of value judgments about the relative importance of the targets. It should be noted, therefore, that the research framework does not eliminate suboptimization by "optimizing" a set of objectives. Policy scientists can, however, avoid the pitfalls of suboptimization by comprehensive planning, that is, by analyzing the global system.

Principles of Justice

In addition to cost-effectiveness, policymakers consider ethical criteria when formulating public policies. Several principles of justice can be used to formulate and evaluate criminal justice policies. *Constitutional rights should be upheld.* Indeed, recent court decisions have emphasized the need for ensuring that offenders be maintained in secure, yet humane, surroundings. Punishments should be *parsimonious.* In other words, the least restrictive and least punitive sanction which will achieve the goals of the system as effectively as other punishments ought to be chosen. Offenders should be treated *uniformly.* Thus, persons committing similar offenses ought to be treated similarly. This fairness principle is aimed, for example, at enhancing justice by reducing unwarranted discretion and disparity in sentencing. The severity of punishment ought to be *proportionate* to the seriousness of the offense, taking into account the harm caused and the culpability of the offender. Finally, the costs and benefits of crime reduction programs ought to be distributed *equitably* among the beneficiaries of the programs. Each of these principles can be used to evaluate the effect of programs on the level of justice in the system.

Conclusion: The Framework in Perspective

As with any scientific endeavor, the analysis in this book is built on the work of many others. The framework was developed by extracting from several disciplines concepts which describe relationships among policy-relevant variables. The theory of relative opportunity, which is in the analysis in later chapters, is a synthesis of economic and sociological opportunity structure theories. The approach to modeling the criminal justice system combines econometrics with systems dynamics. The criteria for evaluating policies include criteria from the social sciences and ethics. Together, these four matters (policy analysis, causal analysis, modeling, and evaluation) form the foundation for the analysis to follow.

The policy science research framework owes much to the work of a few authors.[43] The idea of expressing the relationships among program options and objectives in terms of instruments and targets was first formulated by Jan Tinbergen. He summarizes his framework for analyzing macroeconomic policies as follows:

> As the broadest object of the theory of economic policy we consider the determination of the optimum policy, given the individual preference indicators of the citizens of a community. The object is very broad indeed and implies, among other things:
>
> (i)   the fixation of a collective preference indicator;
> (ii) the deduction, from this indicator, of the targets of economic policy generally;
> (iii) the choice of "adequate" instruments, qualitative and quantitative;
> (iv) the determination of the quantitative values of the instrument variables, as far as such instruments are chosen; and
> (v)   the formulation of the connections between (a) the relation between targets and quantitative values of instrument variables on the one hand and (b) the structure of the economy studied on the other hand.[44]

The framework used in this analysis is in some ways an extension of Tinbergen's. There are, however, a few major differences. First, economists often try to find "the optimum policy." Politics involves competition and compromise over competing values. Therefore, policy scientists must not seek optimum solutions. They must devise comprehensive plans.

Second, Tinbergen takes as given the target variables and "the nature of the instrument variables."[45] Economic policy has a clearly defined set of targets. They are gross national product, balance-of-payments deficit, employment, and the real wage rate. Targets for social policy are often difficult to deduce. Indeed, there may be disagreement over the choice of targets. Variables such as government expenditures and tax rates are standard instrument variables in economic policy analysis. Rules in policy systems are often not obvious; and being qualitative, they are often difficult to measure. An important part of developing a strategic plan is determining the nature of programs and their instruments.

Third, the natural technique for applying Tinbergen's framework to the analysis of macroeconomic policies is econometric simulation. The Council of Economic Advisors forecasts economic conditions from their econometric models. The policy research model used in this analysis (see the appendixes) combines econometric modeling with systems dynamics. Regression analysis is appropriate for testing theories, and systems dynamics is well suited for describing the properties of complex social systems and simulating their behavior.

Finally, Tinbergen's framework was designed specifically for analyzing economic policies. The policy science research framework can be used to analyze any policy system, not strictly economic policy systems. Thus, it is a general framework designed for studying generalized policy systems. In the chapters that follow the general policy science research framework is applied to an analysis of criminal justice policies.

Notes

1. David Easton, *A Systems Analysis of Political Life.*

2. Ibid., p. 350.

3. For a development of the linkages between the two concerns of policy analysts, see Paul R. Eberts and Sergio Sismondo, "A Multilevel Policy Research Paradigm."

4. Kenneth Boulding, "Economics and General Systems," p. 84.

5. Richard A. Cloward and Lloyd E. Ohlin, *Delinquency and Opportunity.*

6. Ibid., p. 78.

7. Sheldon Danziger and David Wheeler, "Economics of Crime and Punishment," pp. 113-131.

8. Cloward and Ohlin, *Delinquency and Opportunity*, pp. 97-101.

9. Christopher Jencks, *Inequality*, pp. 138-141.

10. Danziger and Wheeler, "Economics of Crime and Punishment," p. 117.

11. Llad Phillips, Harold L. Votey, Jr., and D. Maxwell, "Crime, Youth, and the Labor Market," p. 502.

12. Paul R. Eberts and Kent P. Schwirian, "Metropolitan Crime Rates and Relative Deprivation," p. 92.

13. Cloward and Ohlin, *Delinquency and Opportunity*, p. 132.

14. There is a statistical problem which arises out of combining adult and juvenile offenses. Deterrence is usually operationalized as the certainty and severity of sentence, that is, the probability of receiving a prison sentence and

the average length of time served in prison. The standard procedure for measuring the probability of sentence has been to use the ratio of the number of adult first commitments (to prison) to the number of offenses reported. This measure is inaccurate because the numerator excludes juvenile sentences (the denominator includes juvenile reported offenses). This makes the estimated effect of deterrence, a key structural variable in the system, tenuous.

15. Isaac Ehrlich, "Participation in Illegitimate Activities," pp. 537-543.

16. See, for example, Robert Evans, Jr., "The Labor Market and Parole Success"; Phillip Cook, *The Effect of Legitimate Opportunities on the Probability of Parole Recidivism.*

17. James Q. Wilson, *Thinking about Crime*, p. 50.

18. Ibid.

19. Ibid.

20. Paul R. Eberts, "Consequences of Changing Social Organization in the Northeast," pp. 22, 23.

21. Edward C. Banfield, *The Unheavenly City Revisited*, p. 180.

22. See Ehrlich, "Participation in Illegitimate Activities," pp. 556-559.

23. For a collection of econometric studies of crime, see Lee R. McPheters and William B. Stronge, *The Economics of Crime and Law Enforcement.*

24. Ehrlich, "Participation in Illegitimate Activities," p. 558.

25. The "optimal" expenditure could be derived by optimizing an objective function (for example, minimizing the social cost of crime) so that the marginal benefits of the policy equal its marginal cost. Cf. Gary S. Becker, "Crime and Punishment: An Economic Approach," pp. 180-217.

26. Forst explains the specific differences between the two studies by explaining that "Ehrlich estimates the elasticity of the aggregate crime rate with respect to the probability of apprehension and imprisonment to be -0.99, and I estimate it to be -0.02; he estimates the elasticity of the aggregate crime rate with respect to the average time served in prison to be -1.12, and I estimate it at 0.01." Brian Forst, "Participation in Illegitimate Activities: Further Empirical Findings," p. 479. It should be noted that although the variables cited in the quote are important indicators of deterrence, none of the coefficient estimates reported by Forst was statistically significant even at a .6 significance level.

27. Ehrlich, "Participation in Illegitimate Activities," p. 545.

28. Ibid.

29. Forst, "Participation in Illegitimate Activities," p. 485. The coefficient estimate was statistically significant at the .95 significance level.

30. Paraphrased from Danziger and Wheeler, "Economics of Crime and Punishment," p. 127.

31. As of 1974, there were forty-six models in these four categories. See J. Chaiken et al., *Criminal Justice Models: An Overview*, appendix.

32. Ibid., pp. 46-89. Some of these are specialized computer models, and others are dynamic queuing models or linear programming models.

33. Saul I. Gass et al., *A Guide to Models in Government Planning and Operation* (Mathematica, Inc., 1974), pp. 262-268.

34. Ibid., p. 242.

35. Ibid., p. 268.

36. Stephen Stollmack, "Predicting Inmate Populations from Arrest, Court Disposition, and Recidivism Rates," pp. 141-162.

37. Ibid., pp. 141, 142.

38. Alfred Blumstein and Richard Larson, "Models of a Total Criminal Justice System," pp. 199-232.

39. Jacqueline Cohen et al., "Implementation of the JUSSIM Model in a Criminal Justice Planning Agency," pp. 117-131.

40. Blumstein and Larson, "Models of a Total Criminal Justice System," p. 228. Their model includes a "crime-switch" matrix (that is, a matrix describing the probability that an offender will commit another type of crime given he has already committed a particular type of crime). Recidivists and "virgins" enter the criminal justice system. But there are no controls to reduce the number of crimes committed.

41. Jay Forrester, *Industrial Dynamics and Urban Dynamics.*

42. Becker, "Crime and Punishment: An Economic Approach," p. 170.

43. J. Tinbergen, *On the Theory of Economic Policy*; Paul R. Eberts and Sergio Sismondo, "Designing and Managing Policy Research" and "Principles in Design and Management of Policy Research for Public Planning Agencies"; Alice M. Rivlin, *Systematic Thinking for Social Action*; Yehezkel Dror, *Design for Policy Sciences* and *Ventures in Policy Sciences.*

44. Tinbergen, *On the Theory of Economic Policy*, pp. 3 and 4.

45. Ibid., p. 4.

4

The California Juvenile Justice System

This chapter describes the adjudication and correctional processes in the California juvenile justice system. The treatment juveniles receive as they are processed through the justice system is quite different from that of adult offenders. Two philosophical views of children, dating to ancient times, underlie the structure and process of the juvenile justice system. One view is that children, until some legally specified age, lack the maturity to recognize the harm inherent in some acts. Even if they are aware of the harmful nature of crime, the other premise is that juveniles should not be punished as severely as adults.[1] These two views were the philosophical foundation behind the establishment of a separate juvenile court (with a legal procedure quite different, until recently, from that in an adult criminal court) and a separate correctional system for juveniles. In California this distinction may best be seen by the fact that juvenile law, both substantive and procedural, is written not in the penal code, but in the California Welfare and Institutions Code (hereafter W&I Code).

Juvenile Offenses

The Juvenile Court Law first enacted in 1903 and completely rewritten in 1961 placed authority in criminal justice agencies over three types of juveniles. Children under 18 are referred to as dependent and neglected if they are the victims of parental abuse (W&I Code, Sec. 600). If they cannot be controlled by their parents, they are referred to as incorrigibles or "601s" under the Welfare and Institutions Code section of the same number. In other states acronyms such as CHINS (Children in Need of Supervision) are used instead of the label "601." Juveniles who commit felonies or misdemeanors in violation of the Penal Code are labeled delinquents or "602s." The purpose of this chapter is to explain the process 601 and 602 juveniles follow as they pass through the system.

Dependent and neglected children are excluded from further discussion because of the nondelinquent nature of the minors' case. In California, young adults between the ages of 18 and 21 are accorded certain special privileges not given to adults over 21. In some instances they are even treated as juveniles (for example, CYA wards). "Youthful offenders" are considered adults in this study.

The juvenile justice process (adjudication and corrections) may be viewed as a stock-flow process. Figure 4-1a and b presents a schematic representation of the stock-flow process to be discussed in this chapter. The adjudication process

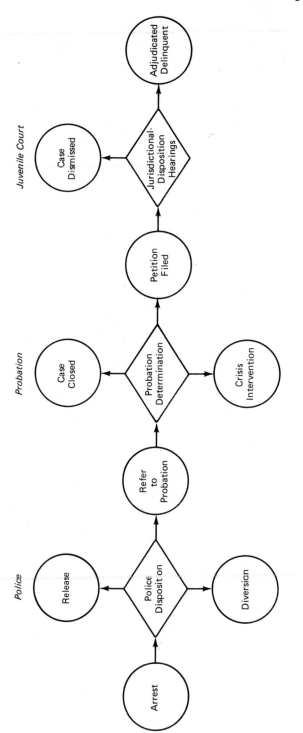

Figure 4-1a. The Juvenile Justice Process: Adjudication.

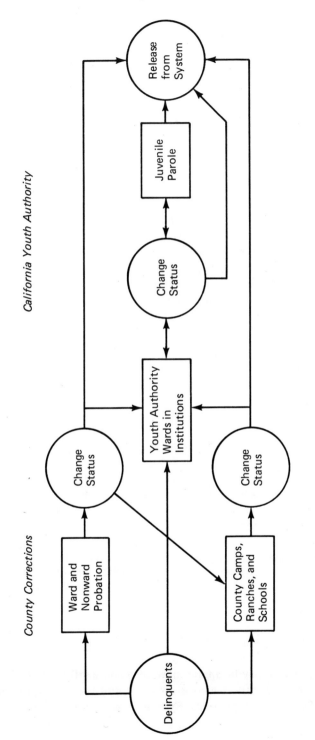

Figure 4-1b. The Juvenile Justice Process: Corrections.

requires that three key decisions be made. The police must refer a youth to probation, the probation officer must file a petition, and the judge must find the youth delinquent (figure 4-1*a*). Each of these decision points is depicted by a diamond. Circles represent juvenile *flows* (for example, the number of juveniles adjudicated delinquent *during the year*). Figure 4-1*b* shows that the correctional process comprises county and state (California Youth Authority) agencies. Rectangles represent juvenile *stocks* (for example, the number of juveniles on parole *on a particular day*).

This chapter is concerned with the decisions that determine whether a youth is adjudicated and the type of corrections program in which he is placed. Appendix A describes mathematically the stocks and flows of juveniles as they pass through the system. Several figures in this chapter are divided into two parts: the decision-making process described in this chapter and the stock-flow process modeled in appendix A. (See figures 4-3 to 4-6.) The top of these figures depicts, in detail, the adjudication process. The bottom represents the stocks and flows of juveniles as they pass through the adjudication and corrections processes. For example, some juveniles are held in juvenile hall while they await disposition. In order to distinguish between the decision-making process and the flow of juveniles, single lines are used to denote flows of information and double lines are used to denote flows of juveniles, respectively. With these preliminaries in mind, the various decisions made at arrest, probation intake, juvenile court, and corrections are now described.

Juvenile Arrests

The police make two major decisions regarding juvenile offenders. These are depicted in figure 4-2 as the field apprehension decision and the police disposition. Although the police are allowed discretion in arresting juveniles, as they are in arresting adults, their disposition decisions are to be guided by the Welfare and Institutions statute. The philosophy of the framers of the juvenile law is set forth in section 625 as follows:

> In determining which disposition of the minor he will make, the officer shall prefer the alternative which least restricts the minor's freedom of movement, provided such alternative is compatible with the best interests of the minor and the community.

Field Apprehension Decision

A juvenile offender may be apprehended by a police officer responding to a call for service or by an officer who is present during the commission of a crime. After a police officer apprehends a youth, he must make a field apprehension

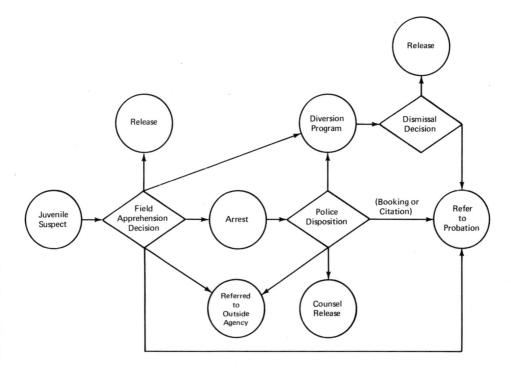

Figure 4-2. Juvenile Apprehension and Referrals.

decision. He has two broad options: he may release the minor in the parents' custody or arrest him. (Technically, juveniles are not arrested, but rather taken into "temporary custody.") If the youth is not taken into temporary custody, the police officer may (1) reprimand him, (2) "counsel and release" him, (3) refer him to an agency participating in a diversion program, or (4) give him a citation to appear at the probation office.

In 1970 California juveniles were arrested for 166,000 delinquencies.[2] If they had been adults, these W&I Code, sec. 602, violations would be felony or misdemeanor arrests. In addition, there were 216,300 arrests for delinquent tendencies (W&I Code, sec. 601). These status offenses refer specifically to juvenile conduct and are not proscribed by the penal code. It is worth noting that the majority of juveniles arrested were arrested for offenses for which adults could not be arrested (for example, runaways, curfew violations). The arrest and subsequent disposition of these 601 juveniles place a heavy load on the justice system. It detracts from the processing of more serious offenders.

Police Disposition

According to W&I Code, sec. 626, there are four possible dispositions after a minor is taken into temporary custody (see figure 4-2). He may be released.

Either he is released to his parents (possibly afte. being enrolled in a diversion program), or he may be referred to an agency outside the juvenile justice system. He may be given a citation to appear before a probation officer, or he may be taken without unnecessary delay directly to the probation officer, usually for booking in the juvenile hall.

The citation, or notice to appear before the probation officer, is much like a traffic summons. The probation officer must receive a copy of the notice so that he becomes aware of the facts (W&I Code, sec. 626). The police provide the probation officer with essentially the same allegations he would provide a district attorney in an adult criminal complaint.[3]

Police Diversion Programs for Juveniles

If the minor is neither taken directly to probation nor given a notice to appear, he is released without becoming a probation case. Some police departments have formal programs to divert juveniles from further processing within the justice system. They may take the form of a specialized juvenile unit which provides counseling to the juvenile and his family or makes referrals to community service organizations outside the juvenile justice system. In addition, officers in the juvenile unit may work in schools to provide crisis counseling and look for early warning signs of delinquency among students. One beneficial aspect of diversion is the greater involvement of community service organizations with problem children.

Diverting juveniles from the adjudication process is an important area of inquiry for a cost-effectiveness study. The amount of resources, primarily workforce, used in diversion programs (including resources outside the justice system) and their effectiveness in treating juveniles must be compared to further juvenile justice processing. As table 4-1 (columns 2 and 3) shows, over 50 percent of minor law violations (the rough equivalent of adult misdemeanors) and delinquent tendencies (that is, 601s) were diverted from further system processing.

(Bureau of Criminal Statistics data cannot be used to ascertain the number of juveniles handled in police departments in formal diversion programs as opposed to counseled and released. Although technically these latter cases are "released," whereas "diverted" cases are referred to some other agency or program, neither moves further into the juvenile justice system.)

The 150,000 cases diverted free up resources in the juvenile system and prevent an overload of cases. This can make existing resources more effective than usual. Furthermore, if the recidivism rate were lower for diverted juveniles, then arrests and juvenile caseloads would decline in the future. Indeed, it is likely that diversion programs would reduce recidivism because patrol officers can admit youths to formal programs instead of merely releasing them. This may

Table 4-1
Police Dispositions of Juvenile Delinquency Arrests, 1969

| | | Percentage of Total Arrests | | |
Offense	Total Arrested (1)	Handled within Department (2)	Referred to Other Agencies (3)	Referred to Probation (4)
Total delinquency	389,394	40.7	3.6	55.7
Major law violations	100,161	18.2	3.3	78.6
Minor law violations	61,883	49.4	1.4	49.2
Delinquent tendencies	227,350	48.2	4.3	47.5

Source: Bureau of Criminal Statistics, *California Crime and Delinquency* (Sacramento: State of California, 1969), p. 143.

be more effective than a few hours of counseling by a patrol officer untrained in the problems of juvenile delinquents.

The savings from diversion programs are significant. As reported in the California Correctional System Intake Study, the Los Angeles Sheriff's Department diverted 689 youths from probation and juvenile court. They estimated a savings of $651,700. Since the diversion program cost the Los Angeles Sheriff's Department $88,762, the net savings to Los Angeles County was $562,938.[4] In addition, the Sheriff's Department reported a reduction in the recidivism rate for diverted youths, down to 40 percent.[5]

Several other counties in California have police-sponsored juvenile diversion programs. They reported similar findings. Over a two-year period, beginning in August 1971, the Sacramento Police Department Youth Services Division received 32 percent of the 9,740 arrested juveniles. The total recidivism rate dropped from 20 percent to 8.5 percent after the program was instituted.[6] The Santa Clara County Pre-Delinquent Diversion Project diverted 1,904 status offenders (601s) during its first year of operation. The recidivism rate for a cohort sample of predelinquents was 48.5 percent whereas the recidivism rate for diverted 601s was only 24.3 percent.[7] Furthermore, the reduction in (projected) probation costs was $492,727. Excluding the costs of the diversion program, net savings totaled $289,716.[8]

Although evaluative findings of diversion programs do not prove that they are more cost-effective than other programs, they are worth citing for a few reasons. Diversion programs offer several benefits. As an alternative to appropriating more resources in an effort to fight crime, legislators can mandate diversion programs. These programs cost less and appear to be more effective than reactive juvenile delinquency programs. Furthermore, it is unlikely that this form of reintegration would be counterproductive toward deterrence or restraint. Diversion programs free up resources in other parts of the system by reducing caseloads. Finally, juvenile diversion is consistent with the values written into the juvenile law. Section 625 of the W&I Code states that "the officer shall prefer the alternative which least restricts the minor's freedom of movement."

Juvenile Probation Intake

The probation officer makes two main decisions after a juvenile is initially referred to him (figure 4-3). First, he decides whether to detain the minor in the juvenile hall or release him to the custody of his parents. Second, he decides whether to file a petition. Filing a petition with the juvenile court officially begins the process of adjudication. These decisions must be made and reevaluated at several points during the juvenile process.

Initial Referral Decision

A minor may be referred to probation by a law enforcement agency, adult court (in the case where a juvenile was erroneously brought before a judge in adult court), school, parents or relatives, or any other citizen including the minor himself. In 1970 law enforcement agencies made approximately 85 percent of the nearly 160,000 initial referrals.[9] Depending on the county, juveniles are brought to probation at a juvenile hall (that is, juvenile jail), probation office, or probation crisis intervention unit. The minor may be transferred from either of the second two units to the juvenile hall. Thus, the important decision is the one made at juvenile hall. At this point, the juvenile may be released, sent to a crisis intervention unit, released in custody of his parents pending an investigation, or detained pending an investigation (see figure 4-3).

Detaining juveniles is different from jailing adults. The general rule for adult felons is to hold them in jail until they make an initial appearance before a judge in the lower court. The judge will make a pretrial detention decision. Adult misdemeanants may be released by the police in accordance with a bail schedule fixed by the courts. Juveniles, on the other hand, must be released unless one of seven legislatively mandated conditions exist (W&I Code, sec. 628). The seven conditions essentially provide for protecting the minor, protecting the court's authority, and protecting the public. But the preponderance of the law is to release the minor. If the minor is detained, a petition must be filed within 48 hours, and a detention hearing must be held the next judicial day.

It is important to note that the holding capacity of the juvenile hall necessarily limits the number detained. (Overcrowded conditions may even decrease the number of police referrals to probation.) The critical issue, then, is

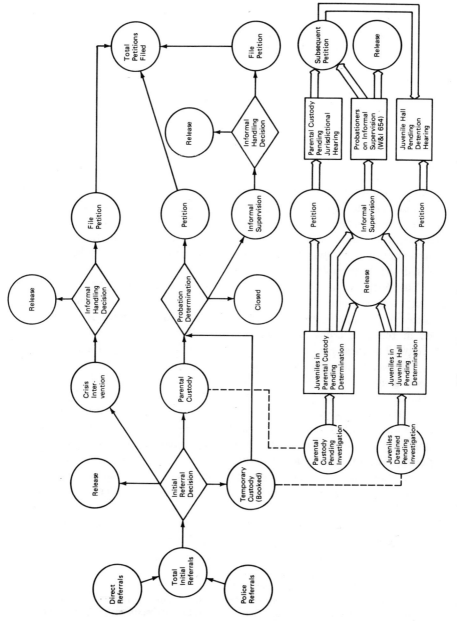

Figure 4-3. Juvenile Probation Intake.

the cost-effectiveness of juvenile detention. As the number of juveniles detained increases, will the number of offenses committed by youths decline? Alternatively, if resources allocated to pretrial detention were used for other programs, such as diversion, would there be a reduction in juvenile delinquency? These questions are answered in the next chapter when the relative cost-effectiveness of diversion and pretrial detention is assessed.

Crisis Intervention

As an alternative to detaining or simply releasing troubled youths, some probation departments have instituted crisis intervention programs. The single most important feature of these programs is that the juvenile receives immediate attention. The decision to file a petition can wait until the crisis is over and the youth and his family have received counseling. (Informal supervision, an alternative to adjudication, does not always have this special feature.) Crisis intervention units in the probation department, as in the case of police juvenile units, divert the juvenile from further criminal justice processing.

The Sacramento Diversion Project has been awarded the "exemplary project" label by the National Institute of Law Enforcement and Criminal Justice.[10] The label is awarded to projects which have demonstrated effectiveness in reducing crime, are adaptable to other jurisdictions, and are cost-effective. For these reasons some details of this diversion project are described.

The Sacramento Diversion Project was designed to handle 601 cases as a test project beginning in 1970. It was adopted in 1972 along with a diversion pilot program for some 602 cases (that is, it excluded violent and some drug offenders). The project was based on two principles. First, the problem should receive immediate attention. Second, the reference group for counseling is the whole family, not just the juvenile offender.[11] Accordingly, staff time is spent primarily in short-term treatment with periodic counseling services, including a 24-hour hot line. The probation staff is given special family counseling training.[12] The pilot project included a control group in order to evaluate its performance.

The project was evaluated on the basis of four criteria. Compared to the 601 control group,

> The number of court petitions was reduced by over 80 percent. Overnight detention was reduced by more than 50 percent. The number of youths involved in repeat offenses of any kind was reduced by more than 14 percent. The number of youths subsequently becoming involved in criminal behavior was reduced by 25 percent. The cost of the new techniques was less than half the cost of the previous procedures.[13]

The results of the 602 project were even more impressive. There was a 90 percent reduction in the number of petitions filed, and the number of repeat offenses declined by more than 40 percent.[14] The detention and cost results were roughly the same as in the 601 project. In short, crisis intervention can be a low-cost, highly effective alternative to adjudication.

Probation Determination

Filing a petition in juvenile court is the first step in the process of declaring a minor a ward of the court. Only the probation officer may file a petition.[15] Thus, in the juvenile justice system the probation officer plays a role similar to that of the adult prosecutor in filing a case with the court; but, unlike the prosecutor, he is a counselor too. He may, alternatively, close the case by outright dismissal or referral to another agency, or he may place the minor under informal probation supervision.

According to the authors of the *California Correctional System Intake Study,* the greatest factor influencing the probation determination decision is the juvenile's threat to the community.[16] Other factors of importance are the nature of the offense, the strength of the evidence, and the juvenile's prior record. All are factors that seem to be of importance in similar stages of the adult criminal justice system.

Without court approval, the probation officer may place a juvenile on informal probation for a period up to six months (W&I Code, sec. 654). In Santa Clara County youths who are charged with petitionable, provable drug cases that are not contested may, if they consent, participate in a drug abuse program.[17] Six two-hour sessions are held with parent and child in an effort to educate them about drugs and help iron out parent-youth communication problems. After the informal supervision period, another determination must be made as to whether to file a petition. In 1970 only 16 percent of all informal supervision cases were petitioned.[18]

In 1970 roughly 33 percent of the nearly 159,000 initial referrals were ultimately petitioned (see table 4-2).[19] The trend during the preceding decade was toward decreasing the percentage of cases petitioned and instead relying more heavily on informal probation (13.5 percent in 1970) and dismissing cases. In comparative terms, although the number of initial referrals to probation nearly tripled since 1960, the number of cases petitioned less than doubled.

Juvenile Court

Juvenile court, a subdivision of the superior court, has original jurisdiction in all matters involving minors (youths under 18 years of age).[20] In 1967 a U.S.

Table 4-2
Probation Determination of Initial Referrals, 1970[a]

	Initial Referrals (1)	Closed (%) (2)	Informal Supervision (%) (3)	Petitions Filed (%) (4)
All offenses	159,978	53.1	13.6	33.4
Major law violations	53,017	48.4	14.9	36.7
Drug law violations	22,367	37.0	15.0	48.0
Minor delinquencies	84,594	60.2	12.4	27.4

Source: Bureau of Criminal Statistics, *Crime and Delinquency in California* (Sacramento: State of California, 1970), p. 88.

[a]This table includes an additional 1,034 initial referrals that did not appear in the original source. These were "cases awaiting probation department determination in Alameda County," p. 88 note c. They are distributed in the same proportion as the "known" determinations for each type of offense.

Supreme Court case radically changed procedural juvenile law for all states. Dating to English federal law, juvenile justice was based on the concept of *parens patriae*; that is, the judge acted, figuratively, as a "surrogate parent of the child."[21] Judges took the position that their purpose was not to find fault and punish, but rather to diagnose the cause of the minor's problem and prescribe treatment.

In California, as Thornton and Rose state,

> The paternalistic, informal atmosphere and unlegalistic approach of the juvenile court started to vanish in 1960. The revision of the entire Juvenile Court Act in 1961 revamped not only the philosophy, but the procedural aspects as well. The "father figure" concept of the juvenile court judge was modified to that of a robed, legalistic figure on the bench.[22]

The Supreme Court, in deciding *in re Gault*, accorded juveniles the same rights as adults. They were given (1) the right to counsel, (2) the right to notice of the charge, (3) a privilege against self-incrimination, (4) the right to cross-examine witnesses, (5) the right to transcript of the proceedings, and (6) the right to appellate review.[23] As a result of *in re Gault*, juvenile court procedure has become almost identical to criminal court procedure.[24]

There are three types of juvenile court hearings (see decision points in figure 4-4). Since juvenile legislation emphasizes keeping the juvenile in the home, only a judge can have him detained for more than two days. Furthermore, only a judge can remove a youth from his family and declare him a ward of the court.

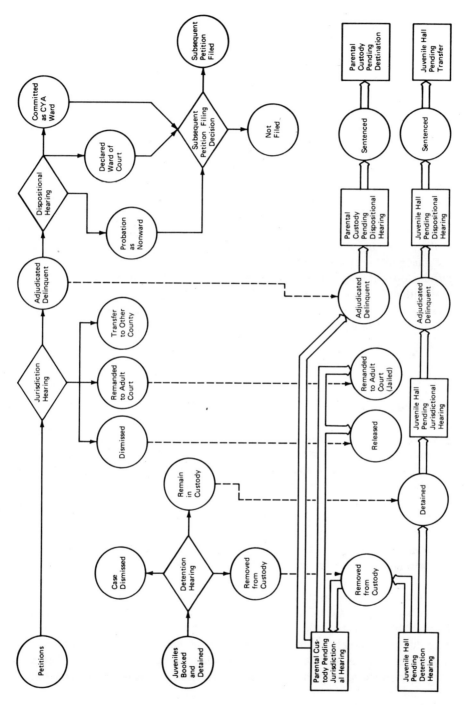

Figure 4-4. Juvenile Court.

These two things are done in a detention hearing and a two-phase adjudication proceeding, the jurisdiction-dispositional hearings.

The Detention Hearing

Within two days after a minor has been detained in a juvenile hall (and a petition has been filed), a detention hearing must be held. He must be represented by counsel, therefore, if he appears without an attorney, the court must appoint one (unless there is an intelligent waiver). If the court determines that the parents can afford an attorney, they must reimburse the county for legal expenses (W&I Code, sec. 634). The judge reviews the probation officer's initial referral decision to detain the minor. The judge uses essentially the same criteria as the probation officer (W&I Code, sec. 635). He may dismiss the case, release the minor to the custody of his parents, or detain him in the juvenile hall until a jurisdictional hearing is held. If he is released, the jurisdictional hearing must be held within 30 days; if he is detained, the hearing must be held within 15 days (W&I Code, sec. 657). The minor may plead to the allegations, waive a jurisdictional hearing, and appear next at a dispositional hearing (W&I Code, sec. 657).

The Jurisdictional Hearing

The purpose of the jurisdictional hearing is to determine whether the minor is actually a 601 or 602 case as alleged in the petition (W&I Code, secs. 701, 702). The minor may admit it and move to a dispositional hearing. Otherwise, the court must hear evidence in support of the petition.

Although the probation officer prepares the petition and evidence against the juvenile, the prosecutor may present the case at the jurisdictional hearing. In fact, the district attorney has come to play an increasing role in the petitioning process (formerly the bailiwick of probation). This is so because of the necessity of "screening cases for sufficiency of evidence."[25] Since the minor has a right to counsel, the court must appoint one if he is not already represented (unless there is an intelligent waiver as stipulated in W&I Code, sec. 700). The proceeding thus becomes much like a criminal trial, with the prosecution trying to prove beyond a reasonable doubt that the evidence supports the allegations while the defense tries to prove otherwise. As a consequence of enforcing juvenile rights (in accordance with *in re Gault*), juvenile adjudication is conducted more like a criminal proceeding even though it does not result in a criminal conviction (W&I Code, sec. 503).

A judge has only two options after the evidence has been heard. He must either find that "the minor is a person described under Sections 600, 601, 602," or else dismiss the petition (W&I Code, secs. 700, 701). In 1963 slightly less than 15 percent of the petitions were dismissed. By 1970 over 25 percent were dismissed.[26] It seems plausible to speculate that this trend was due to the increased enforcement of juvenile rights (for example, the defense attorney requirement) and especially the more stringent requirements for making a 601 or 602 finding. In essence, this implies a tradeoff between procedural justice and criminal deterrence. Just the same, effective policies exist—and to some extent have been used—for handling these (dismissed) cases. As suggested earlier, by diverting cases likely to be dismissed, additional benefits and cost savings would accrue.

The Dispositional Hearing

After a minor has been adjudicated delinquent or predelinquent (602 and 601, respectively), a hearing must be held to determine the minor's status and type of care. The dispositional hearing must be held within 10 days after adjudication if the minor is in custody; 30 days if released (W&I Code, sec. 702). The judge makes his decision on the basis of a social study prepared by the probation department. The social study includes the probation officer's assessment of the minor, the minor's offense, prior record, and recommended disposition. But it is the judge who has authority to decide what status and care the minor should receive.

The judge has three broad dispositional options. First, he may reprimand the minor and dismiss the case (W&I Code, sec. 782). Second, he may place the minor on probation for six months without declaring him a ward of the court (W&I Code, sec. 725). Finally, he may declare the minor a ward of the court (W&I Code, sec. 730). If he is declared a ward, the youth may be (1) returned to his own home under formal probation supervision; (2) placed in a foster home by probation, or an agency outside the juvenile justice system; (3) placed in a private or public institution; (4) placed in a county home, camp, ranch, or school for delinquents (or a juvenile hall if the county does not have a ranch, camp, or school); or (5) committed to the California Youth Authority (CYA). 601 cases may only be committed to the CYA on a supplemental petition if it is ascertained "that the previous disposition has not been effective in the rehabilitation of the minor" (W&I Code, sec. 777). Not only are the judge's options fairly diverse, but, unlike adult dispositions where the length of sentences is prescribed in the penal code, the judge has the authority to decide how long (until the age of 21) the minor must remain a ward of the court.[27]

Subsequent Petitions

Some time after adjudication, it may be necessary or desirable to change the court's dispositional order. Supplemental petitions may be filed if there has been

(1) a violation of the original court order, (2) a probation violation, or (3) generally a failure to adjust (that is, the minor was not rehabilitated under the original disposition).[28] If a minor is to be removed from his home, then the court must go through essentially the same petitioning process as for an initial petition.

According to sec. 778, W&I Code, "any parent or person having an interest . . ." in the child may file a supplemental petition. This filing does not, however, automatically lead to a hearing. The court must first determine whether a hearing is warranted.[29] If there is to be a hearing, it must be done with all the procedural requirements of an original hearing.

Conclusion

Table 4-3 shows the 1970 percentage distribution for juvenile court dispositions of initial petitions. Two very important inferences can be drawn from these data. First, as in the adult criminal justice system, there is a strong filtering process. The process results in the removal of juveniles from the system and tends to avoid the imposition of harsh penalties (that is, commitment to the CYA). (It should be noted that some wards are incarcerated in county camps or schools.) Of the 382,900 juveniles arrested, only 1 percent were adjudicated delinquent. Less than 1 percent of these 39,500 juvenile delinquents were initially committed as CYA wards. All others remained in their community. Second, the type

Table 4-3
Juvenile Court Dispositions of Initial Petitions, 1970

Referral Offense (and Number)	Court Disposition (%)				
	Dismissed or Remanded to Adult Court	Nonward Probation	Declared Ward	Committed to CYA	Total
Major law violations (16,696)	25.6	13.1	60.0	1.3	100
Drug violations (10,229)	34.9	15.8	48.6	0.7	100
Other delinquencies (24,791)	26.7	11.2	61.2	0.2	100
All offenses (less transfers) (54,716)	27.8	12.7	58.7	0.7	100

Source: Bureau of Criminal Statistics, *Crime and Delinquency in California* (Sacramento: State of California, 1970), table III-11.

of offense has an effect on the disposition. Drug cases are dismissed most frequently, while major law violators are most likely to be committed to the CYA.

Both the filtering process and trial outcomes depend on the merits of the individual cases, attorney's skills, and the attitude of probation officers and judges toward punishment. These factors may be viewed as institutional constraints affecting the level of punishment in the juvenile justice system. These constraints make it necessary for policymakers to consider the potential benefits and cost savings of adopting policies which trade off different types of adjudications, for example, emphasizing serious offenses over minor delinquencies. This issue is taken up in the next chapter.

Juvenile Corrections

According to an official report of the California Board of Corrections, "The primary goal of juvenile institutions, as well as that of all corrections, should be the protection of society, i.e., minimizing the probability of recidivism."[30] From the perspective of developing a strategic plan, "minimizing the probability of recidivism" is only one of several means to protecting society. The authors of the report go on to discuss several others:

> [They] include *incapacitation, deterrence,* and, particularly, *rehabilitation* and *reintegration.* It is the position of the Juvenile Institution Task Force that . . . society is best protected by the effective rehabilitation and reintegration of a youth in society.[31]

Although official reports proclaim an emphasis on rehabilitation and reintegration, more money is spent on incapacitation and hence deterrence.[32]

Juvenile corrections in California is a bifurcated system of state and county responsibility. At the county level responsibility for corrections has been invested primarily in probation departments. The California Youth Authority (CYA) is the juvenile counterpart of the California Department of Corrections. It has some authority to intervene in county corrections (for example, setting standards for county homes, ranches, and camps). A special feature of California corrections is that there was a deliberate shift from state-run corrections to county corrections in order to keep juveniles in their communities and to reduce state expenditures. In order to facilitate this, the state subsidizes the counties (according to a legislatively fixed schedule) for reducing commitments to state facilities.[33]

County Corrections

In 1970 there was a total of sixty-eight county facilities (that is, homes, ranches, camps). Figure 4-5 depicts juvenile county corrections. The juvenile law stipulates that at most a facility may hold 100 youths. Some facilities were homes with as few as six youths. Others were at maximum capacity.[34]

Thirty-five counties had no facilities. Fifty-nine facilities were located in twelve counties in the San Francisco Bay area and Los Angeles Basin.[35] Counties without juvenile facilities must place wards in their juvenile hall (if approved by the court), contract with another county for facility space, or commit them to the CYA.

It is important to remember that not all wards are placed in facilities (see figure 4-5). In 1969 less than 20 percent of the court wards were placed in facilities.[36] It must be assumed that all others remained in their homes or foster homes under probation supervision.

The California Youth Authority

The Department of the Youth Authority was created in 1941. Its purpose, according to the Youth Authority Act, was

> ...to protect society more effectively by substituting for retributive punishment methods of training and treatment directed toward the correction and rehabilitation of young persons found guilty of public offenses.[37]

By 1970 there were eleven schools, four conservation camps, three reception centers, and thirty-one parole field offices.[38] In addition, the CYA uses some Department of Corrections facilities for some older wards (generally committed by adult court), and a few wards are jailed or referred to the Department of Mental Hygiene. Figure 4-6 displays these institutions and their population movement by type.

The CYA, part of the state's Human Relations Agency, has five divisions, with the Divisions of Rehabilitation Services and Community Services receiving 98.9 percent of the 1970 fiscal year budget. As far as how this money was spent, 71 percent was allocated to institutions. The remainder was allocated to parole. The cost ranged from $4,648 to $9,000 per inmate per year, depending on the institution.[39] The other divisions handle administrative matters and research and development. In addition, there is the Youth Authority Board, the CYA's parole board.

Rehabilitation programs are primarily geared toward giving CYA wards vocational training and academic education. According to the Department of the Youth Authority, "other programs include remedial education, behavioral modification, aide training, cultural enrichment and recreation."[40] The Division of Community Services' primary function is to aid localities with technical assistance, training, and financial assistance. The last of these functions includes the probation subsidy program, mentioned earlier, youth service bureaus, and delinquency prevention programs sponsored by community organizations and

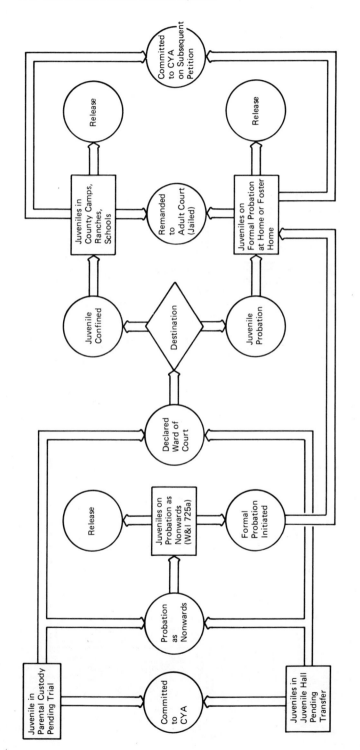

Figure 4-5. Juvenile County Corrections.

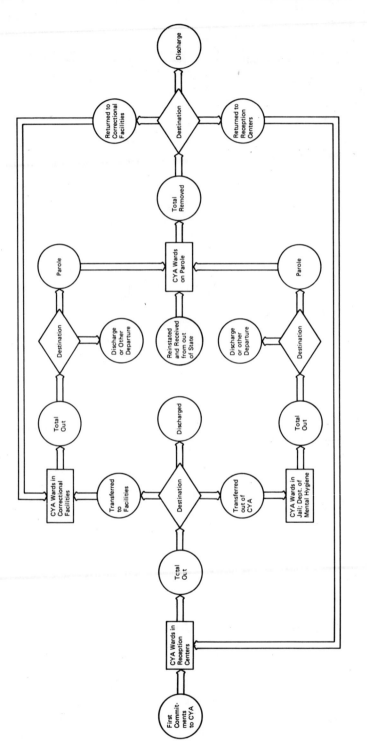

Figure 4-6. California Youth Authority Wards.

probation departments. The research division has influenced CYA policy in the direction of rehabilitation and reintegration into the community and diversion from the system.[41]

Conclusion: Comparing Crime Control Programs

The policy issue that seems to be most important now (at least from the point of view of strategic planning) is what to do with those offenders whose delinquencies were not prevented. The thesis of this book is that crime prevention is the most cost-effective method of crime control and, from the point of view of the potential offender and victim, prevention is the most just. Yet, to deny the necessity of finding cost-effective programs to handle offenders would be to miss one of the most important aspects of developing a strategic crime control plan.

Several strategies are feasible. It is possible to reduce crime by incarcerating offenders (through restraint and deterrence). It is also possible to reduce recidivism by rehabilitating or reintegrating offenders. Although Martinson's study on prison reform discussed in chapter 2 is now often cited as evidence that rehabilitation does not work, there is a fallacy in this argument.[42] The fallacy results from not realizing that although rehabilitation may not work for all offenders, it may work for some. Even more important is that some types of programs may be, in general, more effective than others. The policy research problem, then, is to find the most cost-effective combination or mix of programs for offenders.

Evaluating Correctional Program Performance

Correctional programs may be thought of as falling into one of two broad categories, institutional or noninstitutional, the main difference being the degree of freedom accorded the offender. In California a probation subsidy program was established to keep youths in their community. The state subsidizes county governments for sponsoring probation as an alternative to incarceration. In the interest of evaluating program performance (that is, crime control effectiveness), the degree of restraint is a more meaningful factor than one based on the program sponsor (that is, the county or the state). This latter factor, however, is important insofar as administrative considerations (including efficiency and equity) are relevant.

A correctional program classification based on the degree of freedom and the level of government is depicted diagrammatically in figure 4-7. The classification highlights two points. First, community contact does not depend on the level of government administering the program. Thus, policy recommendations transferring program operation to localities would seem to be based on administrative grounds rather than on performance ideals. In contrast, the intent of the probation subsidy legislation was to improve program performance as well

Freedom of Movement
and Community Contact

		Low	High
Level of Government	Low	1 County camps, ranches, schools	2 County probation (juveniles in homes)
	High	3 State CYA Institutions	4 CYA Parole

Figure 4-7. Correctional Program Classification.

as administration.[43] The second point follows logically. The degree of community contact and freedom of movement are highest in a noninstitutional setting (although there is some variability among types of institutions). Thus, state subsidies to county probation facilities, and the resultant shift of offenders from state-operated facilities to county ones, cannot be justified on performance grounds unless they are *in fact* more effective than state facilities and noninstitutional corrections. The scorecard for these four program types appears in table 4-4.

Cost Comparisons. In conducting this research, it was not possible to find probation cost data for the entire state.[44] On the basis of costs estimated from the Sacramento Probation Department, the yearly cost per formal probation caseload is estimated to be $368.[45] The annual formal probation cost is about half the cost of parole (56.8 percent, to be exact). It is substantially lower than the cost of institutionalizing juveniles. The cost of institutional care is at least ten times the cost of noninstitutional parole and at least seventeen times the cost of noninstitutional probation.[46]

   Column 5 in table 4-4 shows the total cost over the entire time period that first commitments stay in their respective type of corrections. These figures must be analyzed with caution because many wards in county facilities will go on to formal noninstitutional supervision (type 2) after release and others will be sent to CYA facilities. Thus, the total cost of $21,261,000 understates the actual cost before their wardship status is terminated. The total cost for CYA wards is likewise understated because many will become parolees. In short, not only is the annual probation cost per case less than the annual cost of institutionalization, but also more youths can be handled on probation for a longer period for less money.

Table 4-4
Juvenile Corrections, 1970

	Number of First Commitments	Approximate Average Daily Population	Average Length of Stay (Months)	Annual Cost per Ward	Total Cost (Rounded to Thousands) for Time of Stay, All Commitments (5)
	(1)	(2)	(3)	(4)	$(5) = (1) \times \frac{(3)}{12} \times (4)$
Wards in county facilities	6,941	2,500	5.6	$6,564	$21,261,000
Formal probationers in homes	25,217	53,000	12	368	9,280,000
CYA wards in institutions	3,746	6,000	9.2	6,754	19,397,000
CYA wards paroled	6,640	14,000	21.2	648	7,601,000

Sources: Bureau of Criminal Statistics, *Crime and Delinquency in California* (Sacramento: State of California, 1970); Board of Corrections, *California Correctional System Study: Juvenile Institutions Task Force Report* (Sacramento: State of California, 1971), p. v and appendix; Department of Youth Authority, *Annual Report, 1970* (Sacramento: State of California, 1970); R. Baron and F. Feeney, *Juvenile Diversion through Family Counseling* (Washington: GPO, 1976), p. 12.

Performance Comparisons. Proceeding from the premise that institutional care costs considerably more than noninstitutional care, one must ask what that extra money buys that noninstitutionalization cannot. The answer is simple: deterrence and restraint, but nothing more. Rehabilitation programs that can be conducted in institutions can be conducted outside them (with the additional benefit of eliminating the high cost of institutionalization). Furthermore, institutionalization is antithetical to a reintegrative approach to corrections. The ward is taken out of his community; he may, in fact, experience severe problems of adjustment after being released.[47] The policy research issue boils down to this: For the extra cost of institutionalization, how many crimes are avoided that would otherwise be committed? That is, if all those youths incarcerated in 1970 were given probation, how many more crimes would there have been in 1970?

There are two ways to approach this problem. First, one may study recidivism rates over a period of several years for samples of probationers and compare these data with those for former prison inmates (including parolees). Alternatively, one may focus on the total effect of the programs under comparison. (Recidivism accounts for only a fraction of all crime.) Incarceration physically restrains offenders from committing crime outside prison; and prison rehabilitation programs or the unpleasant aspects of prison life (that is, special deterrence) may keep them from committing crime when they are released. Their imprisonment, however, will have the "side effect" of deterring others from committing crime (that is, general deterrence).

Probation and diversion programs may also have "side effects." That is, there may be influences on persons who are not clientele. For example, these programs may reduce general deterrence, as in the case where an individual commits a crime because he does not fear the threat of imprisonment. All he faces is a possible probation sentence. On the other hand, probation and diversion programs that work seriously toward reintegrating the youth into his community and solving family tensions may have positive "side effects." The youth may be a positive influence on other members of his family and community. In addition, there may be less alienation from existing sources of authority. This is because the juvenile justice system may be perceived by members of the community as using its power in a more "legitimate" way. Which of these two tendencies is stronger in the total picture is an empirical question.

The preceding discussion warns that recidivism rates are only a partial measure of a program's performance. One must be cautious in using them for the purpose of program comparisons for two additional reasons. First, most recidivism statistics are based on samples of offenders, case studies, or even pilot projects. The policy conclusions that one makes from these statistics may be unfounded for the entire state. Although the number of offenders in the sample may be statistically significant for the program under study, that program may be quite different (that is, statistically unreliable) from other programs of the same type in the state.

Second, there are numerous definitions of recidivism. These definitions are based on where the offender is in the system when he recidivates (for example, probation, parole, release) and what the outcome of his change of status is (for example, arrest and release, sent to prison with or without a conviction). Because of these differences in definition and because of the problem of selecting a reliable sample, average recidivism rates for alternative programs are not statistically accurate estimates of recidivism. But, as Martinson and Wilks point out, this information is better than no empirical evidence at all.[48] With these caveats in mind, recidivism rates will be reported.

Within 15 months after release from CYA institutions in 1968, 45.3 percent of the parolees committed violations.[49] Youths paroled in 1969 had a recidivism rate of 40.1 percent. Some of these parolees were returned to institutions, their parole being revoked; others were eventually discharged. Roughly half of the offenses were major law violations, and about 10 percent were technical parole violations.[50] Within five years after release in 1968 and 1969, 62.3 percent recidivated.[51]

There are no data published on statewide probation recidivism rates. Several samples are available which can produce a range of estimates. One must keep in mind that probation cases may receive different treatment depending on the program. This treatment, and not probation per se, may have an effect on recidivism.

The recidivism rate for the Sacramento 601 Diversion Project's control group was 54.2 percent, but only 22.1 percent committed serious 602 offenses (that is, felony and drug violations).[52] In the case of the 602 control group, the recidivism rate was 38.1 percent. Only 24.8 percent committed serious 602 offenses.

Martinson and Wilks report recidivism rates for 128 studies. Five of these studies dealt with California delinquents. The mean rates are as follows: 17.83 for 12 delinquents in group homes; 28.13 for 133 youth probationers; 32.56 for 298 youths in a community treatment project; 44.50 for 34 first-time juvenile offenders; and 50.69 for 86 in a rehabilitation project.[53]

On the basis of these statistics, a few tentative conclusions may be drawn. Parolees do *not* have a considerably lower rate of recidivism than probationers. In fact, it appears to be higher.[54] This seems to hold for serious offenders as well as less serious offenders, such as technical parole violators. After the offender is released from an institution, an event that will occur within nine months on the average after admission, it appears that he will be just as likely to recidivate as if he were never incarcerated but placed on probation instead. Thus, the special deterrent and rehabilitative effects of incarceration seem to be, on the basis of these statistics, no greater than their alternative, probation.

If one conclusion can be drawn from these data, it is that the evidence is inconclusive. This indicates that research should be geared toward finding accurate recidivism rates for alternative programs.[55] In any case, recidivism rates give only a partial picture of the total effect of various programs.

Alternatives to Incarceration

The cost and performance comparisons tend to show that incarceration is, relative to probation, less cost-effective. With this in mind, the question that must be raised is, Why adjudicate at all? Three arguments are often cited as justifications for believing that adjudication and incarceration are necessary procedures: (1) some delinquents are so dangerous that to let them return to the streets is to ask for more crime; (2) without the prospect of incarceration, there will be no general deterrence to juvenile delinquency; (3) unless the delinquent is punished for his crime, retributive justice is not done and this may undermine the state's source of control for maintaining social order.

The first two arguments merit discussion here.[56] Incarceration restrains and deters criminals. If reformation is done in a noninstitutional setting, where it costs less, will restraint and deterrence be reduced? First, the restraining effect of incarceration is *not* reduced if there is a *selective process* of noninstitutionalization. If dangerous offenders, offenders with long prior records for serious crimes, are incarcerated, restraint will reduce crime. This becomes apparent by realizing that had the offender been incarcerated after, say, his second offense, all subsequent offenses would have been avoided. If nondangerous offenders are incarcerated, they may be more likely to commit crimes after release. This may occur because of the prison dependency effect discussed earlier or because criminal skills and attitudes may be acquired in prison. In conclusion, restraint may be a valid argument for serious offenders if it is done on a selective basis.[57]

The issue of general deterrence must be analyzed as a tradeoff problem. If more offenders arc given noninstitutional treatment, fewer will be incarcerated. Some would argue that this would reduce the likelihood of imprisonment and weaken the threat of punishment. It is plausible, however, that reducing the number of petitions will also reduce the probability of dismissal. If cases are better screened, the probability of adjudication and commitment becomes greater for serious offenders. If fewer offenders are institutionalized, serious offenders can be confined longer without increasing institutional budgets. The issue of deterrence versus reintegration must be settled on scientific grounds. In conclusion, it must be remembered that corrections, whether institutional or not, and diversion from adjudication are both reactive policies. They handle offenders after the fact, after someone's right to life or property has been violated.

The emphasis in this section has been to point out some of the areas where the relative effects of alternative criminal justice policies should be analyzed. It is equally important to assess the effect of proactive policies designed to prevent crime. Both kinds of policies, those internal to the system, such as deterrence and restraint, and those external to the system, such as prevention, are analyzed in the next chapter.

Notes

1. Warren E. Thornton and Max C. Rose, *Philosophy and Procedures in Juvenile Court,* p. 7.

2. Bureau of Criminal Statistics (BCS), *Crime and Delinquency in California,* 1970, p. 12. Statistics cited in this chapter are for 1970 (unless data for that year were not available) because 1970 was used as the base year for the simulation model. Many of the parameters could only be estimated with 1970 census data and 1970 LEAA data (see appendix B).

3. Thornton and Rose, *Philosophy and Procedures in Juvenile Court,* p. 14.

4. California, Office of Criminal Justice Planning, *California Correctional System Intake Study,* p. 127. Original drafts of the flowcharts in this chapter were improved after studying this report.

5. Ibid., p. 141.

6. Ibid., p. 136.

7. Ibid., p. 139.

8. Ibid.

9. BCS, *Crime and Delinquency,* 1970, p. 86.

10. Roger Baron and Floyd Feeney, *Juvenile Diversion through Family Counseling.*

11. Ibid., p. 5.

12. Ibid., p. 2.

13. Ibid., p. 8.

14. Ibid., p. 18.

15. In the case where a private citizen applies to the probation officer for a petition and then applies to the juvenile court for review because the probation officer did not file a petition, the court may, upon review, order the probation officer to file a petition (W&I Code, sec. 655). If a minor appears in adult court and is certified to the jurisdiction of the juvenile court, the probation officer is required, by sec. 656, W&I Code, to file a petition. Thornton and Rose, *Philosophies and Procedures in Juvenile Court,* p. 19.

16. *California Correctional System Intake Study,* p. 36.

17. Ibid., p. 146.

18. Ibid., p. 30.

19. BCS, *Crime and Delinquency,* 1970, p. 90.

20. Although the prosecutor may not accept a criminal complaint against a person he knows to be a minor, the juvenile judge may remand a case to adult court if the minor was over 16 years old when he committed a criminal violation and the 602 case is not fit for juvenile treatment. Thornton and Rose, *Philosophies and Procedures in Juvenile Court,* pp. 17, 18.

21. Thornton and Rose, *Philosophy and Procedures in Juvenile Court,* p. 8.

22. Ibid.

23. Paul B. Weston and Kenneth Wells, *The Administration of Justice,* p. 217. Gault was denied all these rights and sentenced to six years in juvenile corrections for making an obscene telephone call, an offense carrying a penalty for adults of a $50 fine and two months in jail; *in re Gault,* 387 U.S. 1 (1967).

24. Thornton and Rose, *Philosophy and Procedures in Juvenile Court,* p. 9.

25. *California Correctional System Intake Study,* p. 46.

26. BCS, *Crime and Delinquency,* 1970, p. 93.

27. *California Correctional System Intake Study,* p. 53.

28. Thornton and Rose, *Philosophy and Procedures in Juvenile Court,* p. 35.

29. Ibid.

30. Juvenile Institutions Task Force (JITF), *California Correctional System Study* (Sacramento: State of California, 1971), p. 18.

31. Ibid.

32. Department of the Youth Authority, *Annual Report, 1970*, p. 5.

33. Probation Task Force, *California Correctional System Study* (State of California: Human Relations Agency, 1971), p. 66.

34. JITF, *California Correctional System Study*, appendix.

35. Ibid., p. 8.

36. Calculated from JITF, *California Correctional System Study*, p. 11, and BCS, *Crime and Delinquency*, 1970, p. 95.

37. W&I Code, sec. 1700.

38. Department of the Youth Authority, *Annual Report, 1970*, p.4.

39. JITF, *California Correctional System Study*, p. 14.

40. Department of the Youth Authority, *Annual Report, 1970*, p. 6.

41. Ibid., p. 7.

42. For critiques of the rehabilitative model, see Robert Martinson, "What Works?—Questions and Answers about Prison Reform," pp. 22-54; Ernest van den Haag, *Punishing Criminals*, pp. 190, 191.

43. Probation Task Force, *California Correctional System Study*, p. 66.

44. Probation is administered at the county level, and this information is apparently not reported or published for the entire state.

45. The estimated figure is calculated as follows: 10 hours to place a juvenile in a foster home and 36 hours of placement supervision per year (this higher figure is also used for juveniles supervised in their own homes), for a total of 46 hours per year per case. The Sacramento Probation Department estimates its hourly cost to be $8, producing a total of $368 per case. Data are from Baron and Feeney, *Juvenile Diversion through Family Counseling*, p. 12.

46. JITF, *California Correctional System Study*, p. v. and appendix.

47. Karl Menninger, *The Crime of Punishment*. A classic example of having difficulties adjusting after release from prison was Charles Manson. He became so dependent on his prison environment (in which he spent the better part of his minority) that before being released in 1967, he pleaded with prison officials not to be released. As Manson often said, "Prison is my home, the only home I ever had." Within the next two years he would become responsible for over thirty-five murders. Although Manson is, admittedly, an extreme case, it is not an uncommon phenomenon among ex-convicts who recidivate to do so partly because of a subconscious desire to return to prison. See Vincent Bugliosi and Curt Gentry, *Helter Skelter* (New York: W.W. Norton and Company, Inc., 1974).

48. Robert Martinson and Judith Wilks, *Knowledge in Criminal Justice Planning*. Martinson and Wilks give a pragmatic justification for averaging recidivism rates, even though as they admit, "To research purists this would appear to violate many rules of quality research and constitute a critical flaw in the approach" (p. 25).

49. Department of the Youth Authority, *Annual Report, 1973*, p. 35. Wards in institutions are omitted from this discussion on the basis that they cannot recidivate if they are already incarcerated.

50. Department of the Youth Authority, *Annual Report, 1970,* p. 36. These data are for 1970 parolees.

51. Department of the Youth Authority, *Annual Report, 1973,* p. 34.

52. Baron and Feeney, *Juvenile Diversion through Family Counseling,* p. 10. The control group is the relevant sample for indicating probation recidivism in Sacramento. These statistics are based on a twelve-month follow-up.

53. Martinson and Wilks, *Knowledge in Criminal Justice Planning,* document numbers 0982h, 0984e, 0983h, 2257b, 0809.

54. This seems to be a general finding. In comparing all recidivism rates, Martinson and Wilks report that ". . . probation produces a mean rate which is lower than any other category (21.31). The rate for the max-out category [that is, discharge without supervision] is 31.55, which is higher than the rate for imprisonment plus standard after-care 23.35." Ibid., p. 42. (These rates include adult recidivism.)

55. Experimental and Development (E&D) programs are in their infancy in this area. Although some would argue that rehabilitation is impossible, and therefore E&D budgets should be reduced or eliminated, there is a fallacy to this argument. Although existing rehabilitation programs may perform poorly, that does not imply that redesigning or restructuring them or implementing new ones based on E&D will not perform well. See A. Rivlin, *Systematic Thinking for Social Action,* for a general discussion of experimental design that is consistent with the approach presented here. One use of the simulation model will be to show where E&D monies would be most productive in reducing crime.

56. As defined in chapter 1, retributive justice is a system goal. It would, therefore, be inappropriate to consider this argument in the context of program comparisons. Furthermore, the state's source of control is deterrence. Punishment causes people to follow the law for moral reasons and because they fear the threatened consequences. Thus, the argument that retribution is the state's source of control is a fallacy.

57. Two different approaches to restraint are often proposed. One would keep the offender incarcerated indefinitely until he is rehabilitated. The other would have the sentences fixed (for example, mandatory minimum, flat sentences). The simulation model can be used to assess these alternative programs.

5

Analyzing the Impact of Criminal Justice Policies: Computer Simulation Results

In this chapter, a number of policy research propositions about the behavior of the criminal justice system are examined. The cost-effectiveness of two sets of programs is assessed. First, preventive detention and juvenile diversion programs are evaluated. Second, an attempt is made to develop a cost-effective mix of deterrence and prevention programs. The reader should be warned at the outset that the purpose of this chapter is not to present accurate predictions and prescriptions for criminal justice policymakers. Rather, the purpose is to tie together the material presented in earlier chapters. To this end, propositions about the behavior of the criminal justice system are examined by simulating the California juvenile justice system on a computer. In short, the chapter demonstrates a method of designing a strategic plan to reduce juvenile delinquency.

A Simulation Model of the California Juvenile Justice System

This policy science research has a dual focus. On the one hand, it is concerned with scientific verification of sociopolitical theories of crime control. In this context, the interest is in estimating the effect of crime control programs (deterrence, restraint, reformation, and prevention) on juvenile delinquency. Because scarce resources place limits on policy choices, the economic costs of programs are assessed also. In this way, the cost-effectiveness of policy options can be compared. The second concern is in understanding the structural relationships within the system, particularly those associated with crime control programs. On the basis of such knowledge, policymakers can make informed choices among policy options. Policies can be formulated to guide decisionmakers in implementing the programs. In the end, a strategy for reducing delinquency can be designed by finding a cost-effective mix of programs and a set of rules for improving the system.

These two concerns were accommodated by developing a policy simulation model of the California juvenile justice system. The model was constructed using two mathematical techniques. The direct effect of criminal justice programs on juvenile delinquency was estimated with regression analysis from 1970 cross-sectional data for the fifty states. Systems dynamics was used to model the structural interrelationships among the police, courts, and corrections. By combining these two quantitative techniques, it was possible to compare the cost-effectiveness of a wide range of policy and program options. The simulation model is described mathematically in appendix A. Appendix B reports on estimates of the coefficients in the crime equation and the other variables and parameters used in the simulation model. The remainder of this section describes the simulation model in nontechnical terms.

The dependent variable in this regression analysis is the juvenile victimization rate. This is a measure of the actual number of crimes committed by juvenile delinquents. The number of crimes committed by juveniles depends on the state of affairs in the domains of both punishment (police, courts, corrections) and prevention. In this model, the juvenile victimization rate is a function of three deterrence and three prevention variables. Increases in the certainty and severity of punishment and in the probability of arrest deter crime. A decline in teenage unemployment, income inequality, and urbanization (measured as the percentage of the state's population living in urban areas) prevents juvenile delinquency. A 1 percent change in any of the independent variables produces a change in the juvenile victimization rate somewhere in the range of 3 percent (for income inequality) to less than 0.5 percent (for the severity of punishment). For more information about the hypotheses and findings the reader can refer to the discussion of table B-2 in appendix B. In the simulation model, the number of juvenile victimizations is predicted each month from statistically significant deterrence variables endogenous to the criminal justice system and exogenous prevention variables. The number of crimes committed then serves as the starting point for processing offenders through the system.

In the simulation model, the adjudication and correctional processes are viewed as a stock-flow process (as described in chapter 4). Juveniles flow into the system, reside in various stocks, and at some later point flow out of the system. As an example, juveniles held in juvenile hall, which is a stock, may be sentenced; in other words, they flow into probation, another stock. Systems dynamics was used to model the criminal justice system because it can be used to mathematically describe stocks and flows within a system.

Juveniles flow through the model each month in three aggregate offense categories: major offenses (essentially FBI Part I offenses), drug law violations, and other offenses (which are primarily incorrigibles).[1] Accordingly, a priority scheme was devised. Throughout the model, serious offenses are given priority over minor offenses. For example, a proportion of juvenile court resources is allocated for hearings on each of the three types of delinquencies; and if any court resources originally allocated to hearings on major delinquents remain after all major delinquencies are disposed of, they are used for drug law hearings. Similarly, after hearings on drug violations are held, any remaining resources are added to the resources originally allocated to "other" offenses. The path which juveniles follow through the system is determined at a number of key decision points. These are the police disposition, probation determination, adjudicatory hearings, and parole decision. Each sector was amplified with detailed flowcharts, from chapter 4, and these were converted into equations for the computer.

The technique used to model each sector of the system may be explained by using the juvenile court stage as an example. The court stage is divided into three hearings: detention, jurisdictional, and dispositional hearings. The outcome of the dispositional hearing, for example, is calculated from probability tables based on 1970 data published by California's Bureau of Criminal Statistics. In the simulation model, judges will "desire" to send a certain number (based on the probability tables) of adjudicated delinquents to county camps.

The word *desire* is used because the number of juveniles who actually flow into county camps may be less than the number judges would like to send based on 1970 data. The capacity of county camps—in 1970 the statutory maximum was 100 youths per camp—constrains the number of juveniles admitted. When county camps are full, the inflow into the camps is terminated. In short, scarce resources and legal requirements in one part of the system constrain and influence decisions in other parts.

In order to reduce delinquency, policymakers must be able to control the system. One aspect of this chapter focuses on the variables that can be directly manipulated by policymakers. None of the program variables can be directly manipulated, but policy instruments and parameters (for example, budgets and sentences) can be. By manipulating policy instruments, policymakers can implement a change in the program structure. This leads to a corresponding change in the behavior of the system. The chain of impact from policy instruments to targets (reducing predatory delinquency and enhancing justice) is the central concern of policy research. In addition to instrument variables, the model includes "experimental variables," such as the desired arrest rate, which the researcher may manipulate to facilitate the testing of certain propositions. Performance measures for some agencies are built into the model also. For example, the caseload per probation officer is derived each month the model is iterated.

The technique for modeling the California juvenile justice system may be summarized as follows. Juveniles flow through the system in three offense categories. Each month several decisions are made; the outcomes of these decisions are calculated from 1970 data. In cases where juveniles flow further into the system, the model ascertains whether the next sector can handle the caseload. Cases that cannot be handled within the budget constraint are routed elsewhere. Serious offenses are given priority over less serious offenses. In all, 110 equations track the flow of offenders through the system. The last one predicts the crime rate (see appendixes A and B).

California Criminal Justice System Expenditures

The policy research criterion used to evaluate criminal justice policies in this book is cost-effectiveness. Policymakers can choose to finance programs at various budget amounts. They can also set their targets at any level they desire; that is, they can seek numerous degrees of effectiveness. In other words, they may be willing to spend a lot of money to keep crime at a minimum, or they may be willing to allow a higher crime rate in order to keep taxes down. In using cost-effectiveness as a criterion, policy researchers must compare either the costs of alternative programs, while holding effectiveness constant, or the effectiveness of alternative programs at a fixed budget. Policymakers can either redistribute the budget to the various sectors or increase the size of the budget. Since the possible combinations are infinite, only a few are examined in this chapter.

Figure 5-1 presents California's criminal justice expenditure in fiscal year 1970. Only a portion of this expenditure was spent on the juvenile justice system. It is estimated that 30 percent ($385,146,000) of the money was allocated to the juvenile justice system.[2] Thus, juvenile delinquents accounted for nearly one-third of the workload in the criminal justice system. Juvenile delinquents may have been responsible for as much as 40 percent of the predatory crimes committed in 1970. As many as 547,000 Californians may have been victimized (violent and property crimes) by juvenile delinquents. (This is estimated from a simulation based on 1970 parameter estimates. See appendix B for the assumptions made in estimating the number of juvenile victimizations.) These figures indicate that isolating the juvenile justice system for cost-effective analysis is indeed valid. Furthermore, to the extent that juvenile delinquents become adult criminals, reducing juvenile delinquency will (with a time lag) reduce adult crime.

Preventive Detention versus Juvenile Diversion

Two criminal justice programs, preventive detention and juvenile diversion, work in opposite ways toward the common goal of controlling delinquency. Preventive detention controls crime by confining the accused until their guilt or innocence is established in court. Preventive detention is not, however, a crime "prevention" program. As the discussion in chapter 2 indicates, preventive detention is a restraint program. It must be conceptualized as restraint, not prevention, because it works by incapacitating "potential" offenders. Juvenile diversion works in precisely the opposite way. Instead of detaining the accused within the criminal justice system, the accused are diverted from the system. Juvenile diversion is a reintegrative approach to controlling delinquency. If crime is reduced by expanding diversion programs, it is because the institution of punishment does *not* come into play. In other words, the juvenile is not deterred, restrained, or rehabilitated by the criminal justice system; rather, he is reintegrated into the community. The youth learns to conform to community values.

Crime control is but one goal of the criminal justice system. Preventive

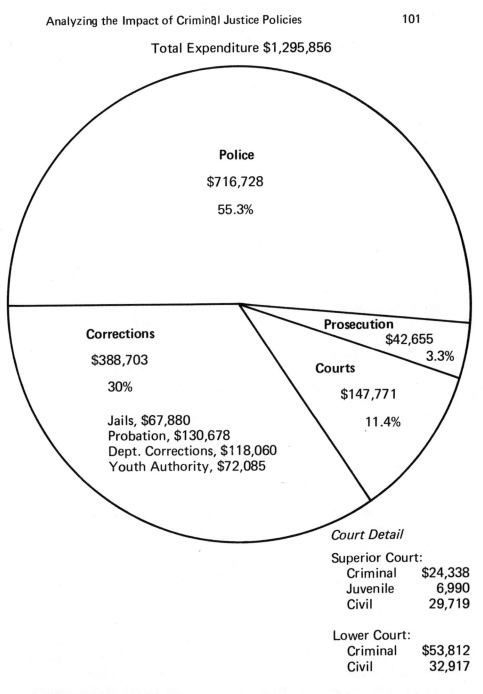

Total Expenditure $1,295,856

Police

$716,728

55.3%

Corrections

$388,703

30%

Jails, $67,880
Probation, $130,678
Dept. Corrections, $118,060
Youth Authority, $72,085

Prosecution
$42,655
3.3%

Courts

$147,771

11.4%

Court Detail

Superior Court:
   Criminal $24,338
   Juvenile   6,990
   Civil   29,719

Lower Court:
   Criminal $53,812
   Civil   32,917

*Excludes building construction.

Source: Bureau of Criminal Statistics, *Crime and Delinquency in California* (Sacramento: State of California, 1974), p. 35.

Figure 5-1. California Criminal Justice Expenditures, Fiscal Year 1970.
          (In thousands)

detention and juvenile diversion have profound effects on the level of justice in the system. Those who argue in favor of a preventive detention policy argue essentially for protective justice. Their view is that if a person has committed one crime, he may commit another. To allow another member of the community to be victimized by someone who has already committed one or more crimes would be an injustice. The fact that an individual has been arrested on probable cause of having committed a crime is justification for believing that he may commit another; it is justification for "preventively" detaining the accused.

Opponents of preventive detention argue that detaining the accused is an unjustifiable deprivation of liberty. Procedural justice, they argue, requires that the accused not be denied the constitutional right to bail. The Eighth Amendment of the Constitution which protects against *excessive* bail has been interpreted by common law as providing a right to bail. As Lewis Katz writes, ". . . it is at present a right supported only by logically persuasive arguments and not by conclusive [Supreme] court decision."[3] The premise behind bail is that anyone accused of a crime is innocent until proved guilty; the state must bear the burden of proof. The accused should be required to give only that amount of surety necessary to guarantee his appearance in court. If he fails to appear as required, bail may be forfeited.

In the juvenile justice system, most youths are released in parental custody after arrest. If they are detained as long as 48 hours, a detention hearing must be held. They may be released on their parents' recognizance. In some cases the youth is temporarily placed in the juvenile hall because the probation officer feels the youth would be worse off at home or because the youth has no home. Those who argue against preventive detention are implicitly arguing that the rights of the accused are more important than the right of the community to safety. In this case, procedural justice and protective justice are competing values, the former considered more important.

Juvenile diversion also affects the level of justice in the system. Diversion and detention programs can be substituted for each other. Every juvenile diverted from the system represents one less youth who can be detained. The same may be said for releasing a juvenile in his parents' custody. There is, however, a difference. The focus of diversion is primarily on removing the youth from the system and reintegrating him into the community. Releasing a juvenile in his parents' custody does not substantially change the focus of the system. The probation department must decide whether to file a petition. The focus is still on adjudication. Although juveniles in detention are more likely to be petitioned than those in parental custody, the fact remains that the latter also face the possibility of being petitioned, and hence adjudicated. Juveniles diverted from the system, for the most part, do not face that. From the point of view of those who want to prevent youths from the indignities of incarceration and the stigma associated with the adjudication process, diversion is perceived as a just treatment.

All the subjective factors previously discussed are amenable to cost-effectiveness analysis. In the following sections, the costs and impact of a preventive detention policy are compared to a juvenile diversion policy. The analysis demonstrates that a policy to detain juveniles prior to adjudication would be quite costly and relatively ineffective in reducing delinquency. On the other hand, if detention resources had been used to divert juveniles from the California system in 1970, the simulation results indicate that California would have experienced a lower crime rate.

The Cost of Juvenile Detention

In 1970 roughly 140,000 juvenile delinquents (excluding dependent and neglected children) were admitted to California juvenile halls. Juveniles are detained for only a few days, and the average daily population was about 3,200. In this subsection, the costs and feasibility of a juvenile detention policy are analyzed. The simulation model demonstrates the physical limitations of expanding juvenile detention. Furthermore, the model makes it clear that hidden costs (associated with detention hearings) must be added to the cost of operating juvenile halls.

In 1970, $16.8 million was spent to finance juvenile detention (table B-15). Approximately 70 percent of the juveniles referred to probation were detained for at least two days. Many of these juveniles (about 150,000) were subsequently released because they were not petitioned or because a juvenile court judge determined that their detention was unwarranted. They spent an average of six to fourteen days in detention depending on the type of offense they were accused of. Youths arrested on drug charges tended to stay longest, major delinquents (that is, predatory crimes) less, and others (that is, primarily delinquent tendencies) the least. But altogether their detention cost the state $16.8 million to operate and maintain juvenile halls.

If every juvenile were detained in California in 1970, it would have cost taxpayers an additional $13 million in custody services. This figure was estimated by simulating a preventive detention policy and comparing its cost to a base policy.[4] In the preventive detention policy, probation officers are required to detain all juveniles referred to probation. This may not be feasible because juvenile hall capacity constrains the number of juveniles who can be detained. Just the same, policymakers may wish to know what such a policy would cost if additional space were available.

The simulation model provided the cost estimate as follows: If probation were to detain more juveniles than juvenile hall capacity allows, there would be a deficit in the juvenile hall budget. The deficit represents the additional resources that would be required to detain juveniles after juvenile halls are filled. As compared to the base policy, the preventive detention policy created an additional $13 million deficit. Thus, the total custody cost of this detention policy would have been $30 million.

California law requires that a juvenile be given a detention hearing if he is detained for 48 hours. Some juveniles do not receive detention hearings because probation does not file petitions in all cases. Thus, some juveniles will be detained for one or two nights but released without a detention hearing because they are not petitioned. Those who are petitioned, however, must receive a detention hearing. Accordingly, a side effect of increasing preventive detention is that the number of detention hearings also increases. In 1970 detention hearings cost $1.2 million (table B-12) in California.

As discussed earlier, juvenile hall capacity restricts probation's decision to detain juveniles. Assume policymakers were willing to provide the additional $13 million in custody services necessary for a preventive detention policy. How much more, in addition to the $1.2 million, would have to be spent on detention hearings? In the simulated preventive detention policy, there were 305,000 juveniles whom probation desired to detain but who were not actually detained because juvenile halls were at capacity. If these juveniles had been detained, only those petitioned would have been given a detention hearing. Given the probability of being petitioned, 47,526 of these juveniles would receive detention hearings. At a cost of $24.73 per detention hearing (see table B-12), detaining every juvenile would have cost *at least* an additional $1.2 million.

The last statement suggests that a preventive detention policy might have cost more than an additional $1.2 million in detention hearings. The cost of detention hearings depends on the number of detained juveniles petitioned. Juvenile court resources allocated to jurisdictional-probation hearings constrain the number of juveniles petitioned. Therefore, if there is no change (from the base simulation) in the amount of resources allocated to jurisdictional-probation hearings, there will not be much change in the number of juveniles petitioned. (There may be a very slight change because there may be a small difference in the number of juveniles in informal supervision petitioned.) Given a constant number of initial referrals, the probability of being petitioned should not vary much from the base policy. This is precisely what occurred in the preventive detention policy simulation. If policymakers increase jurisdictional-probation resources, the number and the probability of juvenile petitions would increase. This would increase the number of detained (petitioned) juveniles requiring detention hearings. The implication is that increasing jurisdictional-probation resources would have, as a result of increasing the probability of petitioning, also increased the total cost of detention hearings under a preventive detention policy.

The probation officer's decision to detain a youth is not without its consequences in other parts of the system. In particular, the cost of his decision must include not only the cost of keeping a youth in custody but detention hearing costs. In 1970 juvenile hall costs totaled $16.8 million; detention hearings cost $1.2 million. In calculating the cost of a preventive detention policy, the additional $1.2 million in detention hearings must be added to the $1.2 million expended on detention hearings in California in 1970. A preventive detention policy would, therefore, cost a total of $2.4 million in detention hearings plus $30 million in custody services. On the other hand, eliminating juvenile detention could have saved taxpayers $18 million. Whether the money would have actually been saved by eliminating juvenile detention or whether it would have been spent on alternative programs is another issue. Policymakers must make such revenue and expenditure decisions on the basis of their priorities.

Some readers may consider the elimination of juvenile detention an absurd idea. There are two reasons for presenting the elimination of juvenile detention as a policy option. First, polar cases bring out certain system principles. For example, eliminating juvenile detention frees up juvenile court (detention hearing) resources. These resources could be used for adjudicatory hearings. Juvenile hall resources could also be put to alternative uses, such as juvenile diversion.

Second, as is explained in the next subsection, on the basis of cost-effectiveness, substantially curtailing juvenile detention may not be as unsound an idea as advocates of preventive detention believe. The important questions are, What effect would eliminating juvenile detention have had on delinquency and could resources allocated to detention have been put into more effective crime reduction programs? These two questions are answered in the following subsections.

The Effectiveness of Juvenile Detention

The preceding discussion demonstrates that a preventive detention policy is quite costly and that eliminating juvenile detention would have freed $18 million for other uses. It is, therefore, imperative to ascertain the effect that eliminating juvenile detention would have had on the juvenile victimization rate. In this book, regression analysis is used to measure the direct effect of causal variables, such as restraint, on juvenile delinquency. The simulation model brings out the indirect effects of juvenile detention on other parts of the system. Accordingly, this subsection focuses on both the direct and the indirect effects in order to assess the impact of a preventive detention policy.

The Direct Effect of Preventive Detention. The direct effect of incapacitation was measured in accordance with the causal model presented in chapter 3. Appendix B discusses the coefficient estimates in the juvenile victimization equation, that is, the change in the juvenile victimization rate resulting from a change in an independent variable, in this case, restraint. The effect of juveniles restrained in public detention and correctional facilities was analyzed. Two measures of juvenile restraint were added separately to the regression equation (appendix B, equation B.15). Neither had a statistically significant (even at an 80 percent significance level) direct impact on the juvenile victimization rate. Furthermore, adding either variable did not significantly change the effect of the other independent variables.

Some researchers argue that statistical significance should not be a substitute for logical theory. In contrast to conventional theory, a positive (though statistically insignificant) relationship was found between juvenile restraint and juvenile crime. In other words, states that detain more juveniles than other states also have higher crime rates. No doubt, some youths are more likely than others to commit a crime after release from juvenile hall. But, in the aggregate, detaining juveniles does not appear to reduce the juvenile victimization rate significantly. This is in complete opposition to the hypothesis that restraint reduces crime.

It is possible to explain the positive relationship between juvenile restraint and crime as follows. States with a greater number of juvenile victimizations also have a greater number of juveniles to restrain. But this alone does not imply that they restrain more juvenile offenders. There may be some factors related to criminal justice policy that create this positive, counterintuitive relationship. Criminal justice policy reflects, to a very great extent, the mood of the people. High crime rates frustrate and anger people. There is a tendency to react by striking back, by seeking solutions that are quick and easy. Locking up criminals is one such solution. Thus, it may be that the causality flows in the opposite direction. The higher the crime rate, the greater the need to seek fast, simple solutions, and hence the more juveniles detained.

Side Effects of Juvenile Detention. Relative to other programs, preventive detention, a restraint program, does not have an appreciable, direct impact on the crime rate. It does, however, have a side effect on the probability of punishment. In the base policy, the probability of punishment for major juvenile delinquents (that is, violent and property crimes) was .00549. This implies that roughly 5 out of every 1,000 delinquents who commit major violations are incarcerated. If every juvenile were detained in California in 1970, the probability of punishment would decline. This is due to the fact that had more detention hearings been held, there would have been fewer resources left for adjudicatory hearings. Conversely, eliminating juvenile detention would have increased the probability of punishment to .006.

Two additional points become apparent from this policy simulation. Although the probability of punishment increased, the number of major juvenile delinquents incarcerated did not. The inflow into correctional facilities was curtailed because the facilities were at capacity. The probability increased, however, because the denominator (that is, the number of victimizations) decreased.

A further point is that the probability of punishment depends on the types of juvenile delinquents detained. In the simulation model, juvenile hall resources are distributed to the three offender categories by giving more serious offenders priority. When the desired rate of detention was increased, all major delinquents and about 75 percent of drug delinquents were detained. None of the other less serious delinquents were detained. The probability of petitioning is higher for major and drug delinquents than for other delinquents. There are two consequences to this. First, the cost of detaining these delinquents is higher because their average stay in juvenile hall is longer. Thus, given a fixed budget, fewer delinquents are detained. Second, although fewer are detained, there are more detention hearings. This results because the proportion requiring detention hearings is considerably higher. Accordingly, the resources remaining for adjudicatory hearings are diminished. This, in turn, reduces the probability of punishment. Although the priority scheme used in the model may not appeal to all analysts, it does point to the fact that different types of offenses must be considered separately because of their differential effects on the system's process.

The Impact of Preventive Detention. Juvenile detention does not have a direct impact on crime, but it does have an indirect effect. The preventive detention policy simulation resulted in a 0.07 percent increase in the number of juvenile victimizations. A side effect of juvenile detention is that court resources are allocated—perhaps one should say misallocated—to detention hearings. These resources could potentially be used for adjudicatory hearings. Since they are not, the probability of punishment is lower, and hence the crime rate is higher than if fewer detention hearings had been held.

It should be noted that the 0.07 percent increase in juvenile victimizations understates the increase that would have occurred if every juvenile were "preventively" detained. As discussed earlier, the juvenile hall capacity constraint made it infeasible to detain every juvenile. If the juvenile hall budget were increased, however, so that all juveniles could be detained, it would have cost an additional $1.2 million in detention hearings. Since detention hearings are given priority over jurisdictional-probation hearings, the additional $1.2 million would have been taken away from adjudicatory hearings. This would have further lowered the probability of punishment and increased the crime rate. The slight increase (0.07 percent) in juvenile victimizations from the base policy is primarily due to the fact that a few additional detention hearings were held even though, as mentioned earlier, fewer juveniles were actually detained.

Table 5-1 is a policy impact matrix. The policy impact matrix was designed to present the results of simulations to policymakers in an easily understandable format. The most pertinent information appears in the policy impact matrix. The variables that policymakers can directly manipulate appear on the left side of the table. The impact of these instruments on the policy targets appears on the right side. One has only to read from left to right to see the values of (a

Table 5-1
Policy Impact Matrix 1: Preventive Detention versus Juvenile Diversion

| | Policy Instruments | | | | Targets | |
Policy Simulation	Juvenile Hall Budget ($)	Police Juvenile Diversion Budget ($)	Probation Crisis Intervention Budget ($)	Adjudicatory Hearings ($)	Juveniles Detained[b]	Juvenile Victimizations (Change from Base Policy)[a,b] (%)
1	16,850,000	0	0	1,500,000	101,322	+.07
2	0	0	0	1,900,000	0	−1.9
3	0	16,600,000	0	1,900,000	0	−2.3 to −2.4[c]
4	0	14,300,000	2,300,000	1,900,000	0	−3.5[d]
5	0	17,000,000	0	1,900,000	0	−1.5[e]
6	0	17,000,000	0	2,400,000	0	−4.9[e]

[a]Major delinquents only.

[b]The base policy had 139,093 juveniles detained; 552,742 juvenile victimizations (budgets were the same as in policy simulation 1).

[c]Two police diversion failure rates (PDFRs) were used. A 10 percent failure rate produced a 2.4 percent reduction in the number of juvenile victimizations; a 25 percent failure rate produced a 2.3 percent reduction. All three types of delinquents were diverted.

[d]The police diversion failure rate was 20 percent; the probation crisis intervention failure rate (PCIFR) was 5 percent. All three types of delinquents were diverted.

[e]Policy simulations 5 and 6 were based on a 20 percent police diversion failure rate. Only "other" delinquents (primarily delinquent tendencies) were diverted.

combination of) policy instruments and their impact on the targets. All extraneous information, such as program structures and social processes, is explained in the text or table notes. Policy simulation 1 (table 5-1) shows that a total preventive detention policy would increase the crime rate by 0.07 percent.

Although the simulation results are not presented as predictions, they do offer some insights as to how the system operates in principle. Policy simulation 2 (table 5-1) shows that eliminating preventive detention reduces the number of juvenile victimizations by 2 percent. Reducing juvenile detention makes available more court resources for adjudicatory hearings. As compared to a preventive detention policy, eliminating juvenile detention increases the probability of punishment, and thereby indirectly leads to a lower crime rate.

Justice, as well as crime, has social indicators. An indicator of procedural justice is the number of juveniles detained while awaiting disposition of their cases. Policy simulations 1 and 2 show that as procedural justice increases, that is, as fewer juveniles are preventively detained, crime declines. Thus, on the basis of these simulation results, protecting the rights of the accused and of the public appear to be complementary objectives. A policy designed to enhance procedural justice may, as a side effect, protect the public.

In conclusion, preventive detention is not a cost-effective policy. First, preventive detention is an extremely expensive policy. Second, it is ineffective. Accordingly, the resources used to provide custody services in California in 1970 could have been put to better use. There are numerous options from which criminal justice policymakers can choose. They could put the money to alternative uses in the criminal justice system, they could use it in other policy systems, or they could simply reduce taxes. These are value judgments that policymakers must make. Policy scientists must show the relative cost-effectiveness of the alternatives. In this book, one alternative, juvenile diversion, is assessed.

Juvenile Diversion: A Cost-Effective Alternative

Juveniles may be diverted from the adjudication process at any point prior to petitioning. Juvenile diversion has a dual purpose. First, diversion virtually eliminates any detrimental effect that punishment may have on a youth. The issue of the youth's culpability is considered less important than the effect which the adjudication process will have on him. In other words, a youth may be diverted because officials believe the petitioning process, court adjudication, and penalty may have a harmful effect on the youth. Juvenile diversion programs include some form of treatment. Youths are counseled, and an attempt is made to reintegrate them into the community.

Second, diversion reduces the workload of agencies further along the process. Some police departments have formal diversion programs. Youths are counseled by police officers trained in juvenile problems, and they may be referred to a community service organization. In either case, they are rarely referred to probation. (If a youth fails to meet the requirements of the diversion program, he can be referred to probation.) Juveniles referred to probation may be petitioned and thus face the possibility of adjudication. Probation may divert juveniles through crisis intervention or informal supervision. Probation diversion programs reduce the juvenile court workload.

Resource Implications. In order to assess juvenile diversion as an alternative to detention, the cost of the two programs must be compared. In the base policy, approximately 140,000 juveniles were detained. The juvenile hall budget was $16.8 million. Thus the average cost was approximately $120 per juvenile detained.

In the simulation model, the cost per juvenile in a diversion program was $150. This was approximated from diversion costs in Los Angeles and Santa Clara. The cost for the Los Angeles Sheriff Department program (cited in chapter 3) was $128 per youth.[5] The cost of the Santa Clara Diversion project was $107 per youth.[6] To assess cost-effectiveness in the simulation model, the higher figure of $150 was used to avoid underestimating the average cost of juvenile diversion for the state.

Based on an average cost of $150, approximately 112,000 juveniles could be diverted by the police. Approximately 30 percent of each of the three types of juvenile delinquents (major, minor, other) were diverted. In other words, the type of offense was not used as a criterion for selecting candidates for diversion. Furthermore, it was assumed that the cost of diversion did not vary by offense.

Compared to the number of juveniles detained in the base policy, 28,000 fewer juveniles were diverted. Fewer juveniles were diverted because the average cost of diversion was higher than the cost of detention. If the average cost was approximately $125, as the Los Angeles and Santa Clara data indicate, then almost as many youths could have been diverted by the police as were detained. In conclusion, if the 1970 juvenile hall budget was reallocated to police diversion programs, almost as many youths could have been diverted as were detained.

Police diversion programs reduce the number of juveniles referred to probation. In the simulated policy, it was assumed that the police would find as many youths warranting diversion as there were slots in the diversion program. Thus, with resources equivalent to the juvenile hall budget, roughly 120,000 youths could have been diverted. If we assume that 20 percent of juveniles in police diversion fail to meet the requirements of the program, then 96,000 juveniles would have been successfully diverted from probation. Every juvenile referred to probation represents an addition to the workload. Thus, at $16 per initial handling, their diversion reduces the probation department's workload by approximately $1.5 million.

Initial handling costs reflect only a part of the total cost of the adjudication process. In the absence of police diversion programs, some juveniles diverted in policy simulation 3 might have been petitioned. Three additional system processing costs would be incurred. The petitioning process cost probation $72 per petition in 1970. Petitioning 96,000 juveniles would have cost probation $7 million. Furthermore, 96,000 petitions represent a juvenile court workload of $6.5 million. Each juvenile would have been given a jurisdictional hearing at $49.47 per hearing; approximately 70 percent of them would have also been given a probation hearing at $25.48 per hearing (see table B-12 for cost figures). Thus, if it is assumed that all 96,000 juveniles would have been petitioned (had they not been diverted), their diversion represents a total probation and court workload reduction of $15 million.

The simulation model prevents the oversight of assuming that an additional 96,000 juveniles could have been petitioned. The juvenile court budget constrains the number of petitions that can be filed. The number of juveniles whom the probation department desired to petition in policy simulation 3 exceeded the juvenile court budget constraint. Accordingly, it would not have been feasible to petition additional juveniles. It is plausible to assume that some of the diverted juveniles might have been petitioned instead of those actually petitioned. The aggregate number of petitions, however, is a function of the juvenile court budget. If all juvenile court resources are used, the number of petitions filed is at a maximum. In this case, diversion does not reduce court costs.

In chapter 4 it was suggested that diversion can "prevent an overload of cases" in the criminal justice system. The volume of resources which are freed by diversion depends on the assumptions that one makes about the probation determination decision. It should be recalled that these policy simulations are based on a special assumption. It was assumed that probation decisionmakers desire to file petitions for all initial referral cases closed. In other words, if juvenile court resources were infinite, probation would not close any cases. This assumption was made in order to force the court budget constraint to become binding.

Alternatively, it can be assumed that in 1970 the actual probabilities for each type of determination (table B-8) were close to probation's desired determination. This model solves for the actual probability of petitioning on the basis of the desired number of petitions and the juvenile court resource constraint. In reality, many cases may be closed because probation officers do not believe certain youths should be petitioned. Even if juvenile court resources were actually increased in 1970, the probability that a case was petitioned may not have been higher (than reported in table B-8). Thus, if 96,000 juveniles were diverted, the number of petitions filed could decrease. Under this assumption, juvenile diversion would indeed "prevent an overload of cases" in juvenile court.

It is clear that diverting 120,000 juveniles at the police stage reduces the probation department's workload by about $1.5 million. Police diversion can, therefore, make existing resources more effective. The $1.5 million can be used to handle the probation caseload (that is, wards and nonwards of the court) instead of deciding whether to file petitions (that is, initial handling costs). This might increase probation performance by decreasing the caseload per probation office.

It was not possible to determine the decrease in the caseload per officer because of confounding factors. Changes in the caseload size contribute to changes in the caseload per probation officer. Nonetheless, probation performance may be improved because probation officers can spend a few more hours on each case. In 1970 the average daily caseload was approximately 65,000 (that is, the sum of informal supervision, nonward, and formal ward population averages from table B-14). On the average, $1.5 million would provide an additional $23 of probation services per case. At $8 per hour (probation cost), probation officers could spend, on the average, about three hours more per case than they did in 1970.

Finally, diverting 96,000 juveniles may, to some extent, reduce the number of petitions filed and hence reduce the cost of filing petitions. Thus, part of probation's $7 million petitioning cost could also be spent on caseload services. Furthermore, reducing the number of petitions makes more juvenile court resources available for other uses. In short, by freeing up resources and improving probation performance, juvenile diversion can make the criminal justice system more cost-effective.

The Impact of Diversion. Policy simulation 3 (table 5-1) shows that substituting most of the juvenile hall budget ($16.6 million) into police diversion programs reduced the number of juvenile victimizations between 2.3 and 2.4 percent. The reduction in delinquency is presented as a range because it was not possible to find published data for the police diversion failure rate. An advantage of the simulation model used in this book is that the effect of a range of failure rates can be examined. A failure rate of 10 percent reduced the number of juvenile victimizations by 2.4 percent; a failure of 25 percent by 2.3 percent. Hypothetically, if all juveniles failed to meet the requirements of the program, the number of victimizations would have been reduced by 2 percent (compare policy simulation 2). Thus, it is safe to say that, no matter what the failure rate, substituting police diversion programs for juvenile detention could have—on the basis of this model—reduced the number of juvenile victimizations between 2 and 2.5 percent.

It is critically important to understand what caused the reduction in the crime rate. This model distinguishes between direct and indirect effects. The direct effect of counseling and other treatments for diverted youths could not be measured in this book. Specifically, data limitations made it impossible to determine the percentage of reduction in crime that would result from a 1 percent increase in expenditures on juvenile diversion programs. In other words, the direct effect of diversion, that is, reintegrating youths into their communities, could not be measured.

It was possible, however, to ascertain the indirect effects of diversion. Diversion increased the probability of punishment and thereby decreased the crime rate. The probability of punishment increased because of several inter-related factors. In order to examine these relationships, the diversion policy must be compared with policy simulation 2. Comparing the diversion policy with the base policy does not isolate the indirect effects of diversion because the diversion policy did not include any juvenile detention. Accordingly, the diversion policy must be compared with the policy that eliminated detention (compare policy simulation 2). In this manner, the only policy change is the addition of diversion.

Compared with policy simulation 2, the nonward and formal ward proba-tion stocks increased at a slower rate. Since the number of subsequent petitions is a proportion of these probation stocks, there were fewer subsequent petitions. In the model, subsequent petitions are given priority over initial petitions. Accordingly, a decline in the number of subsequent petitions makes more resources available for hearings on initial petitions. The probability of punish-ment increased from .006 (in policy simulation 2) to .0063 in the diversion policy (simulation 3, table 5-1). The result is approximately a 1.5 percent decline in the number of victimizations from policy simulation 2. Eliminating juvenile detention and replacing it with juvenile diversion in 1970 could have indirectly reduced the number of juvenile victimizations by nearly 2.5 percent (compare policy simulation 1). Furthermore, it is plausible that the crime rate would have been reduced even more because of the direct effect of reintegrating juvenile delinquents.

A major objective of strategic planning is to find a cost-effective program structure. In an attempt to find a cost-effective mix of programs, juvenile diversion expenditures were allocated to probation crisis intervention as well as police diversion programs. As policy simulation 4 (table 5-1) shows, $2.3 million was distributed to crisis intervention programs. Combined with $14.3 million for police diversion programs, the number of juvenile victimizations was reduced by 3.5 percent. Thus, a program structure which combined police and probation programs is more cost-effective than a police program alone.[7]

As in the case of police diversion programs alone (policy simulation 3), the mix of programs had an indirect impact on the crime rate. The probability of being petitioned increased because more court resources were available for adjudicatory hearings. In this respect, police and probation diversion programs are program complements. A combination of the two programs is more cost-effective than either alone.

It must be reiterated that the decrease in crime was due solely to the indirect effects of diversion. The optimal mix of programs for a given expendi-ture, which would result from this simulation model, does not reflect the different treatments of the reintegration programs. Crisis intervention may be more effective for extremely troubled youths than police counseling. Some methods of crisis intervention are generally more effective than others. The fact that reintegration programs have differentially direct effects means that clientele must be chosen selectively. It also means that a cost-effective mix of programs found by analyzing indirect effects may not be optimum if the direct effect of reintegration were included. Just the same, preventive detention and juvenile diversion are program substitutes. The more resources are reallocated from detention to diversion, the lower the juvenile victimization rate.

Conclusion: Expanding Juvenile Diversion

The previous subsections analyzed juvenile diversion without considering any institutional factors related to its implementation. In this conclusion, an example is given to show how diversion could be instituted as part of a cost-effective strategic plan. The main point is to demonstrate that by diverting juveniles who have committed minor offenses predatory crime can be substantially reduced.

Criminal justice is—and must be—individualized. No two individuals are identical; no two treatment programs are equally cost-effective. Legislators cannot easily fit programs to individual needs. Accordingly, a program structure must be developed which is both comprehensive enough to cover the range of demands on the criminal justice system and flexible enough to allow decision-makers to effectively tailor programs to individual needs. In a system with limited resources, the best way to accomplish this is to set priorities.

Policy simulations 5 and 6 can be used to show the cost-effectiveness of one priority system. In policy simulation 5, $150,000 more than the juvenile hall budget ($16,850,000) was allocated to police diversion programs. Only "other" delinquents (primarily 601s or delinquent tendencies) were diverted. Specifically, 40 percent of "other" delinquents in police custody were diverted; none of the major delinquents nor any of the drug delinquents in police custody were diverted. In practice, some major delinquents and some drug delinquents might be diverted. In addition, probation officers might detain those juveniles who would be safer in custody than at home. Although this example diverts only a portion of "other" delinquents, the program could be designed to provide a wider variety of services.

Policy simulation 5 (table 5-1) shows a 1.5 percent reduction in the number of juvenile victimizations from the base policy. For reasons discussed earlier (that is, an increase in the probability of punishment) diverting "other" delinquents reduces delinquency. It should be noted, however, that this is not a cost-effective policy. Policy simulation 2, in which no juveniles were diverted, was slightly more effective. For a lower expenditure, diverting an equal proportion of each type of offender was more effective (policy simulations 3 and 4). Nonetheless, under certain circumstances spending $17 million for diverting 113,000 "other" delinquents can be extremely cost-effective.

Policy simulation 6 diverted 113,000 "other" delinquents and, in addition, redistributed $500,000 of juvenile court resources. The rationale for this policy is twofold. More serious offenders (major or predatory delinquents) are given priority in allotting court resources to adjudicatory hearings. At the same time, less serious (601) offenders are not neglected. They are given counseling and other aid which not only diverts them from the adjudicatory process but also reintegrates them. Diverting less serious offenders indirectly reduces the crime rate by freeing up resources for adjudicating serious offenders. A policy which combined juvenile diversion for 113,000 minor offenders with redistributing court resources so that an additional 7,000 adjudicatory hearings could be held for major delinquents (policy simulation 6) reduced the number of juvenile victimizations by almost 5 percent.

Policymakers are concerned with reducing drug delinquencies and "other" (601) delinquencies as well as predatory delinquencies. All three are crime reduction targets. This model was not designed to predict changes in the number of drug delinquencies and other delinquencies. Data were not available for estimating the coefficients in these crime equations. Until researchers are able to predict drug and other delinquencies, policies will have to be formulated without the aid of scientific research findings. Policy scientists can, however, clarify issues involved in making these policies.

There are two programs which policymakers can implement in an effort to reduce drug and other delinquencies. Diversion can be used to provide treatment for some of these delinquents. On the other hand, the certainty and severity of punishment could be increased to deter youths from such behavior. The issue is which program, diversion or punishment, has a more cost-effective impact on drug and other delinquencies.

Three theoretical points can provide insight into this issue. First, before becoming drug delinquents, most "retreatists" commit predatory crimes. The implication is that reducing predatory delinquency will reduce drug delinquency to some extent. Furthermore, drug-related crimes (say, robbery) would decline. Second, it is hypothesized that singling out delinquents for punishment strengthens ties with members of delinquent subcultures. Accordingly, punishing minor offenders may not only alienate them but also increase the likelihood that they will commit serious crimes. Finally, modifying delinquent behavior requires that the values of the delinquent subculture be repudiated. It is suggested that reformation could be made more effective by increasing the integrity of the criminal justice system. One way of doing this, it is hypothesized, is to punish juveniles who have committed serious offenses but help minor delinquents solve their problems.

In setting their priorities, policymakers can consider these three propositions. Some policymakers may believe that minor delinquencies can be reduced only by punishment. They must decide how much of the resources available should be used for punishing minor delinquents. They must be aware of the fact that for each minor delinquent punished a certain number of predatory crimes will be committed and the offenders will not be adjudicated. Other policymakers may believe, as the previous propositions suggest, that diverting minor delinquents and punishing major delinquents are complementary objectives. In this case, priorities are easy to set. The more juveniles diverted for drug and other delinquencies, the lower the number of predatory victimizations. Until these propositions are scientifically tested, policymakers will have to make intuitive judgments.

Deterrence and Prevention: Finding a Cost-Effective Program Mix

The purpose of this section is to present an approach that could be used to develop a strategic plan to reduce delinquency. The approach centers on finding a cost-effective program structure. This simulation model cannot be used to find an optimal mix of deterrence and prevention programs. Furthermore, political reality indicates that there is much debate over goals and programs. So it is not likely that one can find a socially optimal policy in a political context. At any rate, this section assesses the cost-effectiveness of a few select policies. In the first subsection, the effect of increasing the severity of punishment is analyzed. The following subsection demonstrates the approach to finding a cost-effective mix of police deterrence and juvenile employment (prevention) programs. Finally, the impact of income redistribution on the dual goals of crime control and justice is examined.

The Severity of Punishment: An Ineffective Deterrent

Claims are often made that delinquency can be reduced by imposing tougher sentences.[8] The argument is that increasing the severity of punishment is an efficacious deterrent. The costs and effects of such proposals are seldom debated for public scrutiny. If for no other reason, discussion is rare because their costs and effects are virtually unknown. Policy science research can explicate the costs and predict the effects of policies that increase the severity of punishment.

Two assumptions must be made before the cost-effectiveness of increasing the severity of punishment is analyzed. First, it is assumed that state policymakers can promulgate rules to guide the severity of punishment. In California the juvenile court is responsible for setting sentences. The California Youth Authority (CYA) is responsible for releasing CYA wards from institutions. Nonetheless, state policymakers and policy planners can influence sentencing decisions by communicating their desires to the judiciary and the parole board. Ultimately, the legislature has authority to mandate sentences.

Second, punishments can be made more severe in a number of ways. More youths can be sentenced to correctional facilities instead of to probation. For those in prison, the amenities that exist can be eliminated, and treatment can deliberately be made unpleasant. In this book, it is assumed that punishment can be made more severe by increasing the average length of stay in correctional facilities. These various methods are differentially cost-effective. The last method, increasing sentence lengths, is analyzed below.

The cost of increasing the average length of stay in correctional facilities cannot be easily assessed. Sentences are changed through a rule-making process. Since rule changes require no budgetary action, published data do not exist for the cost of sentencing changes. Furthermore, as is discussed later, the severity of punishment constrains the certainty of punishment. Therefore, assessing only the correctional costs of detaining juveniles for a longer period is inadequate. Cost changes in other sectors, which result from changes in the probability of punishment, must be attributed to increases in the severity of punishment. An appropriate procedure is to measure the impact of a sentencing policy change and, holding crime constant, calculate the difference in cost with a policy that changes the probability of punishment. The second policy may result in a cost savings or increase. If the former occurs, then increasing the average length of incarceration is cost-effective. In the latter case, the analyst need not be concerned with a precise measure of the cost of the rule change because it is a more costly policy.

Policy impact matrix 2 (table 5-2) compares a number of deterrence and prevention programs. Policy simulation 1 shows that increasing the average length of stay in county camps has a counterproductive effect. In 1970 the average length of stay was six months. Increasing it to 1 1/2 years could have increased the number of juvenile victimizations almost 3 percent. Thus, mandatory minimum sentencing would have been a detrimental policy in the juvenile justice system.

The counterintuitive result may be explained as follows. As the average length of stay is increased, the time (delay) between commitment and release increases. If facilities are full, there will be a delay in the system before additional commitments can be made. (This would occur in the real world if minimum standards for prison space were enforced.) As the number of new commitments declines, the certainty of punishment becomes a weaker deterrent. When the effect of the severity of punishment is analyzed with an econometric model, other independent variables (the probability of punishment) are held constant. On the other hand, the simulation model takes these interdependencies into account. Depending on the *relative magnitude* of the two direct effects (that is, the deterrent effects of the certainty and the severity of punishment), the crime rate may increase or decrease with an increase in the severity of punishment. The simulation experiments demonstrated that an increase in the average length of stay causes the probability of punishment to decline and hence

Table 5-2
Policy Impact Matrix 2: Deterrence and Prevention

Policy Simulation	Policy Instruments				Targets	
	Average Length of Stay in County Camps (%) (1)	Police Budget Increase ($) (2)	Juvenile Employment Programs ($) (3)	Gini Coefficient of Income Concentration (%) (4)	Change in Distributive Justice[a] (%) (5)	Juvenile Victimizations (Change from Base Policy)[b] (%) (6)
1	+300	0	0	0	0	+2.9
2	0	0	10,000,000	0	0	−1.3
3	0	10,000,000	0	0	0	−1.4
4	0	0	20,000,000	0	0	−2.7
5	0	20,000,000	0	0	0	−2.6
6	0	10,000,000	10,000,000	0	0	−2.8
7	0	30,000,000	0	0	0	−3.9
8	0	0	30,000,000	0	0	−4.0
9	0	0	0	−2	+2	−7.9
10	0	0	0	−4.2	+4.2	−16.3
11	0	0	0	−11.2	+11.2	−37.8

[a]A reduction in the Gini coefficient equalizes the distribution of income (column 4) and automatically increases distributive justice (column 5).
[b]The base policy had 546,487 juvenile victimizations, and the Gini coefficient was 0.357 in 1970.

the juvenile victimization rate rises. The implication for strategic planning is that the certainty and severity of punishment must be balanced—tradeoffs must be made—to find a cost-effective mix of deterrence programs.

Some econometric tests of the deterrence hypothesis have lead to the conclusion that crime will decline as the severity of punishment increases. Indeed, the test of this hypothesis, using cross-sectional data, resulted in a statistically significant inverse relationship between these two variables (see table B-2). (While most other econometric studies support this finding, some have produced conflicting results.) In using the estimated coefficients in the simulation model, policy experiments that increased the average length of stay in county camps resulted in higher crime rates. The technical reason for this result is that the simulation model includes capacity constraints for correctional facilities, whereas econometric models do not. Thus, it is plausible that the coefficients estimated from time-series data would have a positive sign.

Police Deterrence and Juvenile Employment

The issue addressed here is developing a cost-effective mix of police deterrence and juvenile employment (prevention) programs. This involves two aspects of expenditure analysis. The level of financing must be determined, and the distribution of budget to various agencies must be analyzed. The former is a political issue; the latter is an economic one. Expenditure analysis can, however, clarify some of the factors involved in the politics of preparing budgets for agencies.

Figure 5-1 shows that the police received more than half of California's criminal justice budget in 1970. Expenditures on prevention programs are not published as part of California's overall criminal justice expenditures. In order to evaluate the effect of police deterrence and youth employment, additional monies were hypothetically allocated to the 1970 budget. The additional resources were dispersed to the police sector and were used to create jobs for teenagers.

The cost-effective mix of police deterrence and youth employment programs depends on the level of financing. Three budget increases were examined. An additional $10 million, $20 million, and $30 million were allocated to police and employment programs. The effect of these disbursements is depicted in policy impact matrix 2 (see policy simulations 2 through 8). The model demonstrates that allocating $10 million solely to the police is more effective than allocating $10 million solely to youth employment programs. At a higher level of expenditure, that is, $20 million and $30 million, the reverse is true—youth employment alone is more effective than police deterrence. Policy simulation 6, however, shows that a program structure which combines police deterrence with prevention programs is more cost-effective than either alone.

A few points should be made about the cost-effectiveness of these policy simulations. The theoretical reasoning for the efficacy of these two programs was discussed in chapter 3. Increasing the policy budget increases the probability of arrest, which is a deterrent. Job programs increase opportunities for participation in legitimate activities. By increasing legitimate opportunities, illegitimate activities become a less attractive alternative. Furthermore, perceptions of relative deprivation are reduced, and sentiments about official norms are improved. As a result, juvenile delinquency declines.

In this model, the number of arrests and the number of youths employed are a function of their average costs (and total program expenditures). The average cost of arresting a perpetrator of a violent crime was estimated to be $855 in 1970. The average cost for a property arrest was $685. These cost estimates were based on the number of hours it takes to make an arrest and total police expenditures per hour. (The procedure for estimating arrest costs is described in appendix B.) The cost of youth employment programs was based on the assumption that $4 per hour would cover administrative costs and wages. A teenager could, therefore, be employed full-time for one year for $8,000.

The relative cost-effectiveness of the two programs depends largely on the accuracy of their cost estimates. Since the output level of both services is a function of average cost, cost-effectiveness comparisons among incremental expenditure increases may not be accurate. An attempt to measure the marginal cost of arrest (using a linear cost function in the range of the expenditure data) produced a marginal cost considerably greater than the average cost. If the marginal cost of arrest is indeed greater than the average estimated cost, then increasing policy budgets in this model may overstate their cost-effectiveness.[9]

On the other hand, the cost-effectiveness of youth employment may be understated. It may not be necessary to employ each teenager full-time for an entire year. The theory of relative opportunity suggests that both opportunities and rewards for employment must be high. This implies that the number of youths employed may be as important as the terms of their employment. Therefore, instead of providing full-time employment to a limited number of youths, it may be more cost-effective to hire more youths for part-time work.

In order to compare the cost-effectiveness of police and employment programs, equal expenditure increments were allocated to each program. Resources were allocated to youth employment programs as if they were used to create public service jobs. Employment programs can be structured so that youths are employed by private industry instead of by the government. This can be done by subsidizing the private sector and instituting training programs. Such a program structure would be considerably less costly than public service jobs. A job program of this type could pay for itself through its contribution to gross national product and tax revenues. Thus, depending on the program structure, youth employment can be considerably more cost-effective than the policy simulations presented in policy impact matrix 2 indicate.

In addition to reducing major delinquencies, both programs have other benefits. They can reduce other crimes and provide other public services as well. Allocating additional resources to the police in this model increases not only the number of juveniles arrested for major law violations but also the number of juveniles arrested for drug law violations, "other" offenses, and the number of adults arrested. Other things being equal, this will lead to an increase in the probability of arrest for other juvenile offenders and adults. To the extent that the probability of arrest is an effective deterrent for these offenders, the number of their offenses will be reduced.

A similar argument may be made for youth employment programs. These programs not only affect the number of predatory crimes, but also reduce drug use and other delinquencies. Expanding opportunities for juveniles will, to the extent that juvenile offenders become adult criminals, reduce the number of predatory crimes committed by adults.

Both programs also have other benefits. The cost of other police functions, such as administrative and community services, was included in arrest costs. (This was done because a detailed breakdown of a police budget was not available.) The implication of distributing the cost of other services over arrest costs is that when arrest expenditures are increased, resources for other public services are automatically increased. Thus, a by-product of increasing the probability of arrest in this model is that the police provide additional community services. Similarly, youth employment has other benefits in addition to reducing delinquency. These are positive externalities. For example, parks may be improved, streets may be cleaned, and refuse may be recycled. In general, the most important difference between spending money on police protection and on prevention programs is that a dollar spent on police protection buys a dollar's worth of crime reduction, whereas a dollar spent on youth employment buys a dollar's worth of crime reduction and other social benefits. These other benefits, to a great extent, influence the political decisions about the level of financing.

The size of the criminal justice budget depends on how much policymakers want to reduce crime and the effect this will have on other political goals. The budget can be distributed to the police and to employment agencies in accordance with the cost-effectiveness criterion. For any budget level, the most effective mix of programs is adopted. Yet, the question remains: How much should be spent on reducing crime? This question can best be answered by analyzing the effect of crime on other political goals. For example, when predatory crime is reduced, insurance costs decline, fewer hospital services are provided, and social well being is improved in general.

This research focused on crime as a dependent variable. Analyzing the effect of crime on other target variables requires that a different policy-affected system be analyzed. Until the cost-effectiveness of reducing crime is analyzed within the context of a more complete policy-affected system, policymakers will have to determine the size of the criminal justice budget on the basis of value judgments.

In conclusion, the criminal justice system's program structure depends not only on its effect on the crime rate, but also on its external effects on other political goals.

Income Redistribution

This chapter concludes with an analysis of the cost-effectiveness of reducing crime by redistributing income. Income redistribution is not specifically a crime reduction program. Rather, it is a program for enhancing distributive justice. It was suggested earlier that distributive justice and crime reduction are complementary goals. In chapter 3 it was hypothesized that reducing inequality is the most cost-effective method of reducing crime. The purpose of this subsection is to examine this rather strongly stated proposition.

There are two reasons for hypothesizing that income redistribution is an extremely cost-effective policy. First, inequality is the key causal variable common to the two main hypotheses of relative opportunity. Social structures manifested by inequality offer few legitimate opportunities for the disadvantaged. Inequalities in the relative position among the various classes produces perceptions of relative deprivation. Relative deprivation alienates youths, and sentiments toward delinquent norms become strengthened. Thus, the thesis of this book is based largely on the relationship between two dimensions of equality (equality of opportunity and equality of results) and crime.

Second, it was hypothesized that reducing inequality is the most cost-effective policy option because it is essentially a "costless" policy. Redistributing income does not necessarily require significant expenditures. Administrative costs can be minimal by making the tax structure more progressive or instituting a negative income tax. Unlike with allocating resources to the police or job programs, no services are provided for the public. Therefore, there are no program operating costs. One might argue that redistributing income will have hidden costs. For example, it may have a detrimental effect on other goals such as gross national product. Until this issue is resolved, policymakers will have to make the necessary value judgments as to the appropriateness of redistributing income.

Policy simulations 9 through 11 (policy impact matrix 2) show the effect of three income redistribution policies. The distribution of income was measured with the Gini index of income concentration. As the distribution of income becomes equalized, the value of the Gini coefficient declines (conversely). The fourth column in table 5-2 shows three changes in the Gini coefficient. Each change equalized the distribution of income.

The simulation results were as follows. A 2 percent change toward equality of income could have reduced the number of juvenile victimizations in California in 1970 by almost 8 percent. A 2 percent reduction in California's Gini coefficient would have made its distribution of income the same as that in Colorado, Idaho, Maryland, and Montana. All these states reported a lower crime rate than California. Changing the distribution of income in California so that it would have been equalized as in Illinois, New Jersey, Vermont, and Oregon (that is, a 4.2 percent decrease in the Gini coefficient) could have reduced the number of juvenile victimizations by over 16 percent. Finally, in policy simulation 11 California's distribution of income was hypothetically changed so that it would have been the most equalitarian state in 1970. This required an 11.2 percent change in its Gini coefficient. The number of juvenile victimizations was reduced by almost 40 percent. These policy simulations demonstrate that income redistribution was the most cost-effective policy option examined.

Income redistribution is a proactive policy. There are several benefits from such a policy. Inequality is an exogenous variable in this policy model, and it can be directly controlled by policymakers. Changes in the income distribution have a direct impact on the crime rate. Without increasing expenditures in the criminal justice system, the number of delinquencies is reduced. As a result, the probability of arrest and punishment increases. They also have a direct impact on the juvenile victimization rate. The result is that income redistribution makes these deterrence programs more effective.

Reducing delinquency by redistributing income is also the most just policy. One measure of retributive justice is the proportion of offenders who receive their "due." Since the certainty of punishment is indirectly increased by redistributing income, this policy improves retributive justice.

Redistributing income enhances distributive justice and prevents social injustices. As stated earlier, equalizing the distribution of income automatically improves distributive justice. Policy impact matrix 2 shows that distributive justice is a target in the policy system. Equalizing the distribution of income, that is, reducing the Gini coefficient (table 5-2, column 4) produces a positive increase in the distributive justice target (column 5). Furthermore, as the distribution of costs and benefits in a community (in particular those associated with crime control) becomes equalized among the various classes, crime is reduced. From the point of view of the potential victim and offender, there are fewer injustices. In contrast, deterrence, restraint, and reformation react to crime. They allow an injustice to be committed in order to avert another. Thus, proactive policies designed to prevent crime by distributing income are most cost-effective and most just.

Conclusion: Reliability of the Simulation Findings

At the beginning of this chapter it was explained that the purpose was *not* to present accurate predictions but rather to demonstrate a method of designing and presenting a strategic plan to reduce delinquency. The simulation results were explained by describing the effect that hypothetical policy changes made in California in 1970 *could have had* in that year. Nevertheless, the question remains: How accurate were the results?

There are a few reasons why the magnitude of the changes in the juvenile victimization rate reported in this chapter may not be accurate. In order to predict crime accurately, the model should be validated by comparing the simulated experience with published crime data for the simulated years. Data limitations made it impossible to validate the model in this manner. (Refer to appendix B for a technical discussion of how the model was validated.) An inability to validate a simulation model would be a serious shortcoming if one were trying to forecast crime.

The changes in the juvenile victimization rate were predicted from a crime equation estimated from cross-sectional data (see appendix B). Coefficients estimated from cross-sectional data represent long-run equilibrium; time-series estimates represent short-run equilibrium.[10] The crime rate predicted from this model may, therefore, reflect factors related to socioeconomic time trends. If the sample period were a few years before or after 1970, changes in socioeconomic factors might have produced different coefficient estimates. Furthermore, since cross-sectional coefficients reflect a long-run equilibrium, the response time from implementing a policy instrument to an equilibrium in the system's behavior may be much faster than would occur in reality. For these reasons, the magnitude of impact in using the victimization equation in this model may not be accurate.

It is plausible, however, that the estimated effect of any independent variable on crime, relative to the other variables, would be approximately the same for cross-sectional and time-series data. If coefficients estimated from the data set used in this book were compared to coefficients estimated from California time-series data, one could ascertain whether the relative effect of the independent variables would be similar. This comparison must await further research. In the meantime, the reliability of the simulation findings must be determined from the quality of the model. All the coefficients in the victimization equation were statistically significant. Furthermore, constraints were built into the system to account for interdependencies among the subsystems. Because of these two attributes of the model, the direction of impact should be accurate for all policy simulations.

Since the purpose of this chapter was to assess the relative cost-effectiveness of a number of policy options, the simulation results must speak for themselves. Substituting juvenile diversion for preventive detention reduces delinquency and enhances procedural justice. Increasing the severity of punishment can be a counterproductive policy. Youth employment programs appear to be as cost-effective as, perhaps more cost-effective than, increasing police budgets. And income redistribution may be the most cost-effective policy for reducing crime and delinquency. On the basis of these simulations, a cost-effective program mix would ensure a "budgetary-balanced" level of deterrence (in other words, resources will be allocated proportionately to the police, courts, and corrections), while emphasizing income redistribution and job programs for teenagers.

Notes

1. The model is iterated monthly for two reasons. First, the mathematical requirements of the technique necessitate that the iteration unit be less than the shortest delay in the system (six months in this model). Stock concepts with less than a one-month delay are treated as flows. Second, the iteration unit should correspond to policy making in the real world. It is not often necessary for decisionmakers to wait a year before changing a rule in the system. It is assumed that the daily decision-making process can be represented in terms of monthly aggregates.

2. The estimate includes the following: $6,990,000 for juvenile court; $75,957,000 for juvenile probation (see table B-15); $72,085,000 for the California Youth Authority; and $230,114,000 for juvenile arrests. The last figure is calculated by multiplying the number of juveniles arrested (in each offense category) times the average cost per arrest (see table B-6).

3. Lewis Katz, *Justice Is the Crime*, p. 139.

4. A few changes from 1970 data were made in the simulated base policy. The desired arrest rates (ARD_i) in the simulation model were set equal to 1. This was done because the juvenile victimization rate (JVRATE) fluctuates in simulations and setting ARD_i equal to 1 forces the police budgets $(POLB_i)$ to become binding constraints regardless of JVRATE. Similarly, in the base policy, police referred all youths to probation; none were counseled and released or referred to other agencies (see table B-7 for comparison with actual 1970 probabilities). The proportion of juveniles that probation desired to petition included the actual proportion of initial referrals that were closed. The probability of informal supervision $P(IS_i)$ remained the same as in table B-8. The purpose of making the changes was to ensure that the constraints further up the system were binding on sectors down system. The preventive detention policy was simulated by setting the desired detention rate $P(DPDD_i)$ equal to 1. This ensures that all juveniles will be detained so long as there is space for them in juvenile hall.

5. Calculated from California Office of Criminal Justice Planning, *California Correctional System Intake Study*, p. 127.

6. Ibid., p. 139.

7. No attempt was made to find the optimal mix of police and probation diversion programs. This would have required a time-consuming and costly computer process. The simulation model could be revised to include optimizing subroutines so that a cost-effective program structure could be computed more economically.

8. For a discussion of the politics of this issue, see Joseph B. Treaster, "Juvenile Criminals, An Increasing Problem," *New York Times,* May 25, 1976, p. 22.

9. This contention finds support in the economic theory of bureaucracy. According to that theory, the output level of government agencies tends to be greater than it would be at an economically efficient level of production. The implication is that the marginal cost of production is likely to be considerably higher than the average cost for the level of services provided by government bureaucracies. For a formal theory of bureaucracy, see William A. Niskanen, Jr., *Bureaucracy in Representative Government* (Chicago: Aldine-Atherton, 1971), pp. 45-77.

10. Cleve E. Willis, "Differential Interpretations of Estimations Based on Time-Series and Cross-Sectional Data," in *Methodological Considerations in Researching Community Services in the Northeast,* New York Agricultural Experiment Station, Bulletin 836, September 1975, pp. 18, 19.

6

Conclusion: Designing a Strategic Plan to Reduce Delinquency

This chapter summarizes the preceding chapters and discusses the future of strategic criminal justice planning. In the first section, the major aspects of the policy science approach to strategic planning are reviewed. Definitions of the essential concepts behind the policy science framework are presented. The simulation model is described by explaining the basic assumptions on which it was built, and the simulation results are summarized. The section concludes with a warning against making unfounded policy recommendations. In the following section, suggestions for further research are made, and some applications of strategic planning are discussed. The chapter ends with a discussion of the role of policy science and strategic planning in the political process.

Summary of Major Points

The preceding chapters presented an approach that could be used to design a strategic plan to reduce crime. Strategic planning is based on coordination, comprehensiveness, causal analysis, and cost-effectiveness. The programs, activities, and decisions of criminal justice agencies must be *coordinated*. All possible courses of action that might be taken to reduce crime must be considered if the plan is to be *comprehensive*. Knowledge of how to reach one's goals, in other words, *causal analysis,* is essential in devising a strategy. As a criterion for selecting the strategy to be implemented, the analyst will choose the mix of programs that most *cost-effectively* reduces crime and enhances justice. In short, strategic criminal justice planning is concerned with determining priorities and developing guidelines to meet the system's goals.

A policy science research framework, designed to systematically analyze and scientifically test the relationships among programs and objectives, integrated three important aspects of crime reduction. First, the nature and causes of crime were discussed. The economic opportunity cost theory and Cloward and Ohlin's theory of differential opportunity were synthesized into a new, more general theory of relative opportunity. The theory of relative opportunity is based on the assumption that criminal proclivities vary among people and that crime can be reduced by increasing rewards and penalties and by changing sentiments about official norms (see chapter 3). The main hypothesis of relative opportunity is that increasing opportunities and rewards for participation in legitimate activities and reducing relative deprivation are cost-effective methods of reducing crime and delinquency.

Second, based on this thesis, the structure and behavior of the criminal justice system were analyzed. The focus of the analysis was, on the one hand, narrowly confined to the California juvenile justice system. But, on the other hand, it was concerned with the broad range of factors that must be considered in such an analysis (chapter 2). In order to handle the complexity, a computer simulation model was constructed (appendix A). It described mathematically the flow of juveniles through the adjudication and corrections processes (chapter 4). The relationships among key decisionmakers and the effect of their actions on the crime rate were incorporated into the model.

Finally, the impact of crime reduction programs on criminal justice goals was analyzed (chapter 5). Specifically, the relative cost-effectiveness of restraint, deterrence, reformation, and prevention programs was assessed. This was done by evaluating the effect of specific programs, such as preventive detention, juvenile diversion, arrest, and youth employment, on the system's performance. The three aspects of criminal justice research were integrated by building a computer model of the California juvenile justice system designed to analyze the cost-effectiveness of a wide range of policy options.

Concepts behind the Policy Science Research Framework

The policy science research framework provides a structure for designing strategic plans. It is general enough to be applied to any policy system. The framework is premised on four beliefs about policy research. First, all public and private affairs in which the government intervenes, including the criminal justice enterprise, can be viewed as a policy-affected system. Second, social science theory and methods can be applied to the pragmatic concerns of policymakers. Third, concepts can be quantified so that subjective hypotheses can be tested and the system's behavior simulated. Finally, the effect of government programs on public and private institutions and their impact on political goals can be ascertained scientifically. The following twelve concepts (from general systems theory and the social sciences) form the basis of the policy science framework.

Policy Science Research. Policy science research combines social science theory and methods with the pragmatic concerns of policymakers. It is a hybrid of policy analysis and the social sciences. Its purpose is to systematically analyze and scientifically test propositions about generalized policy systems.

Generalized Policy Systems. Generalized policy systems are the particular class of systems which deal with the effects of government policies on the social structure and their impact on political goals. Policy systems serve social functions, such as social control and allocation of values, through the intervention of government policy. All decision-making units affecting the system's outputs are included within its boundary. Unless the global system is analyzed, any comparison among public policies would be inadequate.

Public Policy. Public policy was defined as an authoritative ranking of objectives combined with an official set of rules to guide decisionmakers and resources to enable them to achieve the objectives.

Ranking Objectives. Not all objectives can be achieved. Scarce resources limit the extent to which objectives can be attained. Conflicting values bring certain objectives in competition with one another. In short, priorities must be established because not all objectives are attainable.

Policy Instruments. Policymakers implement their policies by manipulating policy instrument variables. They can distribute budgets and promulgate rules. The set of budgets and rules that they establish produces a program structure.

Program Structure. Programs such as organized crime strike forces and concentrated police patrols increase the certainty of arrest. Such programs and others, which increase the certainty and severity of punishment, deter crime. Youth employment and income redistribution prevent crime. Other programs are designed to reform offenders or restrain them from committing additional crimes. The mix of programs, the agencies that must implement them, and the values of the necessary instrument variables form a program structure. The program structure is a part of the system's structure.

System Structure. The pattern of relationships among decision-making subsystems forms the system's structure. Policy systems are complex. Interactions among decisionmakers, side effects of their actions, and constraining factors render the subsystems highly interdependent. Different system structures produce different system behaviors.

System Behavior. Every purposeful system strives toward selected goals. The system can go about meeting its objectives by emphasizing certain programs (such as prevention) and certain objectives (such as reducing violent crime). The system's behavior is reflected in the way it strives toward its goals and in the goals themselves. One may view a system's behavior by looking at the overall conduct of the system.

Chain of Impact. Objectives are achieved through a chain of impact. Establishing a set of policy instruments produces a program structure. The system responds to changes in its structure by exhibiting new behavior patterns. Its behavior affects its goal attainment performance. Thus, implementing policy instruments ultimately has an impact on the system's objectives or targets.

Macrocausal Theory. In order to comprehend the chain of impact, macrocausal theories of the policy system's behavior are formulated. The theories are tested statistically, and then the system's behavior is simulated.

Cost-Effectiveness. The relative merits of programs are determined with cost-effectiveness as the criterion. The costs of a program are assessed, and their impact on the system's targets is predicted. This allows the researcher to determine the effect of rule changes and budget reallocations on objectives while reserving for policymakers the prerogative of setting priorities.

Suboptimization. Unless all significant interrelationships (interactions, side effects, and constraining influences) among decisionmakers are considered, in other words, unless the global system is analyzed, the research effort will produce suboptimal results. A disproportionate distribution of the budget allocated to the subsystems and inefficient rules to guide their behavior will lead to suboptimal system performance. Policy systems are, however, inappropriate candidates for optimizing techniques. Optimums cannot be achieved because what is optimal for one group may be inadequate for another and undesirable from the point of view of still another. For an agreed-on set of objectives, a cost-effective program structure can be implemented for the global system.

A Simulation Model of the California
Juvenile Justice System

The policy simulation model of the California juvenile justice system was constructed using two quantitative techniques. An econometric model statistically tested the delinquency reduction hypotheses of the relative opportunity theory. The dependent variable was the juvenile victimization rate, a measure of the actual number of violent and property crimes committed by delinquents. The coefficients in the juvenile victimization equation were estimated from 1970 cross-sectional data for the fifty states. In addition, properties of systems dynamics were used to model the police, probation, court, and correctional sectors. The statistically verified causal variables (income inequality, urbanization, probability of arrest, probability of punishment, unemployment, and severity of punishment) were used in the simulation model to predict the juvenile victimization rate. Combining statistics with properties of systems dynamics allows the researcher to build a detailed model of the system that can be used to simulate its behavior. As with any model, the one in this book was built on assumptions about the behavior of the "real-world" system. Since the results are reliable only insofar as the assumptions are valid, the major assumptions will be summarized. (It should be noted that the parameters in the model were estimated on the basis of certain assumptions about the data. These are discussed throughout appendix B.)

Juveniles enter the system in large numbers (nearly 400,000 in 1970). Some are petitioned, but most are not. Some of those petitioned are adjudicated delinquent, but most are not. Less than 3 percent of those arrested are finally sent to correctional facilities. In the end, all are released from the system. This filtering process has two broad implications for a model of the juvenile justice process.

First, it was assumed that the process can be realistically described as a stock-flow model. After juveniles are arrested (flow), they are stored in juvenile hall or parental custody (stocks). They remain there (delay) until they are released from the system or sentenced (flow) to probation or a correctional facility (stocks). They may be transferred (flow) from one type of corrections (stocks) to another, and they are ultimately released (flow) from the system. The flow of juveniles from one stock to another makes systems dynamics an appropriate technique for simulating the system's behavior.

Second, it was assumed that the path which juveniles follow through the system is determined at a number of key decision points—the police disposition, probation determination, and adjudicatory hearings. The decisionmakers desire to send a certain proportion of juveniles further into the system. The number of juveniles that actually flows further into the system may be less than the number that the decisionmakers desire to send.

It was assumed that the decision to send a youth further into the system is constrained by resources allocated to sectors further up the system. Juvenile court resources (workforce, capital, time) constrain the number of hearings that can be held. Accordingly, the probation determination is affected by the budget allocated to juvenile court. Similarly, the capacity of juvenile halls and correctional facilities constrains the number of juveniles that may be admitted. Each agency's decisions depend on the decisions of other agents and the distribution of the budget in the global system.

Since juveniles flow through the model each month in three aggregate offense categories, it was necessary to devise a priority scheme. In the real-world criminal justice system, decisions are made on a case-by-case basis. It was assumed that serious offenses are given priority over minor offenses. In the juvenile court sector, for example, a proportion of the resources is allocated for hearings on three types of delinquencies: major law violations, drug law violations, and other offenses. If any court resources originally allocated to hearings on major delinquents remain after all major delinquencies are disposed of, they are used for drug law hearings. Similarly, after hearings on drug violations are held, any remaining resources are added to the resources originally allocated to other offenses. Two additional priority schemes were adopted in the model. It was assumed that detention hearings are given priority over adjudicatory hearings and that subsequent petitions are given priority over initial petitions.

Crime Reduction Findings

This subsection summarizes the analysis in chapter 5 of the four crime reduction programs (restraint, reformation, deterrence, and prevention). These general programs were analyzed by examining the effect of specific programs. For example, restraint and reformation were evaluated by comparing preventive detention with juvenile diversion programs, respectively. Since strategic planning requires that a cost-effective program structure be devised, the following programs were evaluated also: increasing the severity of punishment and increasing the probability of arrest (both are deterrence programs); creating teenage employment programs and redistributing income (both are preventive measures). In addition, the effects of these programs on four types of justice (retributive, restitutive, procedural, and protective) were analyzed. The simulation results point to a number of critical factors about the behavior of the California juvenile justice system. These factors can be generalized to other state systems. The findings are accurate, however, only insofar as the assumptions discussed in the previous section are valid.

Juvenile Diversion and Preventive Detention. Detaining juveniles prior to adjudication is a costly and ineffective method of reducing delinquency. Preventive detention, a restraint program, was not found to have a statistically significant effect on the juvenile victimization rate. On the contrary, juvenile detention indirectly increases the number of juvenile victimizations. A detention hearing is required by law after a youth is detained 48 hours. An increase in the number of detention hearings reduces juvenile court resources which could be used alternatively for adjudicatory hearings. As a side effect of increasing juvenile restraint, therefore, the probability of punishment, an effective deterrent, is reduced. Thus, preventive detention leads to an increase in delinquency.

Juvenile diversion has precisely the opposite effect. Counseling troubled youths instead of putting them through the adjudicatory process can reintegrate them into the community. Although it was not possible to measure the direct effect of diversion on arrested delinquents and their peers, the indirect effects were assessed. Diverting minor law violators frees up resources for adjudicating and punishing juveniles who have committed serious offenses. Furthermore, this policy is consistent with the intent of the framers of the California Welfare and Institutions Code. Procedural justice is enhanced by reducing restriction on minors' freedom of movement. In conclusion, substituting juvenile diversion for preventive detention is a cost-effective means of reducing delinquency and enhancing justice.

The Severity of Punishment. It is often argued that increasing the severity of punishment will deter delinquents. Yet, increasing the average length of stay in correctional facilities was found to lead to an increase in the juvenile victimization rate. This counterproductive result can be explained as follows. Increasing the average length of sentence increases the duration between commitment to and release from correctional facilities. In the model, when facilities are at capacity, there is a delay before new commitments can be made. During this time, the probability that an adjudicated delinquent is punished declines. In short, as the length of stay in facilities increases, the facilities reach capacity faster and the certainty of punishment falls. The decline in the certainty of punishment offsets the increase in the deterrent effect of the severity of punishment. As a result, juvenile victimizations increase.

The inverse relationship between the turnover rate (length of stay) and the inflow rate (probability of punishment) occurs because of the assumption in the model that commitments are terminated until there is space for them. This assumption would be valid in a system which enforces minimum standards for space. It was made to test the effects of mandatory minimum sentencing by controlling the average length of stay in the model. In the real-world system, commitments are still made when facilities are overcrowded. Before facilities reach a saturation point, however, some offenders are released or paroled. Thus, even under this assumption there is an inverse relationship between certainty and severity of punishment. As commitments increase, facilities become over-crowded and authorities release offenders earlier, in effect reducing the length of stay. Thus, a model built on either assumption would demonstrate a reciprocal relationship between the two deterrence variables. So an increase in the length of stay, regardless of how it comes about, would increase crime because of the proportionately greater decline in the certainty of punishment.

Police Deterrence and Teenage Employment Programs. A strategic plan to reduce delinquency requires a cost-effective mix of deterrence and prevention programs. One aspect is finding a balance between police deterrence and teenage employment programs. Increasing police budgets leads to an increase in the probability of arrest. This deters delinquents. Appropriating funds to youth employment programs increases opportunities for participation in legitimate activities. This makes crime a less profitable alternative and strengthens senti-ments toward official norms. Both programs reduce delinquency. The simulation results found the cost-effectiveness of police deterrence and employment programs to be about the same.

There are a number of reasons, however, for believing that the cost-effec-tiveness of employment programs relative to police deterrence is understated in findings based on this model. The effectiveness of allocating resources to the police depends, in part, on the amount of resources allocated to the courts and corrections. On the other hand, employment programs reduce delinquency independently of any activity within the juvenile justice system. In addition to directly reducing delinquency, prevention programs indirectly make deterrence programs more effective. As the crime rate declines (as a result of an increase in employment programs), the probability of arrest increases. This takes place because the number of crimes, which is in the denominator of the probability of arrest, declines as a result of the exogenous influence of employment programs. It should also be noted that reactive criminal justice policies, such as police deterrence, have few, if any, external benefits. Resources allocated to proactive policies, such as teenage employment, can have numerous benefits apart from crime reduction. In short, a cost-effective mix of deterrence and prevention programs would emphasize teenage employment programs while allocating resources proportionately to the police, courts, and corrections.

Income Redistribution. The theory of relative opportunity considers inequality as a key causal variable. Inequality of opportunity makes participation in illegitimate activities relatively more attractive than legitimate opportunities. Furthermore, inequality of results alienates youths. Redistributing income is essentially a "costless" method of preventing crime. Compared to the other policy options, income redistribution was found to be the most cost-effective method of reducing delinquency. Furthermore, income redistribution directly enhances distributive justice. In conclusion, of all the programs studied, income redistribution was found to be the most cost-effective and the most just method of reducing delinquency.

Policy Conclusions

Many policy studies end with a set of recommendations. The recommendations may include a list of policies that ought to be adopted and a discussion of how to implement them. For example, on the basis of these findings one might recommend a negative income tax or increased welfare payments as means of redistributing money. Similarly, one might recommend a strategy for increasing legitimate opportunities by expanding the federal Comprehensive Employment and Training Act (CETA) program, raising the minimum wage, and enforcing affirmative action hiring programs. A strategy to reduce delinquency would also include a mix of deterrence and reintegration (diversion) programs; however, preventive detention and other forms of restraint would be kept at a minimum, based on the findings discussed previously. If policy science research is to have credibility, analysts should answer the following three questions before making policy recommendations such as these: How reliable are the research findings? Has the effect of all relevant variables been tested adequately? Are the proposed programs likely to be as cost-effective in reality as the policy experiments indicate?

The accuracy of these findings depends largely on an assumption about the nature of the data used. The number of juvenile victimizations is predicted in the model from an equation estimated from cross-sectional data. Since cross-sectional data do not reflect time trends, the predicted magnitude of impact from a policy change may be inaccurate. It is, therefore, necessary to make an assumption about the appropriateness of using an equation estimated from cross-sectional data in a simulation model. First, it is assumed that if the estimated coefficients are significant and if constraints are built into the model properly, the direction of the effect should be correct. Second, if the relative effect of two independent variables would be the same using cross-sectional and time-series data, then the relative cost-effectiveness of policy options should be accurate also. As with any assumptions, these matters await further study.

The four policies considered in this book were analyzed both theoretically and empirically. Thus, it would seem that a recommendation to increase pretrial diversion and teenage employment programs, for example, would be well substantiated. Several variables were, however, omitted from the policy simulations. Some variables, such as expenditures on rehabilitation, were omitted because they were not found to have a statistically significant effect on delinquency. In other words, on the basis of statistical tests, rehabilitation programs do not appear to be cost effective (see Hypothesis 2). Other variables, such as reintegration programs, could not be analyzed statistically because of a lack of data. It would obviously not be possible to develop a comprehensive strategy, that is, a cost-effective mix of *all* programs, with the omission of any significant crime reduction variables. Furthermore, even though pretrial diversion was found to reduce delinquency indirectly, its impact is probably understated because its direct effect on crime could not be measured.

On the other hand, urbanization (measured as the percentage of the state living in urban areas) was found to have a relatively large impact on juvenile victimizations. Urbanization is a catch-all variable that disguises crime-generating factors of urban life such as population density, interpersonal tensions, poorly lit streets, and, in general, opportunities for crime. It is impossible to know which (combination) of these structural variables gives urbanization, an aggregate factor, its significant impact on delinquency.

Other variables, which are often theorized to cause crime, were excluded from this analysis. For example, child abuse, learning disabilities, and gun ownership were not analyzed. Variables such as these, which represent individual causal factors, are more difficult for policymakers to control than macrostructural variables. Indeed, people usually resent government intrusions in private matters. The omission of individual causal variables is, therefore, not a serious problem.

Finally, unemployment was measured from aggregate data. It would be misleading, then, to imply that by hiring a particular youth he will be prevented from becoming delinquent. All one can say is that, in the aggregate, juvenile delinquency can be reduced by improving legitimate opportunities for teenage employment.

Even if one were able to find a cost-effective mix of programs through simulated experience, it is possible that the programs would not turn out to be so cost-effective in reality. There are a few reasons for this. First, the method of changing the policy variables may affect the end result. Even though income redistribution was found to have the greatest impact on juvenile delinquency, can one be certain that increasing welfare payments would not have any detrimental effects? Would eliminating tax loopholes and raising tax exemptions in order to make the tax structure more progressive have the same effect on crime as a negative income tax? Second, it may not be feasible to make certain policy changes. If one wanted to recommend reducing urbanization, or increasing the certainty of punishment, how would policy officials go about doing these things? Would it be feasible economically to reduce teenage unemployment? Would it be feasible politically to redistribute income? Third, programs may not be implemented properly, thereby making them less cost-effective than expected. Could one be certain that a newly instituted pretrial diversion program would be managed as well as the programs on which the analyst based his recommendation? In conclusion, before an analyst recommends a strategic plan for reducing crime, he must also develop a strategy for implementing the programs.

Designing a Strategic Plan to Reduce Crime

The purpose of this book was to present a policy science research framework that could be used to design a strategic plan to reduce crime. It was beyond the scope of this book to actually design a detailed strategy. That endeavor would require considerably more research. A list of research subjects which should be investigated in the process of developing a strategic plan is proposed in the following subsection. Then a number of applications of strategic criminal justice planning are discussed.

Suggestions for Further Research

Strategic planning is concerned with the interrelationships among decision-makers which affect the performance of the global system. The policy science research framework focuses on analyzing the impact of their actions on crime. Since the approach combines theory with quantitative methods, further research will have to involve both these aspects of policy research.

A continued effort should be made to improve policy-relevant theories of crime. The theory of relative opportunity was developed for state policies to reduce delinquency. If strategic plans are to consider all types of crime, not just juvenile delinquency, then other theories need to be developed. For example, policy-relevant theories to reduce white-collar crime and organized crime must be developed and tested.

Researchers should experiment with alternative specifications of behavioral equations. Additional measures of the theoretical variables should be constructed. For example, estimates of the number of victimizations could be used to more accurately measure the crime rate. Measures of independent variables, such as rehabilitation, reintegration, housing quality, and median family income, should be statistically tested in the crime equation.

This simulation model could be improved by using offender-specific statistics. The path offenders follow as they flow through the system was based on transitional probabilities at the decision points. Decisions were not made on the basis of offender characteristics. A decision function could be formulated for each decision point. Offender-based transactional statistics (OBTS), a criminal justice data source with the individual as the unit of analysis, could be used to estimate the coefficients in the decision equations. This would allow the researcher to simulate the effect of policies targeted at specific groups.

This simulation model could be improved by adding optimizing subroutines. A limitation of this model, as presently formulated, is that it was not feasible to find the most cost-effective program structure. The model could be redesigned to include optimizing subroutines. This would allow the researcher to find the lowest crime rate for each set of policy inputs.

The simulation model of the California criminal justice system should be expanded to include the adult system. The simulation model was used to analyze a wide range of policy options in the California juvenile justice system. The prosecution, superior court, and adult corrections sectors could be added to the model. Offenders would enter the system at arrest and follow a path to juvenile probation intake or adult prosecution depending on their age. This would allow the researcher to analyze the relative cost-effectiveness of policies targeted at adult and juvenile offenders and tradeoffs among those targets.

In order to develop a strategic plan, the predictive accuracy of the simulation model should be improved. The simulation model could be used for forecasting crime rates and resource requirements. This could be done by estimating the coefficients in the crime equation from California time-series data. Predictions for 1971 to 1975 could be verified by comparing them with data for those years. Once validated, the model could be used for forecasting.

Applications of Strategic Criminal Justice Planning

Strategic criminal justice planning has a number of practical applications. The National Advisory Commission on Criminal Justice Standards and Goals has made a number of recommendations for research and development. Two of its "standards" are as follows:

> Improve the linkage between criminal justice planning and budgeting. Monitor the implementation of the system to determine the cost and performance of the system and its component parts.[1]

Strategic planning can be an ongoing process for ensuring these two standards. The Task Force on Criminal Justice Research and Development recommended a systems perspective for studying the interactive effects among criminal justice organizations:

> Common themes such as discretion in decision making will best be understood by enlarging the scope of study across organizational boundaries rather than by confining such studies to particular types of agencies. Systemwide studies can also be used to investigate unexpected (and compensatory) effects in one part of the system resulting from decisions in another part. Such studies could lead to an increase in knowledge about the functioning of the criminal justice system as a whole.[2]

The strategic planning approach presented in this book satisfies both recommendations. Other advantages of the approach are that strategies are formulated from whatever limited data are available. For example, learning crime reduction principles from cross-sectional data is considered to be better than formulating policies on the basis of intuition alone. Strategic plans can be used to determine the areas that should yield the greatest payoff for experimental and developmental projects. They can also be used as forecasting tools. Daniel Glaser has suggested that a "knowledge-building apparatus" should be institutionalized to provide a feedback on the system's performance to policymakers (chapter 1). Strategic planning could be institutionalized to provide this feedback on a continual basis.

The approach to strategic planning developed in this book has been presented to the U.S. Department of Justice as a framework for designing a strategy for federal corrections. The problem facing the Federal Corrections Policy Task Force was spelled out in a paper proposing a modified version of the policy science framework as follows: The task force must decide how to restructure the criminal justice system so as to best ensure public safety and enhance justice within the confines of available resources.[3] A wide range of corrections-related issues (for example, the efficacy of rehabilitation, the abolition of parole, and sentencing reform) were placed in context by pointing out their interrelationships and their impact on policy goals. Because a fundamental concern in corrections is balancing the rights of inmates with protecting society, policy options to reduce prison overcrowding and improve the quality of correctional services (for example, prison construction and alternatives to incarceration) must be evaluated for their effect on security, deterrence, reformation, and justice. At this writing, the strategy the task force will adopt remains to be seen.

Policy Science Research in the Political Process

Criminal justice policy is formulated through a process of multiple political influences. The outcome of the policy process has tremendous consequences on the well-being of the public. The major premise of this book is that democratic governments could better serve the public by formulating policies after considering all (or most of) their possible consequences. Strategic planning offers such an approach to policy making. Strategic plans would be only one of many influences in the policy process. At least they would demonstrate the effect of a proposed action on public and private institutions and the resultant impact on political goals. The important value judgments would still remain political.

This chapter concludes with a discussion of the influence of policy science research in the political process. The research framework for developing strategic plans stems from a policy scientific approach to policy analysis. The following subsection discusses the major differences between the policy science methodology and another framework, planning programming budgeting systems (PPBS), for analyzing public policies. The chapter ends with a discussion of scientific policy research as a countervailing influence to ideological policy making.

Strategic Planning Compared with Planning Programming Budgeting Systems

In the mid-1960s President Johnson required all federal agencies to use PPBS for budgeting and policy making. PPBS is essentially cost-benefit analysis applied to multiple political objectives. An agency's objectives are categorized, and the costs of programs and their economic benefits (in terms of the objectives) are assessed. The greater the net benefits over costs (or the higher the benefit-cost ratio), the more grounds for implementing the program. The advantage of PPBS (as compared with cost-benefit analysis) is that all the agencies' programs and objectives are incorporated into the analysis.

By 1970 it was apparent that PPBS had failed to systematically improve policy making in the federal social agencies.[4] There are several reasons for its failure. Part of the failure was due to inadequacies in its methodology.[5] Cost-benefit analysis requires that all variables be measured in dollar terms. This automatically precludes any variables from consideration that cannot be quantified with some dollar measure. Policymakers cannot wait for social science methodology to improve. Policy research avoids this problem because the variables are taken directly from a data base without converting the data to monetary—perhaps arbitrary—values. But more important than this, it lets the policymakers make the value judgments about the relative worth of targets.

Another problem is that PPBS and its underlying technique, cost-benefit analysis, as Ida Hoos states, "encourages preoccupation with bits and pieces; suboptimization serves as a useful rationalization for failure or inability to grasp and grapple with large wholes."[6] A more useful way to analyze the relative merits of various programs is to assess their impact on the system's goals. It is more appropriate to analyze the resulting tradeoffs among all relevant system goals rather than to optimize a limited set of (efficiency and equity) goals.

It is essential that policy scientists develop theories about the system's behavior. According to Wildavsky, "Although the system [PPBS] dredges up information under numerous headings, it says next to nothing about the impact of one program [or goal] on another. There is data but no causal analysis."[7] The policy science research framework places great emphasis on scientifically testing theories and simulating a system's behavior.

A compelling explanation for its failure, one made by Wildavsky, is that PPBS is inherently subversive of the politics within government and therefore, one might add, doomed by misuse.[8] Enthoven has suggested ten guiding principles for policy analysis. One of them is that "analysis should be open and explicit. Analysis is not a substitute for debate. It should provide a framework for constructive debate."[9] PPBS does not allow for debate and compromise over political objectives. The framework for strategic planning does.

Ideology versus Policy Science

Formulating public policies on the basis of scientific policy research has the advantage that subjective value judgments can be analyzed objectively. Thus, policy science can be used to minimize the detrimental effects of ideology. The assumptions that people make about the way the world works—primarily political reality—and the way they feel it should work form a loose set of ideas, an ideology on which they base their thinking about political issues. Walter Miller has categorized left and right ideologies along a continuum as they relate to criminal justice. The major contention of his paper is that "ideology is the permanent hidden agenda of criminal justice."[10] In other words, policies are heavily influenced by ideology—both right and left—and that influence is largely unnoticed.

Policy science research can be used to confront ideological predilections. Policymakers who choose to let their ideology control their actions must be put in the position of either blatantly disregarding the results of an analysis or commissioning further study. There is nothing wrong with the latter. The policy conclusions discussed earlier highlight the fact that much research remains to be done. Debate over issues will point to areas where more research must be conducted. But the fact remains that the research is done through a scientific process—where studies can be replicated, theories improved, and fraudulent results uncovered. This lends legitimacy to policy research. Ideological policymakers may be held accountable for disregarding a prediction that their policy would end as a dismal failure. Should a policy simulation—a laboratory experiment—prove wrong, the researcher has only to redo his experiment. Should a government policy be implemented and prove a fiasco, the waste of human life and dignity is all but irreversible. The force of policy science may prove Miller wrong. Perhaps the "permanent hidden agenda," ideology, will be replaced by above-board, objective research—policy science research.

Since ideological influences can be pernicious, it is imperative that policy scientists analyze the merits of the values and assumptions behind left and right ideologies. Social order is the fundamental value for the right; social justice for the left. Social order and social justice are, of course, valued by virtually everyone. The basic disagreement between the right and left is over the relative importance of these two values. Conservative ideology assumes that social order is a prerequisite to social justice; liberal ideology assumes that social order cannot be had without social justice.

The previous discussion warning against making unfounded policy recommendations may leave the reader wondering whether any strategy can be supported on the basis of this research. Stricter enforcement of the law will deter juvenile delinquency. This appeals ideologically to the majority of the public. Yet, the policy science research presented in the previous chapters demonstrates that it is more cost-effective and more just to emphasize proactive policies designed to prevent crime by enhancing distributive justice. Deterrence works after the fact, after an individual has been victimized. It allows an injustice to be committed in order to avert another. Prevention, in this sense, is the more just alternative and should be favored on moral principles. But as demonstrated in this analysis, it is also a cost-effective approach. Policymakers who take seriously their rhetoric that crime must be abated must take action to enhance social justice and human dignity. We can have order. But we cannot have it without great human costs unless we have it with justice.

Notes

1. National Advisory Commission on Criminal Justice Standards and Goals, *A National Strategy to Reduce Crime,* pp. 154, 155.
2. National Advisory Commission on Criminal Justice Standards and Goals, *Criminal Justice Research and Development,* p. 130.
3. U.S. Department of Justice, "A Proposed Framework for Designing a Strategy for Federal Corrections" (Washington: U.S. Department of Justice, 1978). This paper was coauthored by Gregory P. Falkin and Robert J. Comiskey.
4. Walter Williams, *Social Policy Research and Analysis.*

5. Joint Economic Committee, *Analysis and Evaluation of Public Expenditures : The PPB System.*

6. Ida Hoos, *Systems Analysis in Public Policy,* p. 147.

7. Aaron Wildavsky, "The Political Economy of Efficiency," p. 343.

8. Ibid.

9. Alain C. Enthoven, "Ten Practical Principles for Policy Research and Program Analysis," p. 457.

10. Walter B. Miller, "Ideology and Criminal Justice Policy: Some Current Issues," p. 454.

Appendix A
A Simulation Model of the California Juvenile Justice System

This appendix describes the simulation model of the California juvenile justice system.[1] The model is a mathematical representation of the juvenile justice process discussed in chapter 4.[2] It was developed using the theory and methodology presented in chapter 3. The model was programmed for the computer in TROLL, an interactive computer package.[3]

Juvenile Offenses

Most empirical studies of crime use the number of offenses reported to the police as a dependent variable. But the number of reported offenses is a function of both the number of people actually victimized and public attitudes toward the police. Thus, in this book the dependent variable is defined as the juvenile victimization rate. It is a measure of the number of violent and property crimes (per 100,000 population) actually committed by minors. The juvenile victimization rate is expressed as a function of three deterrence and three prevention variables:

$$\ln \text{JVRATE} = \ln \beta_0 + \ln \beta_1 \times \text{URBAN}$$
$$+ \ln \beta_2 \times \frac{\text{UNEMPLOY}}{\text{PJUVPOP} \times \text{POP}} - \ln \beta_3 \times \text{PJPUNISH}_{t-1}$$
$$- \ln \beta_4 \times \text{SJPUNISH}_{t-1} + \ln \beta_5 \times \text{INEQUALITY}$$
$$- \ln \beta_6 \times \text{PJARREST}_{t-1} \qquad (A.1)$$

where	JVRATE	= juvenile victimization rate
URBAN	= percentage of population living in urban areas
UNEMPLOY	= number of juveniles (ages 14 to 17) unemployed
PJUVPOP	= proportion of juveniles in total population
POP	= California population
PJPUNISH	= probability of juvenile punishment
SJPUNISH	= severity of juvenile punishment

INQUALTY = distribution of income inequality

PJARREST = probability of juvenile arrest

The calculation of the deterrence variables is postponed until the end of this appendix.

The number of juvenile victimizations is found from the victimization rate:

$$JVICTIMS = JVRATE \frac{POP}{100,000} \qquad (A.2)$$

For the purposes of reported offenses and arrests, violent offenses are separated from property crimes. The number of offenses reported to the police is as follows:

$$JRO_k = P(JRO_k) \times P(JV_k) \times JVICTIMS \qquad (A.3)$$

where k = 1, 2 = violent, property offenses

JRO   = juvenile reported offenses

$P(JRO)$ = probability that juvenile offense is reported

$P(JV)$ = probability that juvenile victimization is a type K offense

Juvenile Arrests

In this model, juveniles and adults are arrested in the following six offense categories: violent felonies, property felonies, drug violations, other felonies, delinquent tendencies, and misdemeanors.[4] Delinquent tendencies are the juvenile equivalent of adult misdemeanors; hence, juveniles enter the juvenile justice system in only five offense categories.

After an offense is reported to the police, an arrest may be made. In reality, there is a certain probability of being arrested. But this probability, or arrest rate, depends on the amount of police resources devoted to investigating and clearing particular types of crimes. This model allows the analyst to experiment with both the distribution of the police budget and a desired arrest rate for violent and property offenses.

The procedure used is to find the total cost of achieving a desired arrest rate (for violent and property crimes). The desired arrest rate will be achieved to the extent that the police budget is adequate to cover the total cost of the arrests. The total number of arrests is calculated and then separated into its juvenile and adult components.

The total cost of arrests is a function of the average cost.

$$ATC_k = AAC_k \times ARD_k \times (JRO_k + ARO_k) \qquad (A.4)$$

where   ATC = arrest total cost

           AAC = arrest average cost

           ARD = arrest rate desired

           ARO = adult reported offenses (this is an exogenous variable)

It is possible that the analyst may not allocate sufficient resources to reach the desired arrest rate for violent or property crimes. A check is, therefore, built into the model. If the budget distributed to violent or property arrests is insufficient, then the arrestees who would create a potential deficit are not arrested. Thus, the total number of arrests in each category is calculated by ascertaining whether sufficient resources have been allocated to achieve the desired arrest rate:

If $ATC_k > POLB_k$ (A.5a)

then $AT_k = ARD_k \times (JRO_k + ARD_k) - \dfrac{ATC_k - POLB_k}{AAC_k}$ (A.5b)

If $ATC_k \leqslant POLB_k$ (A.5c)

then $AT_k = ARD_k \times (JRO_k + ARO_k)$ (A.5d)

where   POLB = police budget

This model assumes that juveniles and adults face equal probabilities of arrest. Accordingly, the proportion of juveniles (adults) arrested is the same as the proportion of juvenile (adult) offenses reported.

$$JA_k = \frac{JRO_k}{JRO_k + ARO_k} \; AT_k \qquad (A.6)$$

$$AA_k = \frac{ARO_k}{JRO_k + ARO_k} \; AT_k \qquad (A.7)$$

where   JA = juveniles arrested

           AA = adults arrested

The police budget remaining for the last four arrest categories is the total budget less the amount actually used for violent and property arrests. Since it is plausible that the analyst may initially distribute more money to violent and property arrests than is needed to achieve the desired arrest rate, the budget remaining is based on the actual number of arrests.

$$POLBR = POLBT - \sum_{k=1}^{2} (AAC_k \times AT_k) \qquad (A.8)$$

where   POLBR = police budget remaining

POLBT = police budget total

A proportion of the remaining budget is distributed to the last four arrest categories. Based on the budget distribution and the average cost, the number of arrests in each category is found:

$$JA_k = PJA_k \, \frac{PPOLB_k \times POLBR}{AAC_k} \qquad (A.9)$$

$$AA_k = PAA_k \, \frac{PPOLB_k \times POLBR}{AAC_k} \qquad (A.10)$$

where k = 3, 4, 5, 6 = drug, other felony, juvenile tendency, misdemeanor arrests

PJA   = proportion juvenile arrestees[5]

PAA   = proportion adult arrestees

PPOLB = proportion of remaining police budget distributed ($\sum_{k=3}^{6}$ PPOLB = 1)

Finally, juveniles are brought into police custody. The purpose of these equations is merely to recategorize juvenile cases. Juveniles flow through the rest of the model in these revised categories:

$$JPC_1 = JA_1 + JA_2 \qquad (A.11)$$

$$JPC_2 = JA_3 \qquad (A.12)$$

$$JPC_3 = JA_4 + JA_5 \qquad (A.13)$$

where JPC_1 = juveniles in police custody, major delinquents

JPC_2 = juveniles in police custody, drug delinquents

JPC_3 = juveniles in police custody, other delinquents

Police Disposition of Juveniles

After juveniles are taken into police custody, they are disposed of in one of four ways (see figure 4-2, juvenile apprehension). Each outcome is a function of the number of juveniles in police custody and the transition probability that the event in question will occur.

$$JPD_T = \sum_{i}^{I} [P(JPD_i) \times JPC_i] \qquad (A.14)$$

$$ROA_T = \sum_{i}^{I} [P(ROA_i) \times JPC_i] \qquad (A.15)$$

$$JCR_T = \sum_{i}^{I} [P(JCR_i) \times JPC_i] \qquad (A.16)$$

where i = 1, 2, 3 = major, drug, other delinquents (as recategorized in equations A.11 to A.13)

JPD = juveniles in police diversion

$P(JPD)$ = probability of police diversion

ROA = referred to other agency

$P(ROA)$ = probability of referral to other agency

JCR = juveniles counseled and released

$P(JCR)$ = probability of juveniles counseled and released

The fourth possible outcome, referral to probation, includes juveniles referred immediately after arrest and those who fail to meet adequately the requirements of the police diversion program:

$$RTP_i = P(RTP_i) \times JPC_i + PDFR_i \times JPD_i \qquad (A.17)$$

where   RTP = Referred to probation (includes initial and re-referrals)

$P(RTP)$ = probability of referred to probation

PDFR = police diversion failure rate

Police diversion programs require the following expenditure:

$$PDTC = JPD_T \times PDAC \qquad (A.18)$$

where   PDTC = police diversion total cost

PDAC = police diversion average cost

Juvenile Probation

The probation section of the model is divided into the following two parts: probation intake and the initial referral decision, and the probation determination.

Probation Intake and Initial Referral Decision

The initial referral decision involves a two-step procedure. First, juveniles are either booked in juvenile hall or released in custody of their parents.

$$\text{DPDD}_i = P(\text{DPDD}_i) \times (\text{RTP}_i + \text{DIR}_i) \qquad (A.19)$$

$$\text{PCPD}_i = [1 - P(\text{DPDD}_i)] \times (\text{RPT}_i + \text{DIR}_i) \qquad (A.20)$$

where DPDD   = detained pending disposition desired

       $P(\text{DPDD})$ = probability of detained pending disposition desired

       DIR   = direct initial referrals (from courts, schools, etc.)

       PCPD   = parental custody pending disposition

Second, the crisis intervention unit may receive some of the initial referrals who are in parental custody. (Detainees and re-referrals are not eligible for crisis intervention treatment in this model). Initial referrals include direct referrals and police initial referrals:

$$\text{IR}_i = \text{DIR}_i + P(\text{PIR}_i) \times \text{RPT}_i \qquad (A.21)$$

where   IR   = initial referrals

       $P(\text{PIR})$ = proportion of police initial referrals

Some proportion of the initial referrals (who are not detained) will be enrolled in crisis intervention programs:

$$\text{PCI}_i = P(\text{PCI}_i) \times [1 - P(\text{DPDD}_i)] \times \text{IR}_i \qquad (A.22)$$

where   PCI   = probation crisis intervention

       $P(\text{PCI})$ = probability of probation crisis intervention (policy parameter)

It is not always possible for the probation office to detain as many juveniles as they would like to. The desired detention rate is constrained by juvenile hall capacity. Furthermore, it is plausible that juvenile court judges can subtly influence the rate of detention. Thus, even though space may be available in juvenile hall, probation officers may release some juveniles to the custody of the parents even though they would prefer to detain them. The remainder of this section, then, is devoted to finding the actual number of juveniles detained.

The method used to calculate the actual detention rate is to ascertain which of the two constraints, juvenile hall capacity or juvenile court resources, is the more binding one. First, the model calculates the resources required to detain DPDP (that is, the youths whom probation would like to detain). Then the model determines the extent to which the juvenile hall budget meets this resource requirement. If the budget is insufficient, then some of the juveniles cannot be detained. If, however, the budget is adequate, then all may be detained subject to the juvenile court budget constraint.

Second, based on this "potential" number of detainees, the amount of juvenile court resources required for detention hearings is calculated. The model then determines the extent to which the juvenile court budget meets this resource requirement. Finally, the actual number of detainees is determined.

The total juvenile hall detention cost is calculated from the average cost. The cost of detaining a juvenile (that is, the average cost) equals the cost per day times the number of days each juvenile can be expected to stay in juvenile hall. The total number of days in detention can be divided into four phases: (1) from detention to probation determination, (2) after probation determination until a detention hearing, (3) after this hearing until the jurisdictional hearing, and (4) after the jurisdictional hearing until the probation hearing (see figures 4-3 and 4-4). Therefore, the expected time in detention is the number of days between these phases times the probability that a youth passes through each stage.

$$JHAC_i = JHCPD[TDPD + P(PA_i) \times TDPDH + P(D_i \mid PA_i) \times TDPJH$$

$$+ P(AD_i \mid D_i \mid PA_i) \times TDPPH] \tag{A.23}$$

where JHAC   = juvenile hall average cost

  JHCPD = juvenile hall cost per day per detainee

  TDPD   = maximum legal time detained pending probation determination

  $P(PA)$ = probability of being petitioned (see equation A.71)

  TDPDH = maximum legal time detained pending detention hearing

  $P(D \mid PA)$ = conditional probability of being detained after petitioning

  TDPJH   = maximum legal time detained pending jurisdictional hearing

  $P(AD \mid D \mid PA)$= conditional probability of being adjudicated delinquent while detained

  TDPPH   = maximum legal time detained pending probation hearing

In this part of the model, serious offenders are given priority over less serious offenders.[6] Thus, the total cost of detaining major delinquents is subtracted from the total juvenile hall budget:

$$JHBR_1 = JHB - JHAC_1 \times DPDD_1 \qquad (A.24)$$

where   JHBR = juvenile hall budget remaining (after type 1 delinquents are detained)

JHB   = juvenile hall budget

If the budget is sufficient to cover total cost (that is, $JHBR_1 \geq 0$), then all desired detainees are detained. If it is not, a deficit would be incurred. Those juveniles who create the deficit cannot be detained. For $i = 1$,

If $JHBR_i \geq 0$ $(A.25a)$

then $DPDJHB_i = DPDD_i$ $(A.25b)$

If $JHBR_i < 0$ $(A.25c)$

then $DPDJHB_i = DPDD_i + \dfrac{JHBR_i}{JHAC_i}$ $(A.25d)$[7]

where   DPDJHB = detained pending determination given the juvenile hall budget

This procedure is followed for minor and drug delinquents. If $JHBR_1 > 0$, then drug delinquents may be detained within the remaining budget constraint. If it is negative, some major delinquents would not have been detained because the budget was insufficient. Consequently, no drug or other delinquents may be detained. In such a case, the total cost of detaining all drug delinquents is used to create the deficit that would be incurred if all were detained. This ensures that none are detained.

The next step is to subtract the cost of detaining drug and other delinquents from juvenile hall resources available for detaining them. Thus for $i = 2, 3$

If $JHBR_{i-1} > 0$ $(A.26a)$

then $JHBR_i = JHBR_{i-1} - JHAC_i \times DPDD_i$ $(A.26b)$

If $JHBR_{i-1} \leq 0$ $(A.26c)$

then $JHBR_i = - JHAC_i \times DPDD_i$ $(A.26d)$

The model then solves for $DPDJHB_i$ (where $i = 2, 3$) as in equation A.25.[8]

Having found the number of juveniles that may be "potentially" detained within the juvenile hall resource constraint, the model compares the cost of their detention hearings to the juvenile court budget constraint. If the detention hearing budget is adequate to cover the cost of all hearings held for juveniles "potentially" detained, then all are actually held. If the budget is insufficient, then some are not detained. They are released at the juvenile hall in custody of their parents. The same decision rule is used again but essentially in reverse order; that is, least serious delinquents are released first, major delinquents last.

The total cost of detention hearings is subtracted from court resources allocated to detention hearings.

$$EDHB = JHDHB - DHAC \times \sum_{i}^{I} P(PA_i)\, DPDJHB_i \qquad (A.27)$$

where   EDHB   = excess detention hearing budget

   JCDHB   = juvenile court detention hearing budget

   DHAC   = detention hearing average cost

   $P(PA)$ = probability of petition actual (see equation A.42 for calculation)[9]

The detention hearing budget covers costs if $EDHB > 0$. In this case, all juveniles (all $DPDJHB_i$) may be detained. A deficit would arise to the extent that $EDHB < 0$. The juveniles who would create the deficit if detained must be released.

If $EDHB \geqslant 0$ (A.28a)

then $JHDIF_3 = DPDJHB_3$ (A.28b)

If $EDHB < 0$ (A.28c)

then $JHDIF = DPDJHB_3 - \dfrac{-EDHB}{DHAC}$ (A.28d)

where   JHDIF   = juvenile hall/juvenile court budget difference[10]

The difference between juveniles "potentially" detained ($DPDJHB_3$) and those who must be released in order to avoid a deficit is used as a device for releasing delinquents. This device is necessary because three different types of delinquents must be released sequentially. (Using JHDIF prevents a negative solution for the number of delinquents actually detained.) If $JHDIF_3 > 0$, then it represents the actual number detained. If $JHDIF_3 \leqslant 0$, then none of the "other" (type 3) delinquents may be detained. Furthermore, some drug delinquents must be released. Thus, for $i = 3$

If $JHDIF_i \leqslant 0$ (A.29a)

then $DPDA_i = 0$ (A 29b)

If $JHDIF_i > 0$ (A.29c)

then $DPDA_i = JHDIF_i$ (A.29d)

Equations A.28 and A.29 are essentially repeated for drug delinquents. $JHDIF_3$ is used to determine how many drug delinquents must be released.

If	$JHDIF_3 > 0$	(A.30a)
then	$JHDIF_2 = DPDJHB_2$	(A.30b)
If	$JHDIF_3 \leqslant 0$	(A.30c)
then	$JHDIF_2 = DPDJHB_2 + JHDIF_3$	(A.30d)

The actual number of drug delinquents detained is found in accordance with the number that must be released. Thus, equation A.29 is repeated for $i = 2$.

Finally, the actual number of major delinquents detained is equal to the "potential" less any youths who still must be released.

If	$JHDIF_2 > 0$	(A.31a)
then	$DPDA_1 = DPDJHB_1$	(A.31b)
If	$JHDIF_2 \leqslant 0$	(A.31c)
then	$DPDA_1 = DPDJHB_1 + JHDIF_2$	(A.31d)

Probation Determination

The probation determination involves three possible outcomes. The juvenile's case may be cleared, he may be placed on informal supervision, or he may be petitioned. The last possibility includes juveniles who were previously placed on informal supervision or in crisis intervention but failed to meet the requirements of the program. Re-referrals are treated separately if a subsequent petition is filed.

$$IRC_T = \sum_{i}^{I} [P(IRC_i) \times (IR_i - PCI_i)] \tag{A.32}$$

$$ISI_T = \sum_{i}^{I} [P(IS_i) \times (IR_i - PCI_i)] \tag{A.33}$$

$$PD_i = [P(P_i) \times (IR_i - PCI_i) + (PCIFR_i \times PCI_i) + (ISFR_i \times ISO_i)] \tag{A.34}$$

where IRC   = initial referrals closed

$P(IRC)$ = probability initial referrals closed

ISI   = informal supervision inflow

$P(IS)$ = probability of informal supervision inflow

PD   = petitions desired

$P(P)$ = probability petitions desired

PCIFR = probation crisis intervention failure rate

ISFR   = informal supervision failure rate

ISO   = informal supervision outflow (see equation A.64)

Juvenile Court

The actual number of petitions filed is found by calculating the number of desired petitions that may be disposed of within the budget constraint. Since there are three types of offenders, a proportion of juvenile court resources will be used for each type of offense. (This permits the analyst to experiment with alternative resource allocations to each type of adjudication.) Probation will desire to file a certain number of petitions based on the probability that each particular case warrants adjudication (see equation A.34). Limited court resources may make it infeasible for probation to file all the petitions it would like to. In such a case, probation will have to use alternatives to court adjudication (including releasing some of the excess cases). Backlogs are, therefore, not created in this model.[11]

Juvenile Court Intake

In this model, all subsequent petitions take precedence over initial petitions. Thus, the resources available for hearings on initial petitions equal the total juvenile court budget less resources used in hearings on subsequent petitions and detention hearings.

The total cost of hearings on subsequent petitions is a function of the number of hearings and the average cost per hearing:

$$SPTC = SP[JHAC + PHAC] \qquad (A.35)$$

where   SPTC = subsequent petitions total cost

SP   = number of subsequent petitions (see equation A.70 for calculation)

JHAC = jurisdictional hearings average cost

PHAC = probation hearings average cost

The juvenile court budget for initial petitions is the budget remaining after detention hearings (if there is a surplus) and hearings on subsequent petitions.

If	$EDHB > 0$	(A.36a)
then	$JCBR = JCBT - SPTC + EDHB$	(A.36b)
If	$EDHB \leqslant 0$	(A.36c)
then	$JCBR = JCBT - SPTC$	(A.36d)

where   JCBR = juvenile court budget remaining

JCBT = juvenile court budget total (excluding the allocation to detention hearings)

Depending on the total cost of disposing of the desired petitions, there may be a surplus or deficit in the amount of court resources allocated to adjudicatory hearings. The total cost of jurisdictional and probation hearings on (desired) initial petitions is calculated from the same average cost as subsequent petitions.

$$PFTC_i = JHAC(PD_i) + PHAC[P(AD_i) \times PD_i] \qquad (A.37)$$

where   PFTC = petition filing total cost

$P(AD)$ = probability of being adjudicated delinquent (see equation A.49 for calculation)

If sufficient resources are allocated to cover the costs of hearings on major delinquency cases, then all desired petitions are filed and any surplus in the budget is used for the next type of petition (drug violations). If an insufficient amount of resources are allocated, then a deficit would result and some of the desired petitions would not be filed.

The surplus or deficit is measured by subtracting the total cost of disposing of the desired petitions from the court resources allocated to hearings on these cases.

$$PFBR_1 = PJCB_1 \times JCBR - PFTC_1 \qquad (A.38)$$

where   PFBR = petition filing budget remaining (after disposing of type 1 petitions)

PJCB = proportion of juvenile court budget used in disposing of type 1 cases

In the case where court resources are *not* sufficient to handle all desired petitions, the number of desired petitions that will *not* be filed equals the deficit ($PFBR_i < 0$) divided by average cost:

$$PDNF_i = \frac{-PFBR_i}{JHAC + P(AD_i) \times PHAC} \qquad (A.39)$$

where   PDNF = petition desired not filed

Finally, the actual number of petitions filed (in this case for major delinquencies) is as follows:

If $\qquad\qquad\qquad\qquad$ $PFBR_i \geqslant 0$ $\qquad\qquad\qquad\qquad$ (A.40a)

then $\qquad\qquad\qquad\qquad$ $PA_i = PD_i$ $\qquad\qquad\qquad\qquad$ (A.40b)

If $\qquad\qquad\qquad\qquad$ $PFRB_i < 0$ $\qquad\qquad\qquad\qquad$ (A.40c)

then $\qquad\qquad\qquad\qquad$ $PA_i = PD_i - PDNF_i$ $\qquad\qquad\qquad$ (A.40d)

where   PA = petitions actually filed

The procedure is repeated for drug and other delinquents ($i = 2, 3$). The budget remaining requires a slightly different equation (compare equation A.38). If a surplus exists after major delinquency cases are disposed of, then it is added to the court budget for drug delinquents. This procedure is repeated for "other" delinquents. In other words, any resources remaining after drug hearings are held are used for hearings on "other" cases. For $i = 2$ and 3,

If $\qquad\qquad\qquad$ $PFBR_{i-1} > 0$ $\qquad\qquad\qquad\qquad\qquad$ (A.41a)

then $\qquad\qquad$ $PFBR_i = PJCB_i \times JCBR + PFBR_{i-1} - PFTC_i$ $\qquad$ (A.41b)

If $\qquad\qquad\qquad$ $PFBR_{i-1} \leqslant 0$ $\qquad\qquad\qquad\qquad\qquad$ (A.41c)

then $\qquad\qquad$ $PFBR_i = PRCB_i \times JCBR - PFTC_i$ $\qquad\qquad$ (A.41d)

Equation A.40 is repeated (for $i = 2, 3$) in order to find the actual number of petitions filed.[12]

The probability that an initial referral is petitioned was used earlier to determine the juvenile hall detention rate (see equation A.27). It may now be calculated from the actual number of petitions.

$$P(PA_i) = \frac{PA_i}{IR_i - PCI_i} \qquad\qquad\qquad (A.42)$$

Juvenile Court Disposition

There are six possible outcomes after a probation hearing. Adjudicated delinquents receive one of the last four types of sentences.

$$JPRAC_T = \sum_{i}^{I} [P(JPRAC_i) \times PA_i] \qquad\qquad (A.43)$$

$$JPD_T = \sum_{i}^{I} [P(JPD_i) \times PA_i] \tag{A.44}$$

$$NWI_T = \sum_{i}^{I} [P(NW_i) \times PA_i] \tag{A.45}$$

$$FWIP_T = \sum_{i}^{I} [P(FW_i) \times PA_i] \tag{A.46}$$

$$CCID_T = \sum_{i}^{I} [P(CC_i) \times PA_i] \tag{A.47}$$

$$JCYAID_T = \sum_{i}^{I} [P(JCYA_i) \times PA_i] \tag{A.48}$$

where JPRAC   = juvenile petitions remanded to adult court

$P(JPRAC)$= probability juvenile petitions remanded to adult court

JPD   = juvenile petitions dismissed

$P(JPD)$ = probability juvenile petitions dismissed

NWI   = nonward inflow

$P(NW)$ = probability nonward

FWIP   = formal ward inflow partial[1,3]

$P(FW)$ = probability formal ward

CCID   = county camp inflow desired[1,3]

$P(CC)$ = probability county camp

JCYAID   = juvenile court youth authority commitments inflow desired[1,3]

$P(JCYA)$ = probability juvenile court youth authority commitments

The probability of being adjudicated delinquent $P(AD_i)$ was used earlier to calculate the number of probation hearings on initial petitions (see equation A.37). That probability is the sum of several probabilities.

$$P(AD_i) = P(NW_i) + P(FW_i) + P(CC_i) + P(CYA_i) \tag{A.49}$$

Juvenile Corrections

Juvenile corrections is mathematically modeled as six stocks or inventories. Each stock has an average daily population. During each month juveniles are released from a stock in accordance with a turnover rate. Some of these juveniles are sent to other correctional stocks; others are released from the juvenile justice system.

Juvenile Correctional Population Movement

A space-capacity constraint limits the number of juveniles that may enter a facility during the month. Noninstitutional corrections is not so constrained. Thus, the procedure used in this part of the model is to first allocate a budget to the two types of youth correctional facilities (county camps and CYA facilities). The space-capacity constraint is converted into a budget-capacity constraint. Using this constraint and the average cost of confining a juvenile, the "maximum allowable" average monthly population can be found. On the basis of this information, the beginning-of-the-month population, and the turnover rate, the maximum allowable inflow rate can be found. Finally, the desired inflow is admitted until the maximum allowable is reached.[14] If some of the desired inflow must be turned away, they will be sent to another correctional stock.

The section of the model dealing with juvenile correctional population movement is developed in the following phases: (1) based on a budget for correctional facilities, find the usable capacity, that is, existing capacity and newly constructed capacity; (2) for any level of usable capacity, find the actual inflow into the institutions; (3) find the actual inflow into noninstitutional correctional stocks; and (4) find the end of period stocks so that the procedure can be repeated the next time period.

Usable capacity is found through a three-step procedure. First, the total expenditure required to maintain and operate existing facility space is subtracted from the budget:

$$CCBB(t) = CCBT(t) - CCEC(t) \times CCECAC \qquad (A.50)$$

where   CCBB   = county camp building budget

        CCBT   = county camp budget total

        CCEC   = county camp existing capacity

        CCECAC = county camp existing-capacity average (maintenance and operation) cost

Second, the existing capacity during any time period is the capacity that existed in the previous time period plus any additional capacity that is built. If there is money left in the budget, it will be used for building more cells. This procedure ensures that the facility is not filled over capacity and at the same time allows the analyst to expand existing capacity:

If $\qquad$ $CCBB(t-d) > 0$ $\qquad$ (A.51a)

then $\qquad$ $CCEC(t) = CCEC(t-1) + \dfrac{CCBB(t-d)}{CCBAC}$ $\qquad$ (A.51b)

If $\qquad$ $CCBB(t-d) \leqslant 0$ $\qquad$ (A.51c)

then $\qquad$ $CCEC(t) = CCEC(t-1)$ $\qquad$ (A.51d)

where   CCBAC = county camp building cost per unit of space

       d = delay between time that funds are appropriated for construction and time building is completed

Third, the capacity available for use may be thought of as the institution population size that will exhaust the entire budget allocated for maintenance and operation of existing facilities and money earmarked for building or purchasing new facility space. (In this model, concepts such as capacity and overcrowding are defined operationally in terms of the average cost of confinement.) If the budget allocated to county camps is not sufficient to maintain and operate existing capacity, some space must sit idle. Mathematically this occurs if the building budget is a negative value:

If $\qquad$ $CCBB(t) < 0$ $\qquad$ (A.52a)

then $\qquad$ $CCUC(t) = \dfrac{CCBT(t)}{CCECAC}$ $\qquad$ (A.52b)

If $\qquad$ $CCBB(t) \geqslant 0$ $\qquad$ (A.52c)

then $\qquad$ $CCUC(t) = CCEC(t)$ $\qquad$ (A.52d)

where   CCUC = county camp usable capacity

The actual inflow in county camps is the portion of the desired inflow that can be accommodated within the usable capacity. If the desired inflow exceeds the maximum allowable inflow, then some of the desired inflow must be turned away and sent to another correctional stock. The number that must be released is found by subtracting the maximum allowable inflow from the desired inflow rate.

$$RECCID = CCID - [2(CCUC) - CCO + 2(CCPB)] \qquad (A.53)$$

where   CCO   = county camp outflow (see equation A.64)

        CCPB   = county camp population beginning of period

        RECCID = released excess county camp inflow desired[15]

Finally, the actual inflow may be found.

If	$RECCID > 0$	(A.54a)
then	$CCIA = CCID - RECCID$	(A.54b)
If	$RECCID \leqslant 0$	(A.54c)[16]
then	$CCIA = CCID$	(A.54d)

where   CCIA = county camp inflow actual

The procedure just used for county camps is repeated for CYA facilities. First, the budget allocation for building is found.

$$CYABB = CYAFB - (CYAEC \times CYAECAC) \qquad (A.55)$$

where   CYABB   = CYA building budget

CYAFB   = CYA facility (maintenance and operation) budget

CYAEC   = CYA existing capacity

CYAECAC = CYA existing capacity (maintenance and operation) average cost

Second, existing capacity during any time period is the capacity that exists at the beginning of the period including any new construction that is completed.

If	$CYABB(t-d) > 0$	(A.56a)
then	$CYAEC(t) = CYAEC(t-1) = \dfrac{CYABB(t-d)}{CYABAC}$	(A.56b)
If	$CYABB(t-d) \leqslant 0$	(A.56c)
then	$CYAEC(t) = CYAEC(t-1)$	(A.56d)

where   CYABAC = CYA building cost per unit of space

Finally, the model finds the amount of usable space.

If	$CYABB(t) < 0$	(A.57a)
then	$CYAUC(t) = \dfrac{CYAFB(t)}{CYAECAC}$	(A.57b)
If	$CYABB(t) \geqslant 0$	(A.57c)
then	$CYAUC(t) = CCEC(t)$	(A.57d)

where   CYAUC = CYA usable capacity

As in the case of county maps, the difference between the desired inflow and the maximum usable capacity is used to determine the actual inflow. The desired inflow to CYA facilities comes from (1) juvenile and adult courts, (2) wards that the juvenile court desires to transfer on subsequent petitions, (3) parole violators who are returned, and (4) other sources (for example, escapees returned). (Court wards in county camps who, in reality, are transferred directly to the CYA are modeled as passing through formal ward status prior to entering the CYA stock.)

$$CYAID = JCYAID + FWFR \times FWO + ACYAID + P(JPARVR)$$
$$\times JPARO + YAOI \qquad (A.58)$$

where   CYAID   = CYA inflow desired

JCYAID   = juvenile court youth authority inflow desired

FWFR   = formal ward failure rate

FWO   = formal ward outflow

ACYAID   = adult court youth authority inflow desired

P(JPARVR) = proportion of parole outflow returned for violations

JPARO   = juvenile parole outflow

YAOI   = youth authority other inflow

The difference between the desired inflow and the maximum allowable may be rewritten as

$$RECYAID = CYAID - [2(CYAUC) - CYAO + 2(CYAPB)] \qquad (A.59)$$

where   CYAO   =   CYA outflow

CYAPB =   CYA population beginning of period

The actual inflow may now be calculated

If $RECYAID > 0$ (A.60a)

then $CYAIA = CYAID - RECYAID$ (A.60b)

If $RECYAID \leqslant 0$ (A.60c)

then $CYAIA = CYAID$ (A.60d)

Having calculated the actual inflow into institutions, the model computes the inflow into noninstitutional correctional stocks. The inflow into formal ward status comes from several sources. Juveniles may be declared wards of the court on an initial petition. Juveniles who fail to meet the requirements of their nonward status can be placed in formal ward status on a subsequent petition. Juveniles released from county camps remain wards of the court. After county camps or CYA facilities are at capacity, juveniles who cannot be admitted (that is, the excess of the desired inflow over the actual) are also placed on formal probation.

$$FWIT = FWIP + NWFR \times NWO + CCO + (CCID - CCIA)$$

$$+ P(CTA) \times (CYAID - CYAIA) \qquad (A.61)$$

where   FWIT   = formal ward inflow total

         NWFR   = nonward failure rate

         NWO   = nonward outflow

         P(CTA)   = proportion of court turnaways from CYA facilities (see equation A.62 for calculation)

Since juveniles flow into CYA facilities from several sources (courts and parole), a decision rule must be established to determine which juveniles must be turned away from CYA facilities when they are full. The decision rule adopted is that court commitments are turned away from the CYA in the same proportion that the courts (as opposed to the parole board) desire to place them in CYA facilities.

$$P(CTA) = \frac{JCYAID + FWFR \times FWO + ACYAID}{CYAID} \qquad (A.62)$$

The parole inflow comes directly from the outflow from the CYA facilities. It includes parole violators and others who cannot be returned to institutions because they are at capacity.

$$JPARI = P(JPAR) \times CYAO + [1 - P(CTA)] \times (CYAID - CYAIA)$$

$$(A.63)$$

where   JPARI   = juvenile parole inflow

         P(JPAR) = proportion of CYA wards paroled

This section is concluded by solving for the end of period population in each correctional stock. The end-of-period population equals the population at the beginning of the period, plus the inflow, less the outflow. Beginning-of-the-period population is expressed as the population at the end of the previous period, for example, $ISPB(t) = ISPE(t-1)$. The outflow from each correctional stock is the beginning population times the turnover rate. The turnover rate is the reciprocal of the average length of stay.

$$\text{ISPE}(t) = \text{ISPE}(t-1) + \text{ISIT} - \frac{\text{ISPE}(t-1)}{\text{TIS}} \qquad (A.64)$$

$$\text{NWPE}(t) = \text{NWPE}(t-1) + \text{NWIT} - \frac{\text{NWPE}(t-1)}{\text{TNW}} \qquad (A.65)$$

$$\text{FWPE}(t) = \text{FWPE}(t-1) + \text{FWIT} - \frac{\text{FWPE}(t-1)}{\text{TFW}} \qquad (A.66)$$

$$\text{CCPE}(t) = \text{CCPE}(t-1) + \text{CCIA} - \frac{\text{CCPE}(t-1)}{\text{TCC}} \qquad (A.67)$$

$$\text{CYAPE}(t) = \text{CYAPE}(t-1) + \text{CYAIA} - \frac{\text{CYAPE}(t-1)}{\text{TCYA}} \qquad (A.68)$$

$$\text{JPARPE}(t) = \text{JPARPE}(t-1) + \text{JPARI} - \frac{\text{JPARPE}(t-1)}{\text{TJPAR}} \qquad (A.69)$$

where   ISPE   = informal supervision population end of period

NWPE   = nonward population end of period

FWPE   = formal ward population end of period

CCPE   = county camp population end of period

CYAPE   = CYA facilities population end of period

JPARPE = juvenile parole population end of period

TIS   = average length of stay in informal supervision

TNW   = average length of stay on nonward status

TFR   = average length of stay on formal ward status

TCC   = average length of stay in county camps

TCYA   = average length of stay in CYA facilities

TJPAR   = average length of stay on parole

Subsequent Petitions

Subsequent petitions are filed in order to change the status of nonwards and formal wards. Subsequent petitions are incorporated in this model by calculating them as a function of average probation stocks:

$$SP = P(\text{NWSP}) \frac{\text{NWPE}(t-1) + \text{NWPE}(t-1)}{2}$$

$$+ P(\text{FWSP}) \frac{\text{FWPE}(t-2) + \text{FWPE}(t-1)}{2} \qquad (\text{A.70})[17]$$

where $P(\text{NWSP})$ = proportion of nonwards subsequently petitioned

$P(\text{FWSP})$ = proportion of formal wards subsequently petitioned

Correctional Budgets and Performance Measures

At the beginning of each simulation experiment, the model's user allocates a budget to three probation functions: county camp, juvenile hall, and case handling (that is, initial handling, crisis intervention, petition filing, and probation caseload). The entire county camp budget is used for building and maintenance. Any resources in excess of those required for initial handling and juvenile detention are used to handle the probation caseload. The following equation finds the probation budget remaining for the caseload:

$$\text{PROBR} = \text{PROJ} - \left(\text{IHAC} \times \sum_{i}^{I} \text{RTP}_i\right) - \left(\text{PCIAC} \times \sum_{i}^{I} \text{PCI}_i\right)$$

$$\qquad (\text{A.71})$$

$$- \left[\text{PFAC} \times \left(\sum_{i}^{I} \text{PA}_i + \text{SP}\right)\right] + \text{JHB} - \left(\text{JHAC} \times \sum_{i}^{I} \text{DPDA}_i\right)$$

where   PROBR = probation budget remaining after initial handling and detention[18]

PROBJ = probation budget for handling juvenile cases

IHAC   = initial handling average cost

PCIAC = probation crisis intervention average cost

PFAC   = petition filing average cost

The caseload per probation officer is generally used as a measure of probation's performance in handling its workload. Its workload is the sum of three monthly-average noninstitutionalized stocks. Converting the budget remaining for the caseload into its workforce equivalent yields

$$\text{PROCLPO} = \text{PROOW} \left\{ \frac{\text{ISPE}(t-1) + \text{ISPE}(t)}{2} \right.$$

$$+ \frac{\text{NWPE}(t-1)^2 + \text{ISPE}(t)}{2}$$

$$\left. + \frac{\text{FWPE}(t-1) + \text{ISPE}(t)}{2} \right\} \text{PROBR} \qquad (\text{A.72})$$

where   PROCLPO = probation caseload per probation officer

         PROOW   = probation officer's wage (including all overhead costs)

The California Youth Authority budget is separated into two components. The facility budget was previously used to maintain, operate, and build capacity. The parole budget is used to handle the caseload as follows:

$$PARCLPO = \frac{PAROW \times JPARPA}{JPARB} \qquad (A.73)$$

where   PARCLPO = parole caseload per parole officer

         PAROW   = parole officer wage (including all overhead)

         JPARB   = juvenile parole budget

Calculating the Deterrence Variables

The model is concluded by solving for three deterrence variables in the victimization rate, equation A.1, which are endogenous in the juvenile justice system.

The probability of arrest PJARREST is the number of juveniles arrested for violent and property crimes divided by the number of victims (expressed in terms of the victimization rate).

$$PJARREST = \frac{JA_1 + JA_2}{JVRATE(POP/100,000)} \qquad (A.74)$$

The probability of punishment PJPUNISH is the number of first commitments for major delinquencies divided by the number of victimizations.[19]

$$PJPUNISH = \left\{ PCC_1 \times PA_1 - [\frac{PCC_1 \times PA_1}{CCID}(CCID - CCIA)] \right.$$

$$+ PJCYA_1 \times PA_1 - [\frac{PJCYA_1 \times PA_1}{CYAID}(CYAID$$

$$\left. - CYAIA)] \right\} / JVRATE \frac{POP}{100,000} \qquad (A.75)$$

The severity of punishment SJPUNISH is calculated as a weighted index of the average length of stay in county camps and CYA facilities. This measure is weighted by the proportion of commitments (including recommitments) to each type of facility.

$$\text{SJPUNISH} = \text{CCWT} \times \text{TCC} + \text{CYAWT} \times \text{TCYA} \qquad (A.76)$$

where   CCWT   = county camp weight

          CYAWT = CYA weight

Since the victimization rate is a measure of the number of crimes committed by juveniles under 18 years of age, youthful offenders must not be included in the weights. The number of youthful offenders committed to CYA facilities is equal to the number of desired commitments less turnaways from CYA facilities. The decision rule used previously (for the proportion of court turnaways) is used for youthful offenders.

$$\text{YOAI} = \text{ACYAID} - \frac{\text{ACYAID}}{\text{CYAID}}(\text{CYAID} - \text{CYAIA}) \qquad (A.77)$$

where   YOAI = youthful offender actual inflow

The weights for the two facilities are as follows:

$$\text{CCWT} = \frac{\text{CCIA}}{\text{CCIA} + \text{CYAIA} - \text{YOAI}} \qquad (A.78)$$

$$\text{CYAWT} = \frac{\text{CYAIA} - \text{YOAI}}{\text{CCIA} + \text{CYAIA} - \text{YOAI}} \qquad (A.79)$$

By substituting equations A.77 to A.79 into equation A.76, we get

$$\text{SJPUNISH} = \frac{\text{CCIA}}{\text{CCIA} + \text{CYAIA} - \text{YOAI}}\text{TCC}$$

$$+ \frac{\text{CYAIA} - \text{YOAI}}{\text{CCIA} + \text{CYAIA} - \text{YOAI}}\text{TCYA} \qquad (A.80)$$

Notes

1. The simulation model was developed originally in the author's dissertation. See Gregory P. Falkin, "Reducing Delinquency: A Strategic Planning Approach," chap. 4 for a somewhat more detailed explanation of the model.

2. To facilitate the reading of this appendix and appendix B, both follow section by section the description of the juvenile justice system in chapter 4. Substantive and procedural issues of juvenile justice discussed earlier are not reiterated in the appendixes. The reader should, therefore, refer to the appropriate section in chapter 4 to clarify such matters.

3. Computer Research Center for Economics and Management Science, TROLL 1/User's Guide (Cambridge, Mass.: National Bureau of Economic Research, Inc., 1972). The simulation model, symbol definitions, and data (as programmed in TROLL) appear in Falkin, "Reducing Delinquency," appendixes B-D.

4. Arrests are divided into six categories for three reasons. First, the cost of violent arrests is substantially greater than that of other arrests. Second, policymakers may wish to allocate more resources to the control of certain crimes. Third, an original goal of this research was to include a model of the adult system which required the previous categorization. It was not possible to separate JVICTIM into these six categories because some of the independent variables (in equation A.1) could be measured only for the aggregate of these offenses.

5. Since arrests for juvenile tendencies ($k = 5$) include only juveniles, $PJA_5 = 1$ and $PAA_5 = 0$. Conversely, since misdemeanor arrests ($k = 6$) exclude juveniles, $PJA_6 = 0$ and $PAA_6 = 1$.

6. In order to find the desired detention rate, resources are distributed sequentially to the three desired detention rates, priority being given to serious offenders. In the "real world" decisions are made on a case-by-case basis, and status offenders are sometimes detained while dangerous offenders are released. This model was developed, however, with an interest in finding the total number of detainees and experimenting with alternative resource allocations to the three offender categories.

7. To avoid confusion, the reader should recall that the number released in equation A.25d is a negative value. Although the sign is positive, implying addition, $JHBR_i$ is negative.

8. JHBR is a measure of the overallocation or underallocation of juvenile hall resources relative to a desired detention rate. $JHBR_3 > 0$ indicates that some resources are wasted. $JHBR_i < 0$ measures the underallocation of resources for detaining type i delinquents. Ultimately, policymakers must be concerned with the effect that JHBR has on other parts of the system. The important issue is the alternative use of resources. For example, if JHB were initially allocated so that $JHBR_i < 0$ (for all i), how much would crime change as a result of setting one or all $JHBR_i = 0$?

9. Since a detention hearing will be held only after a determination to petition has been made, only a proportion $p(PA)$ of those detained at intake will receive a detention hearing.

10. In equation (A.28d), JHDIF will take on either a positive or a negative

value depending on the number of desired type 3 detainees $DPDD_3$ relative to the total deficit.

11. The approach used to mathematically model the juvenile court process is to find the number of desired petitions that may be filed within the constraint of a one-month budget. Even if probation desires to file more petitions than feasible (within the court's resource constraint), the excess will be released for one of two reasons. First, the law stipulates the maximum number of days that the adjudication process may take (roughly a month for juveniles in detention). Backlogs create delay, and this delay may prevent the timely adjudication of juveniles. Probation may be forced to release them. Second, juvenile court judges may subtly persuade probation to reduce their rate of petitioning.

12. If some of the petitions that probation desires to file cannot be filed ($PFBR_i < 0$), one must conclude that the juvenile courts are underfinanced relative to their potential caseload. In the less likely case where vacancies remain after all desired petitions are filed, then court resources sit idle (this occurs if $PFBR_3 > 0$). Which of these two situations occurs, underallocating court resources ($PFBR_i < 0$) or overallocating court resources ($PFBR_3 > 0$) relative to resources allocated to other subsystems, can be ascertained simply by watching the simulated value of PFBR. In fact, PFBR is a direct measure of the juvenile court's surplus of deficit. It may be interpreted as a measure of the overallocation or underallocation of resources to juvenile court relative to the police or probation.

13. The actual inflow to the last three correctional types may be different from the number that the courts would desire to send if correctional resources were unlimited. This will be taken up in the next section.

14. As an alternative procedure, parole boards can increase the turnover rate (that is, the inverse of the average length of stay) to accommodate a desired rate of inflow. This procedure, which is more in keeping with reality, does not allow the researcher to control the average length of stay. Thus, the turnover rate is used in this model as a policy parameter to facilitate testing of mandatory minimum sentencing policies.

15. The maximum allowable inflow in equation A.53 is the expression in brackets, $2(CCUC) - CCO + 2(CCPB)$. The maximum allowable inflow can be found, in general, as follows. The end-of-period population can be expressed as a function of either the population average ($PE = 2PA - PB$) or the inflow and outflow ($PE = PB + IN - OUT$). Substituting the former into the latter and solving for the inflow, $IN = 2PA + OUT - 2PB$. In the model, the inflow expressed as a function of the average population is the maximum allowable inflow (specifically, $2CCUC - CCO + CCPB$).

16. In the latter case (equations A.54c and d), available space goes unused. Thus, RECCID can be used as a measure for determining the appropriate allocation of resources to county camps. If some of the desired inflow must be turned away from county camps, they will be placed on formal probation.

17. The average population in the previous time period is used in order to expedite the computer solution of SP and to keep computer costs down.

18. It is plausible that a simulation could produce a negative budget remaining for handling the caseload (PROBRR < 0). In reality, this would be absurd. It would result in the simulated experience because the model's user conducted a policy experiment in which the probation budget was much too low relative to the police budget. This situation may arise because as the police budget increases, the number of referrals to probation, and hence the initial handling costs, increases. (Initial handling costs are unconstrained because every case referred to probation must receive some sort of determination.) PROBR can be used as a policy tool to find the appropriate probation budget relative to the police budget. PROBJ would have to be raised until PROBR reaches a positive level sufficient to provide the amount of care for the probation caseload that policymakers wish to implement.

19. A proportion (PCC) of the petitions filed are, for example, potential or desired commitments to county camps. Since there are three types of juvenile delinquents in this model, a decision rule must be used to determine the types of potential commitments that must be turned away if county camps are at capacity (if CCID > CCIA). The decision rule used in this model is that each type of delinquent has an equal probability of being turned away (PCC$_i$ × PA$_i$/ CCID).

Appendix B
Data and Parameter
Estimates for the
Simulation Model

The purpose of this appendix is to explain the methodology used to estimate the parameters in the simulation model (appendix A). Four types of parameters are discussed: (1) the coefficients in the juvenile victimization rate; (2) transition probabilities for police, probation, and court determinations; (3) cost parameters; and (4) time parameters. This appendix concludes with a discussion of the procedure used to validate the model.

Estimating the Crime Equation

This section presents the model, variables, and assumptions used to estimate the coefficients in the simulation model crime equation. Two criteria guided the collection of data and the choice of coefficients. First, the model specification was based on the theory of relative opportunity presented in chapter 3. Second, the variables and coefficients were chosen on the basis of their statistical validity, reliability, and significance. The theory of relative opportunity leads directly to the following general model of crime:

$$\text{CRIME} = f(\text{DETERRENCE, RESTRAINT, REFORMATION, PREVENTION})$$

$$(B.1)$$

The rest of this section explains how these theoretical variables were operationalized, measured, and statistically tested.

An Econometric Model of Crime

Prior to collecting data, the five theoretical variables in equation B.1 were operationalized.[1] Crime was operationalized as the juvenile victimization rate; deterrence, as the certainty and severity of incarceration in juvenile correctional facilities and the probability of arrest; restraint, as the number of delinquents institutionalized; reformation, as expenditures on rehabilitation programs; prevention, as income equality, employment, and urbanization.

These various indicators required several data sources. The unit of observation was the state. Thus, each of the following sources supplied data for the fifty states[2]: The Uniform Crime Report section of the Federal Bureau of Investigation supplied this research project with data on crime (reported offenses) and arrests.[3] Data used for measuring deterrence, restraint, and rehabilitation were taken from Law Enforcement Assistance Administration (LEAA) publications.[4] In addition, the Center for Advanced Computation of the University of Illinois supplied this research project with a computer tape from their data archive of LEAA data.[5] Data used as indicators of crime prevention were collected from Bureau of Census' 1970 census.[6] Expenditure data on juvenile workforce programs were collected from the *Manpower Report of the President*.[7]

In many cases there are numerous ways of measuring operational variables. The definition and construction of each variable used in the econometric model are presented. Two types of variables are discussed. The construction of primary variables, that is, variables explicitly entered in the econometric model, is presented. In addition, the measurement of secondary variables (variables used to construct the primary variables) is explained.

Crime. The dependent variable in this model is the juvenile victimization rate JVICTIM. JVICTIM is the number of people (per 100,000 population) victimized by juveniles each month.[8] Violent victimizations (murder, robbery, rape, and assault) and property victimizations (grand larceny, burglary, automobile theft) are summed.[9] These are defined as major delinquencies in this book.

The number of juvenile victimizations is an unknown quantity; therefore, it must be estimated. Constructing this index involves two steps. First, the number of juvenile delinquencies reported to the police is solved.[10] The number of juveniles arrested is a function of the number of reported offenses. It is assumed that people are just as likely to report a juvenile delinquency to the police as an adult crime. Further, it is assumed that juveniles and adults are arrested with an equal probability.

Accordingly, the number of juvenile delinquencies reported to the police in 1970 may be expressed as follows:

$$\text{JOFFENSE}^{1970} = \sum_{i}^{i=7} \frac{\text{JARREST}_i^{1970}}{\text{TARREST}_i^{1970}} \, \text{OFFENSE}_i^{1970} \qquad (B.2)$$

where $i = 1, \ldots, 7$ = murder, rape, assault, robbery, grand theft, burglary, auto theft[11]

JOFFENSE = juvenile delinquencies reported to the police

JARREST   = juvenile arrestees

TARREST = total arrestees (juveniles and adults)

OFFENSE = total offenses reported to the police

The next step is to find the monthly victimization rate. Since the simulation model is iterated monthly, the dependent variable is an approximation of the monthly victimization rate. The purpose of estimating the crime equation is to predict annual victimization rates from monthly averages. It is assumed that, as a rule of thumb, half of all juvenile victimizations are reported to the police.[12] Thus, the monthly juvenile victimization rate is twice as great as the juvenile reported offense rate.

$$JVICTIM^{1970} = 2 \frac{JOFFENSE^{1970}/12}{POPN/100,000} \tag{B.3}$$

where POPN = state population

By substituting equation B.2 into equation B.3 the monthly victimization for each state may be estimated.

$$JVICTIM^{1970} = \frac{2 \sum_{i}^{i=7} \frac{JARREST_i^{1970}}{TARREST_i^{1970}} \frac{OFFENSE^{1970}}{12}}{POPN/100,000} \tag{B.4}$$

Deterrence. Deterrence was operationalized with three indicators. The probability of arrest is the number of juveniles arrested divided by the number of juvenile victimizations.

$$P(JARREST)^{1970} = \frac{\sum_{i}^{i=7} JARREST^{1970}}{JVICTIM^{1970}} \tag{B.5}$$

where $P(JARREST)$ = probability that juvenile is arrested given he has committed a major delinquency

The average length of stay in juvenile correctional facilities was used to measure the severity of punishment.

$$SJPUNISH^{1971} = ADTCF^{1971}/30 + AMCF^{1971} \tag{B.6}$$

where SJPUNISH = severity of juvenile punishment (average number of months)[13]

ADTCF = average number of days in temporary care facilities (public detention centers, reception and diagnostic centers, and shelters)[14]

AMCF   = average number of months in correctional facilities (training schools; ranches, forestry camps, and farms; halfway houses and group homes).[14]

The certainty of punishment was measured as the probability that a juvenile major delinquent would be sent to a correctional facility as a first commitment given he committed a victimization.

$$P(\text{JPUNISH})^{1971} = \frac{\text{JMFIRSTC}^{1971}}{\text{JVICTIM}^{1971}} \tag{B.7}$$

where $P(\text{JPUNISH})$ = probability of juvenile punishment

JMFIRSTC   = juvenile major delinquency first commitments

Data on the number of first commitments are not broken down by type of offense in *Children in Custody*. The procedure used to estimate the number of major delinquency first commitments was to take the proportion of first commitments (for all offenses) assumed to be major delinquents. The assumption was that major delinquents are committed to correctional facilities in the same proportion that they are found in correctional facilities. Thus, the first step was to find the distribution of delinquents in facilities by type of offense. *Children in Custody* gives a breakdown of delinquents in facilities by type of offense for thirty-nine states.[15] It was possible to estimate the distribution for five additional states from a sample of facilities in the five states.[16]

The number of major delinquency first commitments in forty-four states were calculated as follows:

$$\text{JMFIRSTC}^{1971} = \text{JMDPC}^{1971} \times \text{TFIRSTC}^{1971} \tag{B.8}$$

where   JMDPC   = juvenile major delinquent percentage of the correctional facility population

TFIRSTC = total (all offenses) first commitments to correctional facilities.[17]

These two steps produced a measure of the number of major delinquency first commitments for forty-four states. An estimate for the remaining six states was made by regressing JMFIRSTC on the outflow from correctional facilities. The outflow was the sum of juveniles discharged without supervision and paroled. Table B-1 presents the results of this regression. The t statistic for the coefficient on OUTFLOW is significant at the 99 percent significance level; the F statistic is also significant at the 99 percent level. OUTFLOW seems to be a good predictor of JMFIRSTC (the R^2 was nearly 0.9). This equation was used to estimate the number of major delinquent first commitments for the remaining six states.

Table B-1
Regression Estimates of Coefficients for Juvenile Major Delinquency First Commitments

$\text{JMFIRSTC} = \beta_0 + \beta_1 \text{ (OUTFLOW)}$			
Coefficient	Value	Standard Error	t Statistic
0	−62.986	46.414	−1.357
1	.349	.018	19.300

Number of Observations	Statistics
44	$F_{1,42} = 372.469$
	$R^2 = .899$
	$\bar{R}^2 = .896$

Restraint. Restraint was measured as the percentage of the juvenile population incarcerated. Two related measures were used. In one case, the juvenile population was defined as juvenile ages 1 to 17 inclusive. In the other measure, the relevant population group was defined as juveniles ages 14 to 17 inclusive.

$$\text{JRESTTJ} = \frac{\text{JCFAPOP}^{1971}}{\text{JPOP}^{1970}} \qquad (B.9)$$

$$\text{JRESTSUB} = \frac{\text{JCFAPOP}^{1971}}{\text{JSUBPOP}^{1970}} \qquad (B.10)$$

where   JRESTTJ   = juveniles restrained in correctional facilities as percentage of total juvenile population

   JCFAPOP   = juvenile correctional facility average population[18]

   JPOP   = juvenile population (ages 1 to 17)[18]

   JRESTSUB = juveniles restrained in correctional facilities as percentage of the juvenile subpopulation (ages 14 to 17)

   JSUBPOP   = juvenile subpopulation (ages 14 to 17)[18]

As a proxy for restraint, a measure of the delinquent population at large was constructed. The rationale for this measure is that delinquents not restrained are in the population and may commit another crime.

$$\text{DELTJ} = \frac{\text{OUTFLOW}^{1971}}{\text{JPOP}^{1970}} \qquad (B.11)$$

$$DELSUB = \frac{OUTFLOW^{1971}}{JSUBPOP^{1970}} \qquad (B.12)$$

where   DELTJ   = delinquent population at large as percentage of total juvenile population

OUTFLOW = juveniles discharged and paroled from correctional facilities[19]

DELSUB   = delinquent population at large as percentage of juvenile subpopulation (ages 14 to 17)

Reformation. Reformation was operationalized as expenditures on rehabilitation programs. National data on reitegrative programs are extremely limited.

$$REHAB^{1971} = \frac{TEDEXP^{1971}}{JCFAPOP^{1971}} \qquad (B.13)$$

where   REHAB = rehabilitation expenditures per inmate

TEDEXP = treatment and educational salaries and wages[20]

Prevention. Crime prevention was operationalized in terms of employment, income equality, and urbanization. Several social structure variables were taken or computed from the *Census of Population, 1970.* A list of these variables and their definitions follows:

INEQUALITY = Gini index of income concentration

URBAN   = percentage of state's population living in urban areas

JUNEMP   = percentage of juveniles (ages 14 to 17) unemployed

JNOTSCH   = percentage of juveniles (ages 14 to 17) not enrolled in school

JNOTSNW   = percentage of juveniles (ages 14 to 17) not enrolled in school and not working (unemployed and not in labor force)

AUNEMP   = percentage of adults (ages 18 to 34) unemployed

APARTR   = adult labor force participation rate

Manpower administration expenditures on juvenile job programs were included in this analysis. They were measured as expenditures per juvenile (ages 14 to 17).

$$MANPOWER^{1970} = \frac{MDTA^{1970} + NYC^{1970} + JOBCORP^{1970}}{JSUBPOP^{1970}}$$

(B.14)

where   MANPOWER = 1970 manpower expenditures per juvenile

MDTA   = Department of Labor expenditures on MDTA programs[21]

NYC   = Department of Labor expenditures on Neighborhood Youth Corps programs[21]

JOBCORP   = Department of Labor expenditures on Job Corps programs[21]

The Coefficient Estimates

The coefficients for the simulation model's crime equation were estimated by regression analysis. A few equations, specified in linear and log-log form, were estimated by ordinary least squares. Statistical tests were used as the criteria to determine whether a variable actually explains the crime rate or whether its estimated coefficient was spurious. The research procedure was to include one measure of each theoretical variable in equation B.1.[22] Different measures were substituted into the JVICTIM equation so that hypotheses based on the relative opportunity theory could be statistically tested. Following is the list of hypotheses that were statistically tested.

An increase in each of the deterrence variables P(JARREST), SJPUNISH, and PJPUNISH was hypothesized to have a negative effect on the juvenile victimization rate JVICTIM. Each of the hypotheses was found to be statistically significant at the 95 percent significance level.[23]

The percentage of the juvenile population restrained (JRESTTJ or JREST-SUB) was hypothesized to be inversely related to JVICTIM. This hypothesis was not statistically significant (even at an 80 percent significance level).

The delinquent population at large as a percentage of the juvenile population (DELTJ or DELSUB) was hypothesized to be positively related to JVICTIM. This hypothesis was not statistically significant (even at an 80 percent significance level).

It was hypothesized that, in the aggregate, rehabilitation programs have no significant effect on crime. This hypothesis was statistically tested by determining whether the coefficient on REHAB was significantly different from zero (at an 80 percent significance level). It was not. Thus, the hypothesis that prison rehabilitation has no effect on crime was confirmed.

All the prevention variables (INEQUALITY, URBAN, JUNEMP, JNOTSCH, JNOTSNW, AUNEMP) except APARTR were hypothesized to be positively related to JVICTIM. An inverse relationship between APARTR and JVICTIM was hypothesized. Each of these hypotheses follows from the theory of relative opportunity. Income inequality, according to the theory of relative opportunity, ought to be a powerful explanatory variable (the effect should be significant and with a large magnitude). A few comments will clarify the not-so-obvious rationale for including some of the other variables.

Urbanization is not, strictly speaking, a crime prevention variable. It is, however, a social structure crime causal variable. It is included primarily because the theory of relative opportunity does not include a number of important aspects of modern social life. It is hypothesized that URBAN is a key explanatory variable. Environmental factors of urban life (poorly lit streets, few playgrounds), social interaction patterns among urbanites, and population density may have much to do with high crime rates.

All the measures of unemployment are used to reflect a lack of legitimate opportunities. JUNEMP and JNOTSNW measure the juvenile employment opportunity structure. AUNEMP and APARTR measure the adult opportunity structure. Although adult unemployment does not measure a lack of juvenile jobs, the adult opportunity structure is hypothesized to affect juvenile perceptions of the social system's opportunity structure.

The statistical tests of these hypotheses demonstrated that the opportunity structure is a key explanatory factor of juvenile delinquency. INEQUALITY and URBAN were found to be significant at a 95 percent significance level; JUNEMPLOY, at a 90 percent level. None of the other prevention variables were statistically significant even at an 80 percent significance level.

The following regression equation explained over 70 percent of the variance in the victimization rate:

$$\ln \text{JVICTIM}^{1970} = \ln \beta_0 + \beta_1 \times \ln \text{URBAN}^{1970} + \beta_2 \times \ln \text{JUEMP}^{1970}$$

$$- \beta_3 \times \ln P(\text{JPUNISH})^{1971} - \beta_4 \times \ln \text{SJPUNISH}^{1971}$$

$$+ \beta_5 \times \ln \text{INEQUALITY}^{1970} - \beta_6 \times \ln P(\text{JARREST})^{1970}$$

$$(\text{B.15})$$

Table B-2 presents the coefficient estimates and related statistics.

The regression equation (B.15) is used in the simulation model (see equation A.1). The hypotheses tested in this section substantiate the theory of relative opportunity proposed in chapter 3. In particular, the coefficient values in table B-2 indicate that income inequality has the greatest direct effect on crime. The coefficients from a log-log equation may be interpreted as follows: A 1 percent reduction in the level of income inequality will produce a 2.85 percent reduction in the juvenile victimization rate. Urbanization appears to have the second

Table B-2
Regression Estimates of Coefficients for the Juvenile Victimization Rate

$\ln JVICTIM = \ln \beta_0 + \beta_1 \times \ln URBAN + \beta_2 \times \ln JUNEMP - \beta_3 \times \ln P(JPUNISH) - \beta_4 \times \ln SJPUNISH + \beta_5 \times \ln INEQUALITY - \beta_6 \times \ln P(JARREST)$

Coefficient	Value	Standard Error	Partial	Beta	t Statistic
B1	0.927	0.216	0.548	0.387	4.298*
B2	0.302	0.190	0.236	0.143	1.592**
B3	−0.156	0.053	−0.408	−0.260	−2.927*
B4	−0.443	0.194	−0.329	−0.190	−2.285*
B5	2.851	0.776	0.489	0.348	3.676*
B6	−0.652	0.110	−0.669	−0.512	−5.905*
B0	3,025.570	4,214.130	0.109	7.224E-04	0.718

Number of observations: 50

Statistics: $F_{6,43} = 18.32^*$ $R^2 = .71881$ $\overline{R}^2 = .67957$

*Significant at the 95 percent level.
**Significant at the 90 percent level.

greatest direct effect. One purpose of the simulation model is to ascertain the indirect effects of the deterrence variables and their impact on crime. The thesis of this research is that a cost-effective strategic crime control plan will emphasize income and jobs programs while maintaining a "budgetary balanced" level of deterrence.

Juvenile Arrests

In this section (and the following sections on probation, courts, and corrections) the methodology used to estimate three types of parameters is described. These sections are divided into a discussion of cost estimates, transitional probabilities, and time parameters. In the simulation model, each of these parameters may be changed by the analyst so that the effect of policy changes and changes in subsystem efficiency can be assessed.

The Police Budget and Arrest Costs

A few institutional factors must be considered in estimating the cost of arrest. First, the cost of arrest varies by type of crime according to the amount of resources devoted to the arrest. Violent crimes receive greater resources than misdemeanors. Accordingly, more resources are allocated to arresting perpetrators of violent crimes even though fewer violent offenders are arrested.

Second, the police budget may be divided into two components along functional lines. The detectives' division has responsibility for investigation and clears roughly 50 percent of felony cases.[24] The patrol division makes nearly all misdemeanor arrests, most felony arrests, but has responsibility for patrol and a number of other services such as traffic patrol, emergency services, and other social services.

Finally, a portion of the police budget is allocated to police administration. In addition, a sizable portion of police resources is devoted to other community services not at all related to the police's arrest function.

In an ideal accounting of police arrest costs, resources used for any purpose other than arrest would be excluded. A detailed breakdown of police budgets along divisional or program lines was not available for this book. Accordingly, nonarrest resources are distributed over the resource cost of arrests. Similarly, administrative costs are distributed over all arrests in proportion to the relative workload of the various types of arrest. The implication of this assumption for a simulation model of the police sector is that budgetary figures in any year include a proportion of administrative and other services. This method of estimating arrest costs should and can be justified. Given a certain level or probability of arrest, one may investigate the deterrent effect of the police arrest output. It is unimportant for our purposes to determine precisely which police inputs deter crime. The issue that this book addresses is the relative effect of arrest as compared to other crime control programs.

Table B-3 shows an accounting of police expenditures in 1970. Of police and sheriff expenditures 18 percent is distributed to detectives divisions.[25] This money will be used for felony investigations and juvenile divisions. Since the Highway Patrol makes only traffic arrests, all highway patrol expenditures are included in the patrol budget. Thus, 1970 police expenditures are displayed in table B-4 according to divisional lines.

The detective division's expenditure is distributed over felony and juvenile delinquency arrests (excluding misdemeanors according to a weighting scheme). This must be done because investigating violent crimes takes much longer than other types of crimes. The weights are developed from Greenwood's analysis of the criminal investigation process.[26] The average time per investigation (see table B-5) is used to derive the weighted workload per arrest. The arrest weights are derived by converting the average time for juvenile delinquency arrests (3.4 hours) to a base of 1.

Table B-6 presents the cost of arrest for each offense category. The number of arrests in 1970 (column 1) are weighted by the arrest weights from table B-5 (see column 2). The result is a weighted arrest workload for the detective division (column 3). The cost per (weighted) hour of detectives time is $114.32. This is calculated by dividing the detective budget ($107,063,000 from table B-4) by the total weighted workload ($936,553 from table B-6). The detective's average cost per arrest is displayed for each offense category in table B-6, column 4.

This model does not use a workload measure for the patrol division. It assumes that the patrol budget ($609,665,000 from table B-4) is distributed in an equal proportion over all 1,340,072 arrests (see table B-6, column 1). Thus, the patrol divisions average cost per arrest is $454.95 (table B-6, column 5). The

Table B-3
Police Expenditures, Fiscal Year 1970
(in thousands)

Police and Sheriffs			
Patrol (72%)	$487,732		
Detectives (18%)	107,063		
Total (100%)		$594,795	
Highway Patrol		121,933	
Total			$716,728

Source: Bureau of Criminal Statistics, *Crime and Delinquency in California* (Sacramento: State of California, 1974), p. 35.

Table B-4
Police Expenditures by Division, Fiscal Year 1970
(in thousands)

Patrol divisions	$609,665
Detective divisions	107,063
Total	$716,728

combined average cost (including detective and patrol costs) is presented for each offense in column 6.

The total cost for each category of arrest is presented in column 7. In the simulation model the total police budget is $716,729,640.[27] A budget (based on the total cost in column 7) is distributed to violent and property arrests. The remaining budget is appropriated to the remaining categories according to the percentage distribution calculated from column 7.

Police Disposition of Juveniles

Data on the police disposition of juveniles were not available for 1970. Data were published, however, for 1969.[28] The transition probabilities used in the simulation model are presented in table B-7. Each column represents a disposition, and the probability's symbol used in the simulation model is in brackets.

Juvenile Probation

Based on the transition probabilities in the preceding section, the police refer a certain number of juveniles to probation. Some juveniles referred to probation are police re-referrals. Since some re-referrals are detained, the section of the

Table B-5
Detective Division Weighted Workload

	Average Time per Arrest (hours)	Arrest Weighted
Violent crimes	11.9	3.5
Property crimes	6.8	2.0
Drug crimes	5.1	1.5
Other felonies	6.8	2.0
Juvenile delinquencies	3.4	1.0

Source: Adapted from Peter Greenwood et al., *The Criminal Investigation Process,* vol. 3 (Santa Monica, Calif.: Rand Corporation, 1975), p. 59.

Table B-6
Arrest Cost Estimates, 1970

	Arrests (1)	Weights (2)	Weighted Arrests (3) = (1) × (2)	Detectives' Average Cost per Arrest (4) = (2) × $114.32	Patrol Average Cost per Arrest (5)	Combined Average Cost per Arrest (6) = (4) + (5)	Total Cost (7) = (1) × (6)
Violent crimes	48,535	3.5	169,873	$400.12	$454.95	$855.07	$ 41,500,822
Property crimes	118,671	2.0	237,342	228.63	454.95	683.58	81,121,122
Drug crimes	118,314	1.5	177,471	171.47	454.95	626.42	74,114,255
Other felonies	39,616	2.0	79,232	228.63	454.95	683.58	27,080,705
Juvenile delinquencies	272,635	1.0	272,635	114.32	454.95	569.27	155,202,920
Misdemeanors	742,301	0	0	0	454.95	454.95	337,709,830
Total	1,340,072	–	936,553	–	–	–	716,729,640

Source: Bureau of Criminal Statistics, *Crime and Delinquency in California* (Sacramento: State of California, 1974), pp. 26, 28, 30.

Table B-7
Probability of Police Dispositions of Juvenile Arrests, 1969

Offense	Counseled and Released [P(JCR)]	Referred to Other Agency [P(RDA)]	Referred to Probation [P(RTP)]	Total
Major law violations	.19481	.04363	.76156	1
Drug violations	.15885	.01381	.82734	1
Other delinquencies	.48469	.03675	.47856	1

Source: Bureau of Criminal Statistics, *Crime and Delinquency in California* (Sacramento: State of California, 1969), p. 145.

model dealing with juvenile detention includes re-referrals. (This was done primarily because data were very limited on juvenile detention.) The flow of juveniles through all other sections of the model is based primarily on initial referrals. Subsequent petitions are included as a separate category. Thus, in all sections of the model, except detention, initial referrals are separated from re-referrals.

The probability that a juvenile (including re-referrals) is detained is calculated from two data sources: total referrals to probation and admissions of delinquents to California juvenile halls.[29] The probability was calculated by dividing the former by the latter.

The cost per day of detaining a juvenile in a juvenile hall is $14.75.[30] A discussion of other initial handling costs is postponed until all probation costs are estimated in the section on juvenile corrections.

Probation Determination

Table B-8 presents the transitional probabilities for the probation determination section of the simulation model. As in other tables in this appendix, the parameter's symbol appears in brackets.

Juvenile Court

Estimating juvenile delinquency hearing costs requires a two-step procedure. First, a "juvenile court" budget must be estimated from the allocation of resources to all court operations. This must be done because a separate budget is not published for juvenile courts. Second, the juvenile court budget must be distributed to the three types of juvenile hearings.

Table B-8

Probability of Probation Department Determination of Initial Referrals, 1970

Offense	Initial Referral Closed [P(IRC)]	Informal Supervision [P(IS)]	Petition Filed [P(P)]	Total
Major delinquencies	.48388	.14877	.36735	1
Drug delinquencies	.36953	.15029	.48018	1
Other delinquencies	.60244	.12361	.27395	1

Source: Bureau of Criminal Statistics, *Crime and Delinquency in California* (Sacramento: State of California, 1970), p. 88.

Step 1: The "Juvenile Court" Budget

Juvenile delinquency proceedings come under the auspices of the California Superior Court. In other words, a part of the California Superior Court expenditure is spent on the administration of juvenile cases. In addition, certain court-related expenditures (court reporters, county clerks, law libraries) must be dispersed over the juvenile court portion of the California Superior Court budget. Furthermore, this book also includes public defender expenditures in the court sector. This is done because judges may appoint public defenders to indigent juveniles.

Court costs are calculated on the basis of "a weighted caseload system approved for use by the Judicial Council in 1968."[31] Table B-9 shows the computation of the weighted filings. The weighting system has twenty-six weights. There are two sets of weights, one for Los Angeles and another for the rest of the state. In addition, there are thirteen types of proceedings. To avoid presenting an unnecessarily detailed table, eleven of the proceedings are included in the category labeled "Other." Since each of these categories has a different weight, no weight is presented for "other" proceedings in table B-9. Column 7 lists the weighted filings for the state; column 8, their percentage breakdown. The percentage distribution of the weighted workload is used to distribute the budget to the various proceedings.

In order to find the expenditure on juvenile delinquency proceedings, one must know the expenditure on all superior court proceedings. The Bureau of Criminal Statistics publishes data on direct court expenditures and, as a separate category, "court-related" expenditures. Table B-10 presents the direct court expenditures in column 1. It is not possible to know precisely how much of the court-related expenditure is relevant for an estimate of the superior court budget. Accordingly, the following assumption is made: Court-related expenditures are distributed to the superior and lower courts in proportion to the direct

Table B-9
Superior Court Workload, 1970

Proceedings	State less Los Angeles			Los Angeles			State Total	
	Filings	Weight	Weighted Filings	Filings	Weight	Weighted Filings	Weighted Filings	Weighted Filings Percent of Total
	(1)	(2)	(3) = (1) × (2)	(4)	(5)	(6) = (4) × (5)	(7) = (3) + (6)	(8)
Juvenile delinquency	41,637	54	2,248,398	14,701	80	1,176,080	3,424,478	10.330
Criminal	37,543	150	5,631,450	38,843	136	5,282,648	10,914,098	32.922
Other[a]	257,046	—	10,963,523	137,718	—	7,849,674	18,813,197	56.748
Total	336,226	—	18,843,371	191,252	—	14,308,402	33,151,773	100

Source: Judicial Council of California, *Annual Report of the Administrative Office of the California Courts* (Sacramento: State of California, 1973), pp. 248-263.

[a]Probate; family; motor vehicle; other personal injury, death, and property damage; eminent domain; other civil complaints; other civil petitions; insanity; juvenile dependency; appeals; habeas corpus.

Table B-10
Court Expenditures, Fiscal Year 1970[a]
(in thousands)

Courts	Direct Court Expenditure (1)	Percentage Distribution (2)	Court-Related[b] (3)	Total Court Expenditure (4) (4) = (1) + (3)
Superior court	$34,042	39.17	$16,441	$ 50,483
Lower court	52,857	60.83	25,528	78,385
Total	86,899	100	41,970	128,868

Source: Bureau of Criminal Statistics, *Crime and Delinquency in California* (Sacramento: State of California, 1974), p. 35.

[a]Excluding building construction.

[b]Constables and marshals; court reporters and transcripts; county clerks; law libraries; miscellaneous (crime commissions, juries). *Note:* Grand jury expenditures are excluded.

court expenditures for each court. Column 2 presents this percentage distribution. Court-related expenditures (excluding grand juries) totaled $41,970,000. Column 3 distributes this figure to the two courts. Finally, the total court expenditure for each court is the sum of direct costs and court-related expenditures (see column 4).

The superior court expenditure in 1970 was $50,483,000. This figure must be distributed to the various proceedings discussed earlier (see table B-9). As mentioned previously, this is accomplished by allocating superior court resources according to the workload for each type of proceeding. Table B-11 (column 1) displays the expenditure for each type of proceeding. It is computed by multiplying the superior court expenditure ($50,483,000) by the percentage distribution of the workload (calculated from table B-9, column 8).

As mentioned earlier, in addition to the court expenditure (direct and court-related), public defense resources must also be allocated to each type of proceeding. In 1970, $17,753,000 was spent on public defense. A breakdown of this statewide figure for each type of proceeding does not exist. The public defender of Los Angeles does, however, publish a detailed accounting of his budget.[32] The state expenditure on public defense presented in table B-11 (column 2) is distributed to each type of proceeding in the same proportion as the Los Angeles public defender's budget. As a separate category, all grand jury expenditures are allocated to criminal proceedings (see column 3). Finally, the total expenditure for each type of proceeding (including direct court, court-related, public defense, and grand juries) is presented in column 4. The most important result is that in 1970 juvenile delinquency proceedings cost the state of California $6,990,000.

Table B-11
Court and Public Defense Expenditures, Fiscal Year 1970
(in thousands)

	Court Expenditure (1)	Public Defense (2)	Grand Juries (3)	Total (4) (4) = (1) + (2) + (3)
Superior court proceedings				
Juvenile delinquency	$ 5,212	$ 1,775	$ 0	$ 6,990
Criminal	16,620	6,569	1,149	24,338
Other	28,648	1,065	0	29,713
Lower court	78,385	8,344	0	86,729
Total	128,868	17,753	1,149	147,770

Sources: Bureau of Criminal Statistics, *Crime and Delinquency in California* (Sacramento: State of California, 1974), p. 35; Public Defender of Los Angeles County, *Biennial Report 1973/1974-1974/1975.*

Step 2: The Cost of Juvenile
Delinquency Hearings

The method used to calculate the cost of juvenile delinquency hearings (that is, detention, jurisdictional, probation hearings) is to allocate the "juvenile court" budget to each type of hearing according to their relative workloads. Table B-12 (column 1) presents the number of hearings held in 1970 for each type of hearing.[33] None of the data publications used in this book provided accurate information on the number of hearings. Thus, the number of detention, jurisdictional, and probation hearings was estimated in accordance with the probability that the hearing would be held given a juvenile was detained, petitioned, or adjudicated, respectively. It was assumed that all juveniles subsequently petitioned would receive the combined jurisdictional-probation hearing.

The average time for each of these hearings in fiscal year 1969-1970 appears in column 2.[34] These average times are used as measures of the court workload. The lowest figure (9.2) was chosen as the base and set equal to 1. Column 4 presents the weighted workload for each type of hearing. The juvenile court budget was estimated to be $6,990,236 (see table B-11). The average cost per hearing is estimated by dividing the budget by the total weighted workload (282,571) and multiplying the result by the appropriate weight for each type of hearing (see column 5). Finally, the total cost for each type of hearing is used to allocate resources in the model to the different hearings. The slight discrepancy between the total cost of all hearings in table B-12 (column 6) and the budget (see table B-11) is due to rounding the average cost for each hearing.

Table B-12
Juvenile Delinquency Hearing Costs

Hearings	Number of Hearings (1)	Average Time per Hearing (Minutes) (2)	Weight (Base = 9.2) (3)	Weighted Hearings (4) (4) = (1) × (3)	Average Cost per Hearing (5)	Total Cost (6) (6) = (1) × (5)
Detention hearings	49,296	9.2	1.0	49,296	$24.73	$1,219,090
Jurisdictional hearings	82,044	18.4	2.0	164,112	49.47	4,058,717
Probation hearings	67,149	9.5	1.03	69,163	25.48	1,710,957
Total	280,533	–	–	282,571	–	6,988,764

Juvenile Court Disposition

After a juvenile is adjudicated delinquent on an initial petition, the judge will dispose of the case at a probation hearing. Table B-13 presents the transition probabilities of each offense category for the six possible correctional treatments. They were calculated from raw data by dividing the number sent to each type of correctional program (for each offense) by the number of adjudicated delinquents. In Bureau of Crime Statistics' publications, formal wards comprise wards institutionalized in county camps and wards not institutionalized.[35] In the simulation model these two groups are segregated. Thus, county camp wards are subtracted from total formal wards in order to find the number of noninstitutionalized formal wards.

Juvenile Corrections

The simulation model includes six correctional stocks financed and operated by state and county governments. Table B-14 shows the number of juveniles in each stock on January 1, 1970 (the beginning date of the simulations). These population figures are entered into the model as starting values. The number of admissions to each stock is computed internally with each iteration of the model.

Departures are a function of the beginning-period stock and the average length of stay. The latter is computed in table B-14 (column 6) according to the formula used by Forrester.[36] This figure is reasonably close to published figures for three of the correctional stocks. The legal time for informal supervision and nonward probation is six months. In fact, the computed time is identical. The California Youth Authority reports that in 1970 the mean length of stay in

Table B-13
Probability of Juvenile Court Dispositions, 1970

Offense	Petition Dismissed [P(PD)]	Remanded to Adult Court [P(PRAC)]	Noninstitutionalized				Total
			Non-ward Probation [P(NW)]	Formal Ward Probation [P(FW)]	Committed to County Camp [P(CC)]	Committed to CYA [P(JCYA)]	
Major delinquencies	.23498	.02056	.13089	.44897	.15135	.01325	1
Drug delinquencies	.31333	.03568	.15789	.3843	.10157	.00714	1
Other delinquencies	.26087	.0058	.11177	.50192	.11783	.00181	1

Source: Bureau of Criminal Statistics, *Crime and Delinquency in California* (Sacramento: State of California, 1970), pp. 95, 107.

Table B-14
Juvenile Correctional Populations

	January 1, 1970 (1)	Admissions (2)	Departures (3)	December 31, 1970 (4)	Population Average (5)	Average Length of Stay (Months) (6) (6) = [(1) ÷ (3)] × 12
Informal supervision	11,290	21,704	22,580	10,414	10,852	6
Nonward probation	3,411	6,834	6,822	3,423	3,417	6
Noninstitutionalized formal ward probation	54,282	24,328	31,702	46,908	50,595	20.5
County camps, ranches, and schools	2,605	6,941	6,896	2,650	2,628	4.5
California Youth Authority facilities	5,908	13,768	14,096	5,580	5,744	5.03
Youth parole	14,463	7,061	7,588	13,936	14,200	22.9

Sources: Bureau of Criminal Statistics, *Crime and Delinquency in California* (Sacramento: State of California, 1970), pp. 77, 95, 107, 109, 110; BCS, *Criminal Justice Profile* (Sacramento: State of California, 1976), p. 18.

institutions was roughly ten months and parole was 21.2 months.[37] The calculated time for parole is extremely close, whereas the calculated time for institutional stay is approximately half the reported time. The officially reported average time in county camps is 5.6 months.[38] This is reasonably close to the calculated figure. The average time in probation is not reported separately for noninstitutionalized formal wards.

As mentioned earlier, Bureau of Criminal Statistics' publications do not separate noninstitutionalized formal wards from county camp inmates. Table B-14 shows these two categories separately. They were separated by subtracting county camp population figures from the total formal ward populations. The average population for total formal wards in 1970 was 53,223.[39] The Task Force on Juvenile Institutions reported that the county camp average population in fiscal year 1970 was 2,698.[40] The county camp average population computed from a Bureau of Crime Statistics' publication is 2,625.[41] The discrepancy between these two figures is probably due to different data collection procedures. To be consistent, the county camp population figures (as other data for formal wards) were taken from the Bureau of Crime Statistics.

The California Youth Authority Budget

Correctional financing resides within both state and local authority. Probation is financed by local government with state support. The California Youth Authority budget is used to operate state facilities and youth parole. The California Youth Authority's budget (excluding building construction) for fiscal year 1970 was $72,085,000.[42] The average cost per year per parolee was $648.[43] The average number of parolees per day was 14,200 (see table B-14). Thus, the parole expenditure was $9,201,600. The budget remaining for facilities is $62,883,400.

In 1970 there were 380 parole officers.[44] Distributing the parole budget among all parole officers to include wages and overhead, the allocation of resources per parole officer is $24,215. This is used in the model to find the caseload per parole officer.

The facility budget is similarly distributed over the average population in juvenile facilities. Thus, the average cost of incarcerating a juvenile in a CYA facility in 1970 was $10,944. The model starts with an existing capacity for 6,700 juveniles in the facilities.[45] Above that, more facility space must be built at a cost of $20,000 per unit of space (that is, per juvenile).[46]

Probation Budget and Costs

The expenditure on probation in 1970 was $130,678,000.[47] Table B-15 presents probation costs for five probation functions. Since probation is

Table B-15
Probation Costs and Expenditures, 1970

	Cases	Average Cost	Total Cost
	(1)	(2)	(3) (3) = (1) × (2)
Initial handling, initial and re-referrals	214,267	$16	$ 3,428,272
Petition filing			
Initial petitions	53,382		
Subsequent petitions	29,000		
Total	82,382	72	5,931,504
Juvenile hall detainees	3,172	5,310	16,843,242
County camp inmates	2,650	6,564	17,394,600
Probation caseload			
Informal supervision	10,852		
Nonward	3,417		
Noninstitutionalized formal ward	50,595		
Juvenile subtotal	64,864		32,394,378
Adult superior court	58,633		
Adult lower court	50,936		54,720,949
Adult subtotal	109,569		
Total	174,363	499.42	
Total			$130,678,000

Sources: Roger Baron and Floyd Feeney, *Juvenile Diversion through Family Counseling* (Washington: GPO, 1976), pp. 12, 13; Bureau of Criminal Statistics, *Crime and Delinquency in California* (Sacramento: State of California, 1970).

financed and operated by local government, statewide costs are not available. The approach used to estimate probation costs was to use cost data from available sources for four functions and estimate the caseload cost from the remaining budget.

Cost figures from the Sacramento County Probation Department are available for the first three functions presented in table B-15. The costs are as follows: initial handling was $16 per youth in 1970; petition filing was $72 per juvenile; and detention cost was $14.75 per juvenile per night.[48] The average population in juvenile halls was 3,172.[49] At $14.75 per day, the total cost is $16,843,242. The average cost of confining a juvenile in a county camp was $546 per month, or $6,564 annually.[50] The total county camp cost was $17,394,600.

The total cost of these four functions is $43,597,618. This was subtracted from the total budget. The remaining $87,080,382 was distributed to juvenile and adult probation caseloads. It was assumed that each case demands the same workload. Thus, the average cost per probationer is $499.42. Finally, the total expenditure on juvenile probationers is estimated to be $32,394,378.

Validating the Simulation Model

It was necessary to validate the simulation model for three reasons. First, every simulation model must be pretested to check for typing errors and incorrect starting values and to learn if there were mistakes in the model's design. Second, system dynamics models require that the analyst ascertain that the assumptions of his model are operational. One assumption was that when juvenile institutions are at capacity, the inflow is cut off. Similarly, the probation officer's decision to petition juveniles is affected by the amount of available resources. These and other assumptions were validated by ascertaining that all constraints were binding. Finally, the simulated stocks and flows in this model must be close to actual values for the California criminal justice system in 1970. This is particularly important if the results of policy research are to be trusted.

In order to validate the model, it was first pretested by simulating a constant flow of juveniles through the system. It was estimated that an average of 45,570 juvenile victimizations occurred each month in California in 1970. Based on the probabilities of reporting an offense and arresting an offender, a proportion of juvenile offenders enter the system. Their passage through the system was "tracked." The size of every flow variable and the number of juveniles in a stock at the end of the year (and the yearly average) were compared with Bureau of Crime Statistics annual data. In order to get the model to track the data, two changes were made. First, the maximum allowable population (average) in correctional facilities was set to the highest monthly population for the year. The model was iterated monthly; and if this had not been done, the simulated annual average stock would have been less than the actual. Second, the estimated average length of stay in four of the six correctional stocks (table B-14) had to be changed. Specifically, the average length of stay was changed as follows: county camps was changed from 4.5 to 4.7 months; formal ward probation was changed from 20.5 to 16 months; California Youth Authority was changed from 5.03 to 6 months; youth parole was changed from 22.9 to 28 months. The large change in formal ward time was due to the fact that the model transfers county camp inmates to formal ward status after their incarceration is terminated. Once these changes were made, the model tracked the actual stocks and flows almost perfectly.

As discussed in chapter 5, the absolute magnitude of impact in the policy simulations may not be accurate. The only way one could be certain predictions are accurate is to compare them to data. The model could be simulated from 1970 to 1975, and the crime rate predicted from the model could be compared with published crime data. It was not feasible to validate the model in this manner because values for exogenous variables (inequality, unemployment) were not available after 1970. In conclusion, although the predictive validity of the model could not be verified, the structure of the model appears to be a reasonably accurate representation of the real-world system.

Notes

1. See Peter Abell, *Model Building in Sociology*, pp. 75-101, for a discussion of the methodology of operationalizing theoretical variables.

2. The assumption behind this methodology must be made explicit. The simulation model is iterated monthly. Ideally, the coefficients should have been estimated from California time-series (monthly) data. The data needed to test the theory of relative opportunity in the state of California were not available in time series. Accordingly, it is assumed the coefficients estimated from a cross-sectional analysis are applicable to a time-series simulation. The coefficients are estimated strictly for the purpose of providing parametric values in the simulation model's crime equation. Even though they cannot be used to provide accurate crime predictions, they are valid for experiments aimed at comparing the relative cost-effectiveness of policy options.

3. Federal Bureau of Investigation, *Uniform Crime Reports–1970.* Arrest data are not published by state. The Uniform Crime Report section of the FBI was kind enough to provide the author with needed tables.

4. Law Enforcement Assistance Administration (LEAA), *Children in Custody* (Washington: Government Printing Office, 1971).

5. Center for Advanced Computation, University of Illinois, "Juvenile Detention and Correctional Facility Census of 1971" (University of Illinois: N.I.L.E.C.J. Data Archive and Research Support Center).

6. U.S. Bureau of the Census, *U.S. Census of Population: 1970*, vol. 1, tables 2, 57, 133, 166.

7. U.S. Department of Labor, *Manpower Report of the President, 1971.*

8. Variables are standardized by population in order to avoid serious problems of multicollinearity.

9. Equal weight is given to each type of offense in this index. This approach can be justified. After a comparison of an unweighted index and Sellin and Wolfgang's "seriousness" index, Blumstein found that the two are "almost perfectly linearly correlated." Alfred Blumstein, "Serious Weights in an Index of Crime," p. 864.

10. Phillips, Votey, and Maxwell use this procedure in their model of crimes committed by 18- to 19-year-olds. They were quite successful in predicting crime for this age category as a function of other variables related to the age group (for example, unemployment rate for 18- to 19-year-olds). Most regression models combine juvenile and adult crime and explain the combination primarily in terms of adult variables. Llad Phillips, Harold L. Votey, Jr., and D. Maxwell, "Crime, Youth and the Labor Market," pp. 491-504.

11. The victimization rate in the simulation model excludes nonfeloneous thefts. Uniform Crime Reports include all dollar amount thefts in their larceny data. The Bureau of Criminal Statistics reports show that approximately 18 percent of all thefts in California in 1970 were grand thefts. It was assumed that

this was a constant for all states. Accordingly, 82 percent of the Uniform Crime Report larcenies were removed from the larceny data. Data on arrests and reported offenses are from tables supplied by the Uniform Crime Reports division of the FBI.

12. Doubling JOFFENSE does not alter the estimated coefficients. A victimization rate is used to dramatize the magnitude of the crime control problem. Using reported offenses as a dependent variable understates the severity of the crime problem by roughly 50 percent. It is acknowledged that the 50 percent rule of thumb is an inadequate measure. One way of improving this index would be to use victimization survey data. Based on random samples of a population, one could find the probability that a victimization was reported. The National Crime Panel has conducted victimization surveys in twenty-six cities. National Criminal Justice Information and Statistics Service, *Criminal Victimization in the United States.* It is not a simple matter to generalize from these data to the fifty states used in this regression analysis. Improving this measure would seem a worthwhile endeavor for future research.

13. Another assumption in this model should be made explicit. SJPUNISH and P(JPUNISH) equation B.7 are measured from 1971 data. In using them to explain 1970 crime, it is assumed that these variables did not vary much between 1970 and 1971 in any state. The distribution of these variables across states produces the relevant variance for this equation.

14. Data are from LEAA, *Children in Custody*, pp. 38-41.

15. Ibid., pp. 34, 35.

16. Data were taken from the raw data file for LEAA, *Children in Custody.* The computer tapes were supplied by the Center for Advanced Computation.

17. LEAA, *Children in Custody*, pp. 44, 45.

18. JCFAPOP is from LEAA, *Children in Custody*, pp. 54, 55; JPOP and JSUBPOP are computed from *Census of Population*, tables 133, 166. It is assumed that the JCFAPOP[1970] was close to JCFAPOP[1971].

19. Although OUTFLOW is a flow measure, it is treated as a stock concept in the measure of DELTJ and DELSUB. It is assumed that the number released in 1971 was the same as in 1970.

20. Data are from LEAA, *Children in Custody*, pp. 54, 55.

21. Department of Labor, *Manpower Report to the President*, tables F-3, F-15.

22. This was done to avoid multicollinearity.

23. Percentiles of the student's t distribution are from J. Johnston, *Econometric Methods*, p. 426.

24. Peter W. Greenwood et al., *The Criminal Investigation Process, vol. 3, Observation and Analysis*, p. 73.

25. As mentioned earlier, there is no divisional breakdown of the California police budget. As an approximation of the proportion of the police budget distributed to the detective function, 18 percent is used. The 18 percent figure is

taken from the Berkeley, Los Angeles city and county police departments. For the Berkeley Police Department, see Benson and Lund, *Neighborhood Distribution of Local Public Services*, table 9; for the Los Angeles Police Department see James S. Kakalik and Sorrel Wildhorn, *Aids to Decision Making in Police Patrol*, pp. 3, 21.

26. Greenwood et al., *The Criminal Investigation Process*, vol. 3. A few much more complicated weighting schemes were developed from Greenwood's data. Although more realistic assumptions were used, none of the other weighting schemes differed much from the more parsimonious one presented here. In particular, the scheme presented here distributes detective resources over all arrests. It does not categorize arrests according to whether the detective division actually made the arrests or whether the arrest was made without an investigation by the detective division.

27. As a check to see that the cost estimates are within the 1970 budget, one can see that the total cost of all arrests in table B-6 equals the budget in table B-3.

28. See Bureau of Criminal Statistics (BCS), *Crime and Delinquency in California* (Sacramento: 1969), p. 145.

29. Total referrals were calculated from BCS, *Crime and Delinquency in California*, 1970, pp. 84, 86. Admissions are presented on p. 102.

30. This figure is taken from the Sacramento Diversion Project. See Roger Baron and Floyd Feeney, *Juvenile Diversion through Family Counciling*, p. 13.

31. Judicial Council of California, *Annual Report of the Administrative Office of the California Courts*, 1971, p. 124.

32. Richard S. Buckley, *Biennial Report 1973/1974-1974/1975* (Public Defender of Los Angeles County).

33. It is estimated that there were approximately 28,700 subsequent petitions filed in 1970. Estimated from Bureau of Criminal Statistics, *Adult and Juvenile Probation, 1972*, p. 112.

The number of initial petitions was taken from a simulation of the computer model, so that the cost estimates would be internally accurate. The simulated number of initial petitions was nearly identical to the number reported by the Bureau of Criminal Statistics.

34. Judicial Council of California, *Annual Report of the Administrative Office of the California Courts*, 1971, p. 125. The average time for jurisdictional hearings (see column 2) is the average time for uncontested and contested dispositions of both initial and subsequent petitions.

35. See BCS, *Crime and Delinquency in California*, 1970, annual.

36. Jay Forrester, *Industrial Dynamics*, p. 78.

37. Department of Youth Authority, *Annual Report, 1970*, pp. 32, 34.

38. Board of Corrections, *California Correctional System Study: Juvenile Institutions Task Force Report*, p. 10. The slight discrepancy may be due to the fact that the officially reported time is based on a different population size.

39. Calculated from BCS, *Crime and Delinquency in California,* 1970.

40. Board of Corrections, *California Correctional System Study: Juvenile Institutions Task Force Report*, p. 9.

41. BCS, *Criminal Justice Profile*, p. 18.

42. BCS, *Crime and Delinquency in California*, 1974, p. 35.

43. Board of Corrections, *California Correctional System Study: Juvenile Institutions Task Force Report*, p. v.

44. BCS, *Crime and Delinquency in California*, 1974, p. 33.

45. During the preceding five years, the peak population was 6,542. See BCS, *Crime and Delinquency in California*, 1970, p. 109. A slightly higher figure is used in the simulation model to account for the possibility of overcrowding juveniles prior to building.

46. See Board of Corrections, *California Correctional System Study: Juvenile Institutions Task Force Report*, p. v.

47. BCS, *Crime and Delinquency in California*, 1974, p. 35.

48. Baron and Feeney, *Juvenile Diversion through Family Counseling*, pp. 12, 13. The first two costs are estimated by multiplying the number of hours required per juvenile times the cost per hour ($8).

49. The average population calculated from BCS data is 3,820. Calculated from *Crime and Delinquency in California*, 1970, p. 102. But this figure includes juveniles excluded from this model (dependency, transfers). They comprise approximately 18 percent of the inflow.

50. Board of Corrections, *California Correctional System Study: Juvenile Institutions Task Force Report*, appendix A. The existing capacity is 3,707, which is the average of the county camp capacity for fiscal year 1969-1970 and February 1971 (ibid., p. 9). Facility space is built at a cost of $20,000 per unit.

Bibliography

Books

Abell, Peter. *Model Building in Sociology.* New York: Schocken Books, 1972.

American Enterprise Institute for Public Policy Research. *The Economics of Crime and Punishment.* Washington: American Enterprise Institute for Public Policy Research, 1973.

Banfield, Edward C. *The Unheavenly City Revisited.* Boston: Little, Brown, and Company, 1974.

Bauer, Raymond, ed. *Social Indicators.* Cambridge, Mass.: The M.I.T. Press, 1966.

Benson, C.S., and Lund, P.B. *Neighborhood Distribution of Local Public Services.* Berkeley, Calif.: Institute of Governmental Services, 1969.

Berliner, Joseph S. *Economy, Society and Welfare.* New York: Frederick A. Praeger, Inc., 1972.

Blalock, Hubert M. *Theory Construction.* Englewood Cliffs, N.J.: Prentice-Hall, Inc., 1969.

Blumstein, Alfred, et al. *Deterrence and Incapacitation : Estimating the Effects of Criminal Sanctions on Crime Rates.* Washington: National Academy of Sciences, 1978.

Braybrooke, David, and Lindblom, Charles E. *A Strategy of Decision.* New York: The Free Press, 1970.

Buckley, Walter. *Sociology and Modern Systems Theory.* Englewood Cliffs, N.J.: Prentice-Hall, Inc., 1967.

Burkhead, Jesse, and Miner, Jerry. *Public Expenditure.* Chicago: Aldine Publishing Company, 1971.

Chapman, Jeffrey I. "A Model of Crime and Police Output." Ph.D. dissertation, University of California, 1971.

Cho, Yong Hyo. *Public Policy and Urban Crime.* Cambridge, Mass.: Ballinger Publishing Company, 1974.

Church, Albert. "Econometric Model of Crime in California." Ph.D. dissertation, Claremont College, 1970.

Clark, Ramsey. *Crime in America.* New York: Pocket Books, 1971.

Clinard, Marshall B., and Quinney, Richard. *Criminal Behavior Systems.* New York: Holt, Rinehart and Winston, Inc., 1967.

Cloward, Richard A., and Ohlin, Lloyd. *Delinquency and Opportunity.* New York: The Free Press, 1960.

Cohen, Albert K. *Delinquent Boys.* Glencoe, Ill.: The Free Press, 1955.

Cole, George F. *Politics and the Administration of Justice.* Beverly Hills, Calif.: Sage Publications, Inc., 1973.

Cook, Phillip. *The Effect of Legitimate Opportunities on the Probability of*

Parolee Recidivism. University of California: Institute of Industrial Relations, 1971.

DeGreene, Kenyon. *Sociotechnical Systems.* Englewood Cliffs, N.J.: Prentice-Hall, Inc., 1973.

Dershowitz, Alan M. *Fair and Certain Punishment.* New York: McGraw-Hill Book Company, 1976.

Dror, Yehezkel. *Design for Policy Sciences.* New York: American Elsevier Publishing Company, Inc., 1971.

_____. *Ventures in Policy Sciences.* New York: American Elsevier Publishing Company, Inc., 1971.

Easton, David. *A Systems Analysis of Political Life.* New York: John Wiley & Sons, Inc., 1965.

Eisenhower, Milton S. *The Rule of Law.* Nashville, Tenn.: Aurora Publishing, Inc., 1970.

Falkin, Gregory P. "Reducing Delinquency: A Strategic Planning Approach." Ph.D. dissertation, Cornell University, 1977.

Felice, Laurence G. "Community Structure and Social Control: A Study of Municipal Police Force Size." Ph.D. dissertation, Cornell University, 1971.

Fleisher, Belton M. *The Economics of Delinquency.* Chicago: Quadrangle Books, 1966.

Forrester, Jay. *Industrial Dynamics.* Cambridge, Mass.: The M.I.T. Press, 1961.

_____. *Principles of Systems.* Cambridge, Mass.: Wright-Allen Press, Inc., 1968.

_____. *Urban Dynamics.* Cambridge, Mass.: The M.I.T. Press, 1969.

Glaser, Daniel. *The Effectiveness of a Prison Parole System.* New York: Bobbs-Merrill Company, Inc., 1964.

Goldfarb, Ronald. *Jails.* Garden City, N.Y.: Anchor Books, 1976.

Greenwood, Peter W. *An Analysis of the Apprehension Activities of the New York City Police Department.* New York: The New York City Rand Institute, 1970.

Greenwood, Peter, et al. *The Criminal Investigation Process.* Santa Monica, Calif.: Rand Corporation, 1975.

_____. *Prosecution of Adult Felony Defendants.* Lexington, Mass.: Lexington Books, D.C. Heath and Company, 1976.

Henry, Andrew F., and Short, James F., Jr. *Suicide and Homicide.* New York: The Free Press, 1968.

Hoffman, Mark. *Criminal Justice Planning.* Chicago: American Society of Planning Officials, 1972.

Hoos, Ida. *Systems Analysis in Public Policy.* Berkeley: University of California, 1972.

Jencks, Christopher. *Inequality.* New York: Basic Books, Inc., Publishers, 1972.

Johnston, J. *Econometric Methods.* 2d ed. New York: McGraw-Hill Book Company, 1972.

Kakalik, James S., and Wildhorn, Sorrel. *Aids to Decision Making in Police Patrol.* Santa Monica, Calif.: Rand, 1971.

Katz, Lewis. *Justice Is the Crime.* Cleveland, Ohio: The Press of Case Western Reserve University, 1972.

Lasswell, Harold. *A Pre-View of Policy Sciences.* New York: American Elsevier Publishing Company, Inc., 1971.

Lerner, Daniel, and Lasswell, Harold, eds. *The Policy Sciences.* Stanford, Calif.: Stanford University Press, 1951.

Lewin, David, et al. *The Urban Labor Market.* New York: Frederick A. Praeger, Inc., 1974.

Martinson, Robert, and Wilks, Judith. *Knowledge in Criminal Justice Planning.* New York: The Center for Knowledge in Criminal Justice Planning, 1976.

McPheters, Lee R., and Stronge, William B. *The Economics of Crime and Law Enforcement.* Springfield, Ill.: Charles C. Thomas, Publisher, 1976.

Menninger, Karl. *The Crime of Punishment.* New York: The Viking Press, Inc., 1968.

Messinger, Sheldon, et al. *The Aldine Crime and Justice Annual, 1973.* Chicago: Aldine Publishing Company, 1973.

Miernyk, William H. *The Elements of Input-Output Analysis.* New York: Random House, Inc., 1965.

Mitford, Jessica. *Kind and Unusual Punishment.* New York: Vintage Books, 1974.

Morris, Norval, and Hawkins, Gordon. *The Honest Politician's Guide to Crime Control.* Chicago: The University of Chicago Press, 1969.

Moynihan, Daniel P. *Maximum Feasible Misunderstanding.* New York: The Free Press, 1969.

Nagel, Stuart S. *The Legal Process from a Behavioral Perspective.* Homewood, Ill.: The Dorsey Press, 1969.

————. *Improving the Legal Process.* Lexington, Mass.: D.C. Heath and Company, 1975.

The National Urban Coalition. *Law and Disorder II.* Washington: The National Urban Coalition, 1971.

Neiderhoffer, Arthur. *Behind the Shield: The Police in Urban Society.* Garden City, N.Y.: Doubleday & Company, Inc., 1969.

Newman, Oscar. *Defensible Space: Crime Prevention through Urban Design.* New York: The Macmillan Company, 1972.

Oaks, Dallin H., and Lehman, Warren. *A Criminal Justice System and the Indigent.* Chicago: University of Chicago Press, 1968.

Ostrom, Elinor, et al. *Community Organization and the Provision of Police Services.* Beverly Hills, Calif.: Sage Publications, Inc., 1973.

Posner, Richard A. *Economic Analysis of Law.* Boston: Little, Brown and Company, 1972.

Quade, E.S., and Boucher, W.I., eds. *Systems Analysis and Policy Planning.* New York: American Elsevier Publishing Company, Inc., 1968.

Radzinowicz, Leon. *Ideology and Crime.* New York: Columbia University Press, 1966.

_____, and Wolfgang, Marvin. *Crime and Justice.* The Criminal in Society, Vol. 1. New York: Basic Books, 1971.

Rawls, John. *A Theory of Justice.* Cambridge: Harvard University Press, 1971.

Rivlin, Alice M. *Systematic Thinking for Social Action.* Washington: The Brookings Institution, 1971.

Schultze, Charles L. *The Politics and Economics of Public Spending.* Washington: The Brookings Institution, 1968.

Sharkansky, Ira. *The Politics of Taxing and Spending.* New York: Bobbs-Merrill Company, Inc., 1969.

_____. *Policy Analysis in Political Science.* Chicago: Markham Publishing Co., 1970.

Shoup, Donald C., and Mehay, Stephan L. *Program Budgeting for Urban Police Services.* University of California: Institute of Government and Public Affairs, 1971.

Skolnick, Jerome H. *Justice without Trial.* New York: John Wiley & Sons, Inc., 1966.

Sutherland, Edwin H. *On Analyzing Crime.* Chicago: The University of Chicago Press, 1973.

_____, and Cressy, Donald. *Principles of Criminology*, 9th ed. Philadelphia: J.B. Lippincott Company, 1974.

Taggart, Robert. *The Prison of Unemployment.* Baltimore: The Johns Hopkins Press, 1972.

Tinbergen, J. *On the Theory of Economic Policy.* Amsterdam: North-Holland Publishing Company, 1966.

_____. *Economic Policy.* Amsterdam: North-Holland Publishing Company, 1967.

van den Haag, Ernest. *Punishing Criminals.* New York: Basic Books, Inc., 1975.

van Gigch, John P. *Applied General Systems Theory.* New York: Harper & Row Publishers, 1974.

Viano, Emilio C., and Cohn, Alvin W. *Social Problems and Criminal Justice.* Chicago: Nelson Hall, Inc., 1975.

von Hirsch, Andrew. *Doing Justice.* New York: Hill and Wang, Inc., 1976.

Wallace, Walter L. *The Logic of Science in Sociology.* Chicago: Aldine Publishing Company, 1971.

Weston, Paul B., and Wells, Kenneth. *The Administration of Justice.* Englewood Cliffs, N.J.: Prentice-Hall, Inc., 1973.

Williams, Walter. *Social Policy Research and Analysis.* New York: American Elsevier Publishing Company, Inc., 1971.

Wilson, James Q. *Varieties of Police Behavior.* New York: Atheneum Publishers, 1972.

_____. *Thinking about Crime.* New York: Basic Books, Inc., 1975.

Wolfgang, Marvin E., and Ferracuti, Franco. *The Subculture of Violence.* London: Tavistock Publications, 1967.

Zimring, Franklin E., and Hawkins, Gordon J. *Deterrence.* Chicago: The University of Chicago Press, 1973.

Articles

Bechdolt, B.V., Jr. "Cross Sectional Analyses of Socioeconomic Determinants of Urban Crime." *Review of Social Economics* 33, no. 2 (October 1975):132-140.

Becker, Gary S. "Crime and Punishment: An Economic Approach." *Journal of Political Economy* 76 (March/April 1968):169-217.

Belkin, Jacob; Blumstein, Alfred; and Gloss, William. "Recidivism as a Feedback Process: An Analytical Model and Empirical Validation." Carnegie-Mellon University, Urban Systems Institute, 1972.

Bennett, L.A. "Should We Change the Offender or the System?" *Crime and Delinquency* 19 (July 1973):332-342.

Biderman, Albert D. "Social Indicators and Goals." In Raymond Bauer, *Social Indicators.* Cambridge, Mass.: The M.I.T. Press, 1967.

Block, Michael K., and Lind, Robert C. "An Economic Analysis of Crimes Punishable by Imprisonment." *Journal of Legal Studies* 4 (1975):479-492.

_____ and _____. "Crime and Punishment Reconsidered." *Journal of Legal Studies* 4, no. 1 (January 1975):241-247.

Blumstein, Alfred. "Seriousness Weights in an Index of Crime." *American Sociological Review* 39 (December 1974):854-864.

_____, and Larson, Richard. "Models of a Total Criminal Justice System." *Operations Research* 17 (March/April 1969):199-232.

Boulding, Kenneth. "Economics and General Systems." In *The Relevance of General Systems Theory*, edited by E. Laszlo. New York: George Braziller, 1972, pp. 77-92.

Center for Advanced Computation, University of Illinois. "Juvenile Detention and Correctional Facility Census of 1971." University of Illinois: N.I.L.E.C.J. Data Archive and Research Support Center.

Cho, Yong Hyo. "A Multiple Regression Model for the Measurement of the Public Policy Impact on Big City Crime." *Policy Science*, December 1972, pp. 435-455.

Cohen, Jacqueline, et al. "Implementation of the JUSSIM Model in a Criminal Justice Planning Agency." *Journal of Crime and Delinquency*, July 1973, pp. 117-131.

Danziger, Sheldon, and Wheeler, David. "Economics of Crime and Punishment: Punishment or Income Redistribution." *Review of Social Economics* 33, no. 2 (October 1975):113-131.

Eberts, Paul R. "Consequences of Changing Social Organization in the Northeast. *Papers of the Workshop on Current Rural Development Regional Research in the Northeast.* Northeast Regional Center for Rural Development, July 25-28, 1972, pp. 20-68.

_____. "Trend Analysis: An Overview, With an Illustration on Homicide Rates in New York and the Northeast." Ithaca, N.Y.: Cornell University, 1977.

_____, and Schwirian, Kent P. "Metropolitan Crime Rates and Relative Deprivation." In ed. Daniel Glaser, *Crime in the City.* New York: Harper & Row, Publishers, 1970, pp. 90-97.

_____, and Sismondo, Sergio. "Designing and Managing Policy Research." Paper presented to the Conference on Alternate Methods for Public Policy Research in Rural America. Ames, Iowa: North Central Regional Center on Rural Development, 1975.

_____ and _____. "Principles in Design and Management of Policy Research for Public Planning Agencies," in David W. Rogers and Larry R. Whiting, eds., *Rural Policy Research Alternatives.* Ames, Iowa: Iowa State University Press, 1978.

Ehrlich, Isaac. "Participation in Illegitimate Activities: A Theoretical and Empirical Investigation." *Journal of Political Economy* 81, no. 3 (June 1973):521-565.

Elkin, S.L. "Political Science and Analysis of Public Policy." *Public Policy,* Summer 1974, pp. 399-422.

Enthoven, Alain C. "Ten Practical Principles for Policy and Program Analysis." *Aldine Annual Benefit Cost and Policy Analysis.* Chicago: Aldine Publishing Company, 1975.

Evans, Robert, Jr. "The Labor Market and Parole Success." *The Journal of Human Resources* 3, no. 2 (Spring 1968):201-212.

Falkin, Gregory P. "Finding a Cost-Effective Policy to Reduce Juvenile Delinquency." Paper presented to the 1977 Annual Meeting of the American Society of Criminology, Atlanta, November 1977.

Fleisher, Belton M. "The Effect of Unemployment of Juvenile Delinquency." *Journal of Political Economy* 71 (December 1963):543-553.

_____. "The Effect of Income on Delinquency." *American Economic Review* 56 (March 1966):118-137.

Forst, Brian. "Participation in Illegitimate Activities: Further Empirical Findings." *Policy Analysis* 2 (1976):477-492.

Frank, James, and Faust, Frederic L. "A Conceptual Framework for Criminal Justice Planning." *Criminology* 13, no. 2 (August 1975):271-295.

Gass, Saul I. "Models in Law Enforcement and Criminal Justice." In eds. Saul Cass, and Roger L. Sisson, *A Guide to Models in Governmental Planning and Operations.* Potomac, Md.: Sauger Books, 1975, pp. 231-276.

Gordon, David. "Capitalism, Class and Crime in America." *Crime and Delinquency* 19, no. 2 (April 1973):163-186.

Greenwood, Peter W. "Long-Range Planning in the Criminal Justice System: What State Planning Agencies Can Do." Santa Monica, Calif.: Rand Corporation, 1970.

Harris, John R. "On the Economics of Law and Order." *Journal of Political Economy* 83 (January/February 1970):165-175.

Holahan, John. "Measuring the Benefits from Prison Reform." In *Benefit-Cost and Policy Analysis*. Chicago: Aldine Publishing Company, 1973.

Landes, William M. "An Economic Analysis of the Courts." *Journal of Law and Economics* 14, no. 61 (1971).

_____, and Posner, Richard A. "The Private Enforcement of Law." University of Chicago: unpublished manuscript, September 3, 1974.

Lasswell, Harold. "The Policy Orientation." In eds. Daniel Lerner and Harold Lasswell, *The Policy Sciences*. Stanford, Calif.: Stanford University Press, 1951.

Levine, James P. "The Ineffectiveness of Adding Police to Prevent Crime." *Public Policy* 23, no. 4 (Fall 1975):523-545.

Lind, Robert, and Lipsky, John. "The Measurement of Police Output: Conceptual Issues and Alternative Approaches." *Law and Contemporary Problems*, Autumn 1971, pp. 566-588.

Lowi, Theodore. "Decision-Making vs. Policy Making: Toward an Antidote of Technocracy." *Public Administration Review* 30 (1970):314-325.

Martinson, Robert. "What Works?—Questions and Answers about Prison Reform." *The Public Interest*, Spring 1974, pp. 22-54.

Miller, Walter B. "Ideology and Criminal Justice Policy: Some Current Issues." *The Aldine Crime and Justice Annual, 1973*. Chicago: Aldine Publishing Company, 1973. Reprinted from *Journal of Criminal Law and Criminology* 64, no. 2, pp. 141-162.

Moynihan, Daniel P. "Policy vs. Program in the 1970's." *The Public Interest*, Summer 1970, pp. 90-101.

Packer, Herbert L. "Two Models of the Criminal Process." In ed. Jeffrie G. Murphy, *Punishment and Rehabilitation*. Belmont, Calif.: Wadsworth Publishing Company, Inc., 1973. Reprinted from Herbert L. Packer, *The Limits of the Criminal Sanction*. Stanford, Calif.: Stanford University Press, 1968.

Palmer, Ted. "Martinson Revisited." *Journal of Research on Crime and Delinquency* 12, no. 2 (July 1975):133-152.

Palmore, Erdman, and Hammond, Phillip E. "Interesting Factors in Juvenile Delinquency." *American Sociological Review* 29 (December 1964):848-854.

Phillips, Llad. "The War on Crime." In Harold Votey and Llad Phillips, *Economic Analysis of Pressing Social Problems*. Chicago: Rand McNally & Company, 1974.

_____, and Votey, Harold. "Crime Control in California." *Journal of Legal Studies* 4, no. 2 (June 1975):327-349.

_____ and _____. "An Economic Analysis of the Deterrent Effect of Law

Enforcement on Criminal Activity." *The Journal of Criminal Law, Criminology and Police Science* 63, no. 3 (1972):330-342.

_____ ; _____ ; and Maxwell, D. "Crime, Youth and the Labor Market." *Journal of Political Economy*, May/June 1975, pp. 149-504.

Plattner, Marc F. "The Rehabilitation of Punishment." *The Public Interest* no. 44 (Summer 1976):104-114.

Rottenberg, Simon. "The Social Cost of Crime and Crime Prevention." In Joseph Clark et al., *Crime in Urban Society*. New York: Dunellen, 1970.

Schaefer, Guenther F. "A General Systems Approach to Public Policy Analysis." *Policy and Politics* 2, no. 2 (June 1974):331-346.

Schuessler, Karl, and Slatin, Gerald. "Sources of Variation in United States City Crime, 1950 and 1960." *Journal of Research Crime and Delinquency*, July 1964, pp. 127-148.

Sharkansky, Ira. "Government Expenditures and the Public Services in the American States." *American Political Science Review*, December 1967, pp. 1066-1077.

Sjoquist, David L. "Property Crime and Economic Behavior: Some Empirical Results." *The American Economic Review* 63, no. 3 (June 1973):439-446.

Slivka, Ronald T., and Cannavale, Frank. "An Analytical Model of the Passage of Defendants through a Court System." *Journal of Research in Crime and Delinquency*, July 1973, pp. 132-138.

Stigler, George J. "The Optimum Enforcement of Laws." *Journal of Political Economy* 78, no. 3 (May/June 1970):526-535.

Stollmack, Stephen. "Predicting Inmate Populations from Arrest, Court Disposition, and Recidivism Rates." *Journal of Research in Crime and Delinquency*, July 1973, pp. 141-162.

Sullivan, Richard F. "The Economics of Crime: An Introduction to the Literature." *The Aldine Crime and Justice Annual, 1973*. Chicago: Aldine Publishing Company, 1973. Reprinted from *Crime and Delinquency*, April 1973, pp. 138-150.

Swimmer, Eugene. "Measurement of the Effectiveness of Urban Law Enforcement—A Simultaneous Approach." *Southern Economics Journal* 40, no. 4 (April 1974):618-630.

Tittle, Charles R., and Logan, Charles H. "Sanctions and Deviance: Evidence and Remaining Questions." *The Aldine Crime and Justice Annual, 1973*. Chicago: Aldine Publishing Company, 1973. Reprinted from *Law and Society Review* 7, no. 3 (Spring 1973):371-392.

Tullock, Gordon. "An Economic Approach to Crime." *Social Science Quarterly* 5, no. 1 (June 1969):59-71.

_____ . "Does Punishment Deter Crime?" *The Public Interest*, Summer 1974, pp. 103-111.

Vandaele, Walter. "Participation in Illegitimate Activities I. Erlich Revisited." Cambridge, Mass.: Harvard University, Graduate School of Business Administration, 1976.

van Gigch, John P. "The Contribution of Systems Analysis to the Study of the Criminal Justice System." Paper presented to the Criminal Justice Symposium, Monterey, Calif., California Council on Criminal Justice, Nov. 20, 1969.

Wildavsky, Aaron. "The Political Economy of Efficiency." *Public Administration Review* 26, no. 4 (December 1966):292.

_____. "Rescuing Policy Analysis from PPBS." *Analysis and Evaluation of Public Expenditures: The PPB System.* Joint Economic Committee. 91st Cong. 1st Sess., 1969.

Wilson, James Q., and Boland, Barbara. "Crime." In eds. William Gorham and Nathan Glaser, *Urban Predicament.* Washington: The Urban Institute, 1976, pp. 179-230.

Wolfgang, Marvin E. "Urban Crime." In ed. James Q. Wilson, *The Metropolitan Enigma.* New York: Anchor Books, 1970, pp. 270-311.

Government Publications

Baron, Roger, and Feeney, Floyd. *Juvenile Diversion through Family Counseling.* Washington: Government Printing Office (GPO), 1976.

Belkin, Jacob, et al. *Performance Measurement and the Criminal Justice System.* Washington: GPO, 1976.

Board of Corrections. *California Correctional System Study: Juvenile Institutions Task Force Report.* Sacramento: State of California, 1971.

_____. *California Correctional System Study: Probation Task Force Report.* Sacramento: State of California, 1971.

_____. *California Correctional System Study: Systems Task Force Report.* Sacramento: State of California, 1971.

Bureau of Criminal Statistics. *Crime and Arrests, 1970.* Sacramento: State of California, 1970.

_____. *Crime and Delinquency in California.* Sacramento: State of California, 1970.

_____. *Adult and Juvenile Probation, 1972.* Sacramento: State of California, 1972.

_____. *Crime and Delinquency in California.* Sacramento: State of California, 1974.

_____. *Criminal Justice Profile.* Sacramento: State of California, 1976.

California: Welfare and Institutions Code.

California Council on Criminal Justice. *Synopsis of the 1972 California Comprehensive Plan for Criminal Justice.* Sacramento: State of California, 1972.

California Office of Criminal Justice Planning. *California Correctional System Intake Study.* Sacramento: State of California, 1974.

Chaiken, J., et al. *Criminal Justice Models: An Overview.* Washington: GPO, 1976.

Chelimsky, Eleanor. *High Impact Anti-Crime Program*, vol. 2. Washington: GPO, 1976.

Cohen, Lawrence E. *Delinquency Dispositions.* Washington: GPO, 1975.

_____. *Juvenile Dispositions.* Washington: GPO, 1975.

_____. *New Directions in Processing of Juvenile.* Washington: GPO, 1975.

_____. *Pre-Adjudicatory Detention in Three Juvenile Courts.* Washington: GPO, 1975.

_____. *Who Gets Detained?* Washington: GPO, 1975.

Department of Youth Authority. *Annual Report, 1970.* Sacramento: State of California, 1970.

Federal Bureau of Investigation. *Uniform Crime Reports—1970.* Washington: GPO, 1970.

Glaser, Daniel. *Strategic Criminal Justice Planning.* Washington: GPO, 1975.

Hindelang, Michael, et al. *Sourcebook of Criminal Justice Statistics, 1973.* Washington: GPO, 1973.

Judicial Council of California. *Annual Report of the Administrative Office of the California Courts.* Sacramento: State of California, 1972.

Klein, Malcolm W., and Teilmann, Kathie S. *Pivotal Ingredients of Police Juvenile Diversion Programs.* Washington: GPO, 1976.

Ku, Richard, and Blew, Carol H. *The Adolescent Diversion Project.* Washington: GPO, 1977.

Law Enforcement Assistance Administration (LEAA). *First Annual Report of the National Institute of Law Enforcement and Criminal Justice, Fiscal Year 1974.* Washington: GPO, 1974.

_____. *Sixth Annual Report of LEAA.* Washington: GPO, 1974.

Joint Economic Committee, *Analysis and Evaluation of Public Expenditures: the PPB System.* 91st Cong., 1st Sess., 1969.

National Advisory Commission on Criminal Justice Standards and Goals. *A National Strategy to Reduce Crime.* Washington: GPO, 1973.

_____. *Children in Custody.* Washington: GPO, 1970.

_____. *Criminal Justice Research and Development.* Washington: GPO, 1976.

_____. *Criminal Victimization in the United States.* Washington: GPO, 1976.

Oberlander, Leonard, ed. *Quantitative Tools for Criminal Justice Planning.* Washington: LEAA, 1975.

President's Commission on Law Enforcement and the Administration of Justice. *The Challenge of Crime in a Free Society.* Washington: GPO, 1967.

_____. *Task Force Report: Science and Technology.* Washington: GPO, 1967.

Rutherford, Andrew, and Bengur, Osman. *Community-Based Alternatives to Juvenile Incarceration.* Washington: GPO, 1976.

Taggart, Robert. "Manpower Programs for Criminal Offenders." *Monthly Labor Review*, August 1972, pp. 17-24.

Thalheimer, Donald. *Cost Analysis of Correctional Standards: Halfway Houses.* Washington: GPO, 1975.

Thornton, Warren E., and Rose, Max C. *Philosophy and Procedures in Juvenile Court.* Sacramento: State of California.

U.S. Bureau of the Census. *U.S. Census of Population: 1970.* Washington: GPO, 1972.

U.S. Department of Labor. *Manpower Report of the President, 1971.* Washington: GPO, 1971.

Watkins, Ann M. *Cost Analysis of Correctional Standards: Pretrial Diversion.* Washington: GPO, 1975.

Zimring, Franklin E. *Perspectives on Deterrence.* Washington: GPO, 1973.

Index of Names

Index of Subjects

About the Author

Gregory P. Falkin is a policy analyst with the U.S. Department of Justice. He assisted in preparing the attorney general's "Policy and Program Guidelines" and has been responsible for the background work for the Federal Corrections Policy Task Force. To aid the task force in its deliberations, he modified the approach to strategic planning developed in this book in writing a paper entitled, "A Proposed Framework for Designing a Strategy for Federal Corrections." As a graduate student at Cornell University, he studied public policy from an interdisciplinary perspective with a major in applied economics and public policy. While doing his graduate work, he taught courses in consumer protection and criminal justice at Elmira College. He received the M.S. from Cornell University in January 1975 and the Ph.D. in August 1977.